Avian Aesthetics in Literature and Culture

Ecocritical Theory and Practice

Series Editor: Douglas A. Vakoch, METI

Advisory Board

Sinan Akilli, Cappadocia University, Turkey; Bruce Allen, Seisen University, Japan; Zélia Bora, Federal University of Paraíba, Brazil; Izabel Brandão, Federal University of Alagoas, Brazil; Byron Caminero-Santangelo, University of Kansas, USA; Chia-ju Chang, Brooklyn College, The City College of New York, USA; H. Louise Davis, Miami University, USA; Simão Farias Almeida, Federal University of Roraima, Brazil; George Handley, Brigham Young University, USA; Steven Hartman, Mälardalen University, Sweden; Isabel Hoving, Leiden University, The Netherlands; Idom Thomas Inyabri, University of Calabar, Nigeria; Serenella Iovino, University of Turin, Italy; Daniela Kato, Kyoto Institute of Technology, Japan; Petr Kopecký, University of Ostrava, Czech Republic; Julia Kuznetski, Tallinn University, Estonia; Bei Liu, Shandong Normal University, People's Republic of China; Serpil Oppermann, Cappadocia University, Turkey; John Ryan, University of New England, Australia; Christian Schmitt-Kilb, University of Rostock, Germany; Joshua Schuster, Western University, Canada; Heike Schwarz, University of Augsburg, Germany; Murali Sivaramakrishnan, Pondicherry University, India; Scott Slovic, University of Idaho, USA; Heather Sullivan, Trinity University, USA; David Taylor, Stony Brook University, USA; J. Etienne Terblanche, North-West University, South Africa; Cheng Xiangzhan, Shandong University, China; Hubert Zapf, University of Augsburg, Germany

Ecocritical Theory and Practice highlights innovative scholarship at the interface of literary/cultural studies and the environment, seeking to foster an ongoing dialogue between academics and environmental activists.

Recent Titles

Avian Aesthetics in Literature and Culture: Birds and Humans in the Popular Imagination, edited by Danette DiMarco and Timothy Ruppert
Shamanism in the Contemporary Novel, by Özlem Öğüt Yazıcıoğlu
Modernism and the Anthropocene, edited by Jon Hegglund and John McIntyre
The End of the Anthropocene: Ecocriticism, the Universal Ecosystem, and the Astropocene, by Michael Gormley
Trees in Literatures and the Arts: Humanarboreal Perspectives in the Anthropocene, edited by Carmelina Concilio and Daniela Fargione
Lupenga Mphande: Eco-critical Poet and Political Activist, by Dike Okoro
Environmental Postcolonialism: A Literary Response, edited by Shubhanku Kochar and M. Anjum Khan
Reading Aridity in Western American Literature, edited by Jada Ach and Gary Reger
Reading Cats and Dogs: Companion Animals in World Literature, edited by Françoise Besson, Zelia M. Bora, Marianne Marroum, and Scott Slovic
Turkish Ecocriticism: From Neolithic to Contemporary Timescapes, edited by Sinan Akilli and Serpil Oppermann
Avenging Nature: The Role of Nature in Modern and Contemporary Art and Literature, edited by Eduardo Valls Oyarzun, Rebeca Gualberto Valverde, Noelia Malla Garcia, María Colom Jiménez, and Rebeca Cordero Sánchez

Avian Aesthetics in Literature and Culture

Birds and Humans in the Popular Imagination

Edited by
Danette DiMarco and Timothy Ruppert

LEXINGTON BOOKS
Lanham • Boulder • New York • London

Published by Lexington Books
An imprint of The Rowman & Littlefield Publishing Group, Inc.
4501 Forbes Boulevard, Suite 200, Lanham, Maryland 20706
www.rowman.com

86-90 Paul Street, London EC2A 4NE

Copyright © 2022 by The Rowman & Littlefield Publishing Group, Inc.

All rights reserved. No part of this book may be reproduced in any form or by any electronic or mechanical means, including information storage and retrieval systems, without written permission from the publisher, except by a reviewer who may quote passages in a review.

British Library Cataloguing in Publication Information Available

Library of Congress Cataloging-in-Publication Data

Names: DiMarco, Danette, editor. | Ruppert, Timothy, 1969- editor.
Title: Avian aesthetics in literature and culture : birds and humans in the popular imagination / edited by Danette DiMarco and Timothy Ruppert.
Description: Lanham : Lexington Books, [2022] | Series: Ecocritical theory and practice | Includes bibliographical references and index.
Identifiers: LCCN 2022001941 (print) | LCCN 2022001942 (ebook) | ISBN 9781666901818 (cloth) | ISBN 9781666901832 (paperback) | ISBN 9781666901825 (ebook)
Subjects: LCSH: Birds in literature. | Human-animal relationships. | Nature (Aesthetics) | LCGFT: Essays. | Literary criticism.
Classification: LCC PN56.B56 A94 2022 (print) | LCC PN56.B56 (ebook) | DDC 809/.933628—dc23/eng/20220124
LC record available at https://lccn.loc.gov/2022001941
LC ebook record available at https://lccn.loc.gov/2022001942

*For the birds . . .
and, naturally, for Harold and Heather.*

Contents

Acknowledgments ix

Introduction: The Continuous Line between Birds and Humans in Animal Studies Today 1
Danette DiMarco and Timothy Ruppert

SECTION 1: THE AVIAN-NESS OF AESTHETICS 7

1 Birdwatching and Wordwatching: The Avian Aesthetics of Virginia Woolf's *Mrs. Dalloway* 9
Jemma Deer

2 Birds as Character, Motif, Allusion, and Symbol in Meir Shalev's *A Pigeon and a Boy* 25
Laura Major

3 "With an Aviary Inside Its Head": Surrealist Sensibilities and Avian Ontologies in the Work of J. G. Ballard and Ted Hughes 37
Declan Lloyd

4 The Optimism of Flight: Magical Realism in *Little Nemo in Slumberland* 53
Mark O'Connor

SECTION 2: WRITING ABOUT/LIKE BIRDS 73

5 The Fate of Birds in Anatole France's *Penguin Island* 75
Timothy Ruppert

6	Of Curlews and Crows: Representations of Avian Cognition in North American Animal Stories *Jennifer Schell*	89
7	What Is It Like to Write (Like) a Bird?: Rethinking Literary Practice to Support Avian Subjectivity *Joshua Lobb*	105
8	Margaret Atwood's Bird Narratives *Danette DiMarco*	121

SECTION 3: ENTANGLED WORLDS — 137

9	*The Peregrine*: At the Intersection of Ecocriticism and New Nature Writing *Debarati Bandyopadhyay*	139
10	Helen Macdonald, T. H. White, and Hawks: H is [also] for *History* *Louis J. Boyle*	153
11	Across So Wide a Sea: Humans, Seabirds, and the Kinship of Mortality *Keri Stevenson*	165
12	Window Collisions in Contemporary American Poetry *Calista McRae*	181

SECTION 4: CONSUMERS CONSUMING BIRDS — 197

13	"Their Little Brethren of the Air": Rhetoric of Youth Birding in the United States, 1890s–Present *Laura McGrath*	199
14	Birds Aren't Real: Narrative and Aesthetic Irony in For-Profit Conspiracy *Lauren Shoemaker*	215
15	Laying Eggs: Ludothematic Resonance and the Birds of *Wingspan* *Christopher Moore*	229

Index	249
About the Editors and Contributors	259

Acknowledgments

This project's nascent stages were supported through a sabbatical research leave for Danette, and we are most appreciative to Slippery Rock University for the time granted to her because it helped us to lay a strong foundation for imagining the collection. We extend our thanks to our colleagues in our English Department who have demonstrated care and interest as our endeavor unfolded. Dan Bauer, dean of the College of Liberal Arts, and Nancy Barta-Smith, emeritus professor of English, have also provided unwavering encouragement. The collection benefits inestimably through the artwork of Rebecca E. W. Thomas and Keith Reimink. To our contributors, we extend our deep appreciation for expediting the process. We made many demands quickly, and you responded with alacrity. Finally, we thank Douglas Vakoch for seeing the potential of this project, and Kasey Beduhn for her indefatigable efforts shepherding this book into print.

Introduction

The Continuous Line between Birds and Humans in Animal Studies Today

Danette DiMarco and Timothy Ruppert

Late September 2021 brought an unusual story to news sources in Pittsburgh, Pennsylvania: a Steller's sea eagle named Kodiak, or Kody, flew away from the National Aviary, located in the city's northern section. Soon enough, residents of nearby neighborhoods sighted Kody on front lawns and cobblestone streets, watching him as he made himself as still as an Anthony Smith bronze sculpture. By the time he was found and returned to the aviary in early October, many people had spotted Kody and shared stories of their contact. Not surprisingly, most of these accounts acknowledged how exceptional and strange their experiences with Kody seemed.

While metropolitans seldom see a bird like Kody beyond the mesh netting of a man-made enclosure, it is true nevertheless that human encounters with birds of all sorts have a special influence on our imaginations and hearts alike. Consider, for instance, the case of Mary Oliver's poem, "Winter and the Nuthatch" (2008), in which the speaker laments the shifting loyalties of a bird whom she has hand-fed over several blustery mornings when, early one day, she spots the creature eating from someone else's palm. Hurt at first, Oliver's speaker soon reaches an insight: "Nobody owns the sky or the trees"—a thought reminiscent of the Shawnee leader Tecumseh's admonishment some two centuries ago that no one can "sell the air, the great sea, [or] the earth." But the speaker aligns this idea with a telling qualification: "Nobody owns the hearts of birds." The nuthatch in Oliver's poem lives at a point of intersection with human beings, on the cusp between sky and earth: immediate and elusive, a familiar enigma.

Thom van Dooren's concept of multispecies entanglements underlies the conceptual imaginings of this collection. An entanglements approach serves as a means for challenging human exceptionalism, instead focusing on the necessary intermixing and connecting that implicates humans in the lives of "disappearing others" (van Dooren 5), including birds. Van Dooren turns to stories of diminishing and/or extinct bird populations in *Flight Ways* and *In the Wake of Crows* (2020) to connect humans and birds so that the former are brought "to genuine care and concern" (*Flight* 9) about the latter. Telling stories about birds, for van Dooren, is a way to forge new connections with them.

In *The Bird Way* (2020), Jennifer Ackerman studies birds to reconceive human interpretations of both avian and human lives. With the ability for "complex cognition," birds, according to Ackerman, have been frequently misunderstood by humans due to our own biases, including sensory and geographic ones. More, though, Ackerman's purpose is to get humans to rethink bird intelligence by scrutinizing some intriguing cases of "behavioral flexibility" (15). This flexibility is both an avian and human trait; it is what van Dooren hopes for as he lays bare the human need to better develop and sustain an ethics of care for multispecies intermingling.

The bird-interested chapters within invoke environmental humanities perspectives to say something of value about avian and human lives. Presenting research that bridges their subdisciplinary areas of study (e.g., literature, creative writing, popular culture, and rhetoric) with the study of the environment, the contributing authors expand our current considerations in Animal Studies to include birds, which are the most neglected or marginalized classification. Take, for example, New Zealand's recent decision to name the long-tailed bat as its bird of the year (Gamillo 2021). Good intentions notwithstanding, this choice captures the privileging of the mammal over the avian. This species centrism is changing, especially now that more of the general population recognizes the need for a biodiverse ontology. To close the gap between ornithological and humanities knowledge, this volume of fifteen essays focuses on avian aesthetics to amplify transformations in textual practices in literary, rhetorical, and cultural studies and the environmental humanities.

The book comprises four sections, the first of which, The Avian-ness of Aesthetics, engages questions of both definitional and theoretical merit. In chapter 1, Jemma Deer invites readers to think about the multiplicities inherent in this collection's title. For Deer, aesthetics—here meaning human perceptions of art—might not be arrested in form, but might always be in flight, elusive. By identifying avian aesthetics as the point where birdwatching and wordwatching converge, Deer considers this proximal relationship through examination of Virginia Woolf's *Mrs Dalloway*. Informed by insights from narrative theory, Laura Major investigates, in chapter 2, the textual function of homing pigeons in the intimation of ambivalent national desire as Meir Shalev's *A Pigeon and a Boy* articulates it. Like chapter 2, chapter 3 assesses the significance of symbolic birds, but this time in the literary imaginations of J. G. Ballard and Ted Hughes. Declan Lloyd studies how Ballard and Hughes reperceive and even recalibrate human reality by seeing through birds' eyes, inhabiting their ontologies, or adopting their forms, seeking to discover some unconscious notion of the artistic self. Dreams, myths, and magical realism are cohesive agents in Deer, Major, and Lloyd's chapters, and Mark O'Connor rounds out the section in a study of Winsor McCay's airship series in *Little Nemo in Slumberland*, where McCay makes an ontological shift that fundamentally changes the structure of the comic by celebrating American cities and industrialist profit, to the loss of critical aspects of the environment, including birds.

The volume's second section, Writing About/Like Birds, emphasizes the environmental consequences of bird and human encounters when played out on the imaginative stage, particularly in light of the failures or successes of integrating scientific insight into such transactions. Timothy Ruppert's chapter resuscitates Anatole France's satire *Penguin Island* through a twenty-first-century conservation and nature studies lens, reading the text as a generative entry in the ongoing literary examination of the character of human power and its effects on nonhuman sentient life, as well as on the global ecosystems upon which all life relies. Jennifer Schell carries forward the notion that something of the animal in its real self is compromised by the narrative act or its textual manifestation. In her chapter, she discusses Fred Bodsworth's *The Last of the Curlews* and Kira Buxton's *Hollow Kingdom* with an eye to the inescapable fact that the scientific and narrative elements of avian animal stories do not always cohere. Joshua Lobb reaches a like insight in chapter 7 when he investigates how creative writers access animal consciousness through linguistic means. Implementing Linda Alcoff's definition of *others* to include nonhuman animals, Lobb explores an ethical framework to overcome the power imbalance between human and nonhuman characters in fictional spaces, namely in Philip Temple's *Beak of the Moon*, Daphne du Maurier's "The Birds," and Lobb's own work, *The Flight of Birds*. The character of human and avian relationships receives a slightly different cast in Danette DiMarco's chapter. She examines how bird activist and literary superstar Margaret Atwood negotiates the dilemma of simultaneously providing narrative pleasure as well as educating readers about avian populations in her children's book *For the Birds* and her young adult graphic novel *The Complete Angel Catbird*.

Notions of entanglement take an even more salient position in section 3, Entangled Worlds. In this section, the reader will find four chapters that further journey into questions of the interrelatedness of birds and people. Debarati Bandyopadhyay articulates how John Alec Baker's *The Peregrine* serves as a composite piece that synthesizes New Nature Writing and ecocriticism. Louis J. Boyle analyzes textual intersectionality through the lens of history in Helen Macdonald's *H is for Hawk* and T. H. White's *The Goshawk*. Boyle pays particular attention to the matter of elision in these two works, noting how the authors reconfigure history in different ways in what seems a shared textual practice. This concern with elision intensifies in Keri Stevenson's chapter, in which she reclaims the place of birds in the Blue Humanities from which they have too long been excluded. To accomplish this aim, Stevenson looks at environmental journalist Deborah Cramer's *The Narrow Edge: A Tiny Bird, an Ancient Crab, and an Epic Journey* and the seabird ecologist Carl Safina's *Eye of the Albatross* and *Song for the Blue Ocean*, works in which the intertwined destinies of human communities and seabirds come to the fore. Calista McRae treats a similarly pernicious aspect of bird and human convergences in her chapter on window collisions as depicted in contemporary American poetry. In this way, McRae unpacks the ethical implications engendered when human beings encounter birds in the man-made milieu.

The book's closing section, Consumers Consuming Birds, interrogates the appropriation of birds into the sphere of popular culture. These three chapters address distinct topics of cultural import, beginning with Laura McGrath's look into the rhetoric of youth birding in the United States over the last century. McGrath's chapter expounds on myriad social and political issues that Lauren Shoemaker's chapter addresses in its own overview of the contemporary Birds Aren't Real conspiracy movement. The commodification of birds that Shoemaker describes has a partial corrective in the *Wingspan* board game to which Christopher Moore devotes his chapter on ludothematic resonance. While profits continue to be made, Moore, using game theory, draws the reader's eye to the potential benefits to conservation offered by the entertainment under consideration.

Taken together, these chapters draw necessary attention to the significance and dignity of avian life and invite us to consider, through literary and cultural perspectives, how we can ameliorate our understanding of and disposition toward birds of all sorts. We hope that the title of our collection, and the contents therein, spark insights into the undeniable connectedness between birds and people, what Louise Glück might express as "the one continuous line / that binds us to each other." Through academic approaches to ethical issues, these chapters give flight to the idea that we now must rethink our relationships with birds, lest a creature like Kody continues to exist as a conundrum, at home when in a cage and an anomaly when in the sky.

REFERENCES

Ackerman, Jennifer. 2020. *The Bird Way*. New York: Penguin.

Gamillo, Elizabeth. "New Zealand's Bird of the Year Is . . . a Bat." *Smithsonian Magazine*, November 3, 2021. https://www.smithsonianmag.com/smart-news/new-zealands-long-tailed-bat-is-crowned-bird-of-the-year-180978979/

Glück, Louise. 1992. *The Wild Iris*. New York: ECC.

Guza, Megan. "Stellar's Sea Eagle Kody 'Content to be Back' at National Aviary after 9 Days on the Loose, Officials Say." October 4, 2021. https://triblive.com/local/stellers-sea-eagle-kody-content-to-be-back-at-national-aviary-after-9-days-on-the-loose-officials-say/

Oliver, Mary. 1978. *American Primitive*. New York: Back Bay.

Tecumseh. 1810. "Address to William Henry Harrison on Selling a Country." *American Rhetoric*. Accessed November 27, 2021. https://www.americanrhetoric.com/speeches/nativeamericans/chieftecumseh.htm

van Dooren, Thom. 2014. *Flight Ways: Life and Loss at the Edge of Extinction*. New York: Columbia University Press.

———. 2019. *The Wake of Crows: Living and Dying in Shared Worlds*. New York: Columbia University Press.

Section 1

THE AVIAN-NESS OF AESTHETICS

Chapter 1

Birdwatching and Wordwatching
The Avian Aesthetics of Virginia Woolf's Mrs. Dalloway

Jemma Deer

Avian aesthetics: this is a murmuration of starlings dancing a symphony of shape in waves and curtains of densities and thinnings, metamorphoses of shadow against the sunset sky. Their art is not in total synchrony, nor in total discord, but rather in a graceful tension between the two, followings and stretchings and turnings, like the wayward dynamism that flocks under the surface of what you call your "self." Avian aesthetics: this is the exquisite iridescence of a peacock's plumage, the play of surface and depth like glimmering sunlight on a forest pool, the panache of turquoise, indigo, and gold a product not of pigment but of structure: photons sent on chromatic detours, arriving at your eye transformed by the micro-sorcery of feathers, manipulators of light. Avian aesthetics: this is the song of a nightingale, embroidering the heavy blanket of spring night with threads of piercing color, a stunningly broad spectrum that moves poets to write of its "wild, unquenched, deep-sunken, old-world pain" (Arnold 1877, 48). Avian aesthetics: this is a house-proud bowerbird's exacting display; the shimmering hover of a hummingbird; the staccato choreography of a manakin's dance; the regal glide of a swan on still water, and the rippling train of its wake.

David Abram (2010) recognizes some of the ways in which birds have been "crucial allies for our kind":

> Watching them swoop and glide and carve their way through the air surely ignited many of our human aspirations toward freedom and flight. Their bewildering array of colors and chromatic patterns probably provoked many of our earliest acts of self-adornment, while their feathers figured prominently in human rituals and dances frequently influenced by avian courtship displays.

> Birds have ceaselessly inspired us with their mellifluent voices and polyphonic exchanges, undoubtedly instilling some of our earliest impulses toward song and spoken language. (197)

Birds—creatures that have been making music, visual art, and aesthetic judgments[1] for far longer than humans have—flaunt their aesthetic sense and sensibility and provide the blueprint or muse for much human artistic production. And the parallels between human language and birdsong go beyond poetic metaphor: "songbirds learn their songs the way we learn languages and pass these tunes along in rich cultural traditions that began tens of millions of years ago"; the two learning processes, though independently evolved, rely on "startlingly similar gene activity" (Ackerman 2016, 4, 12).

Human aesthetics follow avian aesthetics, releasing flights of imagination through the mind's sky. But what if we were to read the title-phrase of this book the other way, not as referring to the aesthetics *of* avians, but rather to the avian-ness of aesthetics? What if *aesthetics*—the perception of the arts and the acts and arts of perception—are also continually in flight, airborne, always eluding the grasp of our earth-bound concepts? What if our experience of art is animated by a more-than-human form of life, and moves, like birds, in a mode of which we can only dream?

A figurative link between birds and human language or thought traverses time periods and cultures. We can soar across centuries from Homer's "winged words" to Paul de Man's (1979) remark that meaning is "incessantly [. . .] in flight" (78), and then observe, with novelist George Moore (1936), a graceful, impromptu speaker who "thr[ew] winged phrases into the air that, rising with rapid wing-beats, floated, wheeled, and chased each other like birds," before "perch[ing] with a flutter of wings on a full stop" (268). We can listen to the call of the great horned owl, the Koyukon name for which is *nodneeya*, meaning "tells-you-things" (Griffiths 2000, 223), or watch out for the Norse god Odin's ravens, named Thought and Memory, who "fly every day / the whole world over" (Crawford 2015, 64). We can pay our respects to Thoth, the Egyptian god of writing, speech, and the alphabet, often depicted with the head of an ibis—a monochrome wading bird with a slender neck and down-curving bill, whose pale body and pitch-black head make it appear to have been dipped, beak-first, in ink. Perhaps Hélène Cixous (1998) was recalling the ibis-head of Thoth when she wrote of "the pen's beak" and of the way a sentence "swooped down" on her (12, 130). Or perhaps it is an association I'm only landing on now. "Who is to foretell the flight of a word?" as Virginia Woolf (1931) asks (76).

Avian aesthetics: this is the place where birdwatching and wordwatching meet, where feathers or quills let birds or words fly, where wayward meanings hatch out of human words and take to the skies, eluding our grasp.

Watching birds and words calls for a particular form of attentiveness: an attentiveness that traces flight without arresting it, that listens and looks with patience and receptivity, and that is open to the dynamism of a more-than-human form of life. In what follows I will set three watches, three places from which to perceive and attend to the songs and flights of that form of aesthetics we call literary fiction.

FIRST WATCH: BIRDWATCHING WRITING

Woolf was a writer who saw how "when words are pinned down they fold their wings and die," who described unread books as having "put their heads under their wings, and gone to sleep" (Woolf 2009, 90, 75), who wrote of "the packed and fluttering birds' wings, many feathered, folded, of the past," who saw a sentence cross "the empty space between us" "like a fluttering bird" (Woolf 1931, 62, 67). She wrote in a letter how she would "like to tell myself a nice little wild improbable story to spread my wings" (Woolf 1953, 318), characterized herself as "a flight of green birds alighting now and then" (Woolf 2021, n.p.), and, as her mental health declined, says she heard the birds singing to her in Greek choruses (Lee 1997, 195). One of Woolf's characters is "given to increasing the bounds of the moment by flights into past or future" (Woolf 1941, 11), while another sees words as "mov[ing] through the air in flocks, now this way, now that way, moving all together, now dividing, now coming together" (Woolf 1931, 10). Birds are everywhere in Woolf's writing, when you start watching for them. You could follow the lines of flight and rhythms of song that birds trace between Woolf's texts, but here we will restrict ourselves to *Mrs Dalloway*: a text that is concerned with birds, words, and various kinds of watching. This is a novel that follows the thoughts, memories, and interactions of a small cast of characters through a single day in London, in June 1923—including the eponymous Clarissa Dalloway, a high-society woman preparing to host a party, and Septimus Warren Smith, a World-War-I veteran suffering from what we would now call PTSD.

In his introduction to the Oxford edition of the text, David Bradshaw (2000) remarks on the "insistent parallels" drawn between Clarissa and Septimus, including parallels in their experiences and appearances, in their ventriloquizing of each other, in their homoeroticism, but "most important," he says, is in "the projection of both characters as birds":

> Septimus is "beak-nosed" and reminds Lucrezia of "a young hawk", while Clarissa's face is "beaked like a bird's" [. . .]. The screen in Septimus's room has "blue swallows" on it and is matched by Clarissa's drawing-room curtains

depicting "a flight of birds of Paradise". Septimus is described as "hopping [. . .] from foot to foot" before taking flight through his open window, and [. . .] in the first reference to Clarissa's curtain, we read that it "blew out and it seemed as if there were a flight of wings into the room." (xxxvi–xxxviiii)

While, as Bradshaw attests, there are clearly numerous symbolic and structural connections between Clarissa and Septimus, the notion that this birdishness is the "most important" parallel between them is undone by the fact they are not the *only* characters described as birds. Septimus's wife Lucrezia thinks of herself as "like a bird sheltering under the thin hollow of a leaf" and is envisaged by Septimus as "like a bird, falling from branch to branch, and always alighting," or "like a little hen, with her wings spread" (56, 124, 126). William Bradshaw preys, raptor-like, on the vulnerable: "Naked, defenceless, the exhausted, the friendless received the impress of Sir William's will. He swooped; he devoured" (86–7). Peter Walsh is said to be "a little hawk-like" and to "haunt and hover [. . .] swoop and taste" (139, 134). Other characters are described as a "poor goose" (155); having "the eyes of a bird" (150); being "feathered, evanescent, [. . .] alight[ing]" (47); being likely to "die like some bird in a frost gripping her perch" (138); and having "the birdlike freshness of the very aged" (70). Even nonliving and nonmaterial things are swept up in the flock of bird imagery: a newspaper placard "paused, swooped, fluttered" and the buses "swooped, settled, were off" (96, 114) (the asyndetons here miming the perching, hopping movements described); "mystery [. . .] brushed them with her wing" (12); emotion "rose and fluttered away, as a bird touches a branch and rises and flutters away" (37); and Peter sinks "into the plumes and feathers of sleep" (48). Real birds also move through the novel: "the rooks rising, falling" in the sky over Clarissa's remembered past (3); "the slow-swimming happy ducks; the pouched birds waddling" in Regent's Park (5); the "flight of gulls [that] crossed the sky, first one gull leading, then another" (18); the "sparrows fluttering, rising, and falling in jagged fountains" (19); the "swallows swooping, swerving, flinging themselves in and out, round and round" (59); and the birds that "sing freshly and piercingly in Greek words" to Septimus (21), just as they had done to Woolf.

This, then, is a novel of birdwatching: of watching birds and watching people and things that are seen or described *as* birds. But what is the significance of this for making sense of the text? To answer this question, consider a passage from Nicholas Royle's (2017) novel *An English Guide to Birdwatching*, in which one of the characters admits that he would "like to write a novel that would try to do justice to the reality of birds" (54):

Only it couldn't be a novel. [. . .] I dream about the idea of a hide [. . .] the idea of a *text* that would hide, that would *be* a hide, a place from which to look out and look in, a secret place from which it would be possible not only to observe the activity and behaviour of birds and humans, say, but also to observe the novel itself, a kind of screened-off or embedded space within a novel in which it would be possible to explore the relations between birds and words, birdwatching and wordwatching. (54–5)

Various aspects of the novel indicate that the dream-text of which the character speaks is the text in or through which he speaks: the one we are now reading. The novel comprises two parts, "The Undertaking" and "The Hides." Like physical hides (huts from which to watch birds), these textual hides offer a kind of space from which to "observe the activity and behaviour of birds and humans" and to "explore the relations between birds and words, birdwatching and wordwatching," "imagin[ing] literature reconceived through flights, songs and visions of birds" (Royle 2017, 292).

The division of the book into two parts is, however, somewhat misleading. For it is not only "The Hides" that offers us "a *text* that would hide, that would *be* a hide, a place from which to look out and look in." Rather, this describes the singular experience of reading the novel itself, whether *An English Guide to Birdwatching*, *Mrs Dalloway*, or any other novel. As Royle's character recognizes, to think of a text as a hide is to recognize the uncanny space that fiction inhabits, renders, or constitutes: a space from which you see all sorts of things—not just characters and events, but also internal realities, thoughts and feelings, as well as non- or more-than-human forces and agencies—but are yourself not seen. Being in a hide, or a book, affords you a temporary relief from visibility, from the modifications of behavior required to moderate your outward presentation. Your attention is free to settle in fullness on what is perceived. The hide (textual or physical) enables a particular form of attention, a hallucinatory, filmic, or dreamlike watching, in which one's sense of self sinks into the dark.

Watching the birds and humans of *Mrs Dalloway*, we find ourselves in one of Royle's textual hides, "a secret place from which [. . .] to observe the activity and behaviour of birds and humans." But such a hide, you remember, is also a place from which "to observe the novel itself," "a place from which to look out and look in" (Royle 2017, 55): that is, two strange and intertwined modes of watching that *Mrs Dalloway* also affords. What is "the novel itself" when it comes to *Mrs Dalloway*? Who or what is "looking out" and "looking in," and from where?

In 1892, William James coined the phrase that would come to define literary modernism's distinctive narrative technique: stream of consciousness. But when we look at the original passage from James's essay, we find that the "stream" quickly metamorphizes into the flight of a bird—or the flight of a sentence: "When we take a general view of the wonderful stream of our consciousness, what strikes us first is the different pace of its parts. Like a bird's life, it seems to be an alternation of flights and perchings. The rhythm of language expresses this, where every thought is expressed in a sentence, and every sentence closed by a period" (James 1892, 75).

The plentiful bird imagery of *Mrs Dalloway* might, then, point to the very form of its narrative, which does not inhere in one character (as a stream of consciousness or otherwise), nor in some unifiable narrative voice (what has problematically been called an "omniscient" narrator[2]), but that rather traces one continuous line of "flights and perchings" through a single day in post-war London, looping and diving through people's thoughts and memories. The novel opens with fifty-one-year-old Clarissa Dalloway stepping outside ("what a morning—fresh as if issued to children on a beach"), before diving, with a "lark" (the playfulness, that is, of *Alauda arvensis*, the skylark) and a "plunge" into her memories of being an eighteen-year-old at Bourton, her family home (3). These recollections are brought to rest for a moment as "she stiffened a little on the kerb, waiting for Durtnall's van to pass"—evidently she is walking somewhere—and then the line of narration hops over for a moment to look out from the eyes of a passerby: "A charming woman, Scrope Purvis thought her [. . .]; a touch of the bird about her, of the jay [. . .]. There she perched, never seeing him, waiting to cross" (3). As Clarissa walks on, we take off with her and alternate between what she sees and what she thinks as she goes about her morning's tasks: more memories of Bourton triggered by seeing an old friend, and the reflections set off by passing various shops (5–12). In the florists, her absorption in the "delicious scent, the exquisite coolness" of the flowers is interrupted by the "violent explosion" of a motorcar outside (11, 12). The narration too is dragged outside, and zooms out to a bird's-eye view of the cloud of rumor that spreads through the streets regarding the identity of the car's passenger, before landing with and following Septimus and his wife Lucrezia, who also heard the explosion. So the line of narrative continues, tracing a path through the day that dips in and out of various characters as they come into contact, plunges into the past via their memories, and follows what they see, hear, feel, and think.

We find ourselves both "looking out" (of various characters' eyes, seeing what they see) and "looking in" (tracing their thoughts and memories). But, caught up in the flow of the text, we can fail to register the strangeness of the experience, fail to observe "the novel itself" and the uncanny space it renders. In his seminal essay on Woolf's *To the Lighthouse*, Erich Auerbach (2013) reflects on the elusive nature of the narration: it is a voice, he says, that cannot be identified with Woolf herself, nor with an objective narrator, nor with any of the characters in the novel, perhaps not even with a human person. "It verges upon a realm beyond reality," he writes, "the speakers no longer seem to be human beings at all but spirits between heaven and earth [. . .] capable of penetrating the depths of the human soul [. . .] but not of attaining clarity as to what is in process there" (Auerbach 2013, 532). Auerbach's imagery is ethereal rather than avian, but it does figure the narration as both more-than-human and in flight ("between heaven and earth")—particularly in the way that it untethers itself from the present time and space of the novel: "an insignificant exterior occurrence *releases* ideas and chains of ideas which cut loose from the present of the exterior occurrence and *range freely* through the depths of time" (540, emphasis added). While this style of narration was a modernist innovation—and one for which, as Auerbach recognizes, Woolf demonstrated a particular "insight and mastery" (552)—the flighty stream of consciousness that it aimed to render is as old as humans. Perhaps the many birds and bird images that flock through the pages of *Mrs Dalloway* signal not only the form of the novel itself, but the form of human imagination to which she was so sensitive: the airborne quality of what thinks, imagines, dreams, writes, and reads.

SECOND WATCH: READING AUGURY

Augury is the ancient practice of "predicting the future, revealing hidden truths, or obtaining guidance" from the observation of birds (*OED*). But the notion that one might find "special providence in the fall of a sparrow" (Shakespeare, *Hamlet* 5.2.166–7) might today appear at best archaic and at worst ridiculous. Augury finds or makes meaning where there is none. It is a practice, as Dale Pendell (2009) writes in *The Language of Birds: Some Notes on Chance and Divination*, of "divining, glimpsing, seeing forms in chaos" (13), a practice estranged from a world of so-called "modern" thinking and "enlightened" science, where to cloud causation with correlation is an inexcusable lapse.

Yet are we immune to the inspired or hallucinatory madness of such divinations? Or do we too see forms in chaos, find or create meaning where there is none? As a reading practice, augury links birdwatching to wordwatching. When you see meaning in a text, you participate in a process of creative invention not entirely different from the work of augurs: "Meaning is not in words. Meaning lies between the lines, between the sheets, embedded in sentence. Or sentience" (Pendell 2009, 63). Meaning does not lie dormant in the text, waiting for the spring warmth cast by a reader's gaze to awaken it from hibernation. Rather, the act of reading—the encounter between sentence and sentience—produces and creates meaning, which therefore inheres in the *relation* between the text and reader, not in the text itself. Reading augments texts, augments reality ("augment" and "augur" come from the Latin *augēre*, "to increase"): we are all augurs when we read. This is why we cannot say, finally, what a word or a text means; we cannot exclude the possibility of other meanings, other readings: new forms hatching or emerging, escaping our grasp.

Mrs Dalloway is a text caught up in the reading of birds and signs—and in their resistance to reading. It shows how meaning-making is a creative process: an effect of context, of relation; it might be a trick of the light. Ambiguity—a freedom of meaning—is cast as generative, while there is a precipitate danger in capturing absolute and final meaning: a cage from which the only escape is death. The novel's various scenes of reading include: the aforementioned motorcar explosion, which gives rise to speculation over the passenger's identity; an airplane writing letters in the sky, and the attempts to read its message; Septimus's cryptic drawings and his interpretation of the Greek-singing birds; the "battered" woman's "ancient song," which, though it is said to have an "absence of all human meaning," gives rise to her epic story of "love which has lasted a million years" (68–9); and the news of Septimus's suicide reaching Clarissa's party, which she reads as "her disaster—her disgrace" (157).

Some of these instances have explicit or implicit relations to birds. When the "violent explosion" of the motorcar draws attention, "passers-by [. . .] had just time to see a face of the very greatest importance against the dove-grey upholstery, before a male hand drew the blind and there was nothing to be seen except a square of dove grey" (12). The slightly awkward repetition of "dove grey" serves to underline the elusively avian aspect of the sighting, and ties together both the framing and the obscuring of meaning—"a face of greatest importance" is seen *against* "the dove-grey upholstery," before that same "dove grey" *covers* the face and forecloses certainty as to its identity, releasing ambiguity and speculation to the wind:

> Rumours were at once in circulation from the middle of Bond Street to Oxford Street on one side, to Atkinson's scent shop on the other, passing invisibly, inaudibly, like a cloud, swift, veil-like upon hills, falling indeed with something of a cloud's sudden sobriety and stillness upon faces which a second before had been utterly disorderly. But now mystery had brushed them with her wing; they had heard the voice of authority; the spirit of religion was abroad with her eyes bandaged tight and her lips gaping wide. But nobody knew whose face had been seen. Was it the Prince of Wales's, the Queen's, the Prime Minister's? Whose face was it? Nobody knew. (12)

The narration then follows the car through London, and any assurance about the face behind the blind—Clarissa's belief that it is the Queen; Moll Pratt's that "it was the Prince of Wales for certain" (15, 16)—is diluted in the variousness of opinion. But the mystery and ambiguity *augment* the significance of the occasion, which is therefore cast as transcendent, mystical: "the spirit of religion was abroad," bringing "sobriety and stillness upon faces." In contrast to the image of the cloud-like dispersal of rumor experienced by most of the characters, Septimus experiences a "gradual drawing together of everything to one centre before his eyes," and interprets the commotion caused by the car as concerning him: "It is I who am blocking the way, he thought. Was he not being looked at and pointed at; was he not weighted there, rooted to the pavement, for a purpose?" (13). His reading is without ambiguity, but it is a conviction that claws at his sanity.

Shortly after this scene, attention is drawn upward by an airplane writing in the sky, tracing a cursive that summons onlookers to an act of reading cast as a kind of modern augury:

> the aeroplane soared straight up, curved in a loop, raced, sank, rose, and whatever it did, wherever it went, out fluttered behind it a thick ruffled bar of white smoke which curled and wreathed upon the sky in letters. But what letters? A C was it? an E, then an L? Only for a moment did they lie still; then they moved and melted and were rubbed out up in the sky, and the aeroplane shot further away and again, in a fresh space of sky, began writing a K, and E, a Y perhaps?
>
> "Glaxo," said Mrs Coates in a strained, awestricken voice, gazing straight up [. . .].
>
> "Kreemo," murmured Mrs Bletchley, like a sleepwalker. With his hat held out perfectly still in his hand, Mr Bowley gazed straight up. All down the Mall people were standing and looking up into the sky. As they looked the whole world became perfectly silent, and a flight of gulls crossed the sky, first one gull leading, then another, and in this extraordinary silence and peace, in this pallor, in this purity, bells struck eleven times, the sound fading up there among the gulls.
>
> The aeroplane turned and raced and swooped exactly where it liked, swiftly, freely, like a skater—
>
> "That's an E," said Mrs Bletchley—
>
> or a dancer—
>
> "It's toffee," murmured Mr Bowley [. . .]. (17–18)

The words "fluttered" and "ruffled" lend a feathered birdishness to the plane's trail, while the people watching it seem to be in a trance-like state, as if engaged in the divination of something profound: the reverence of Mrs Coates's "strained, awestricken voice" and the "murmur[ing]" of Mrs Bletchley and Mr Bowley is echoed in the apparent "pallor" and "purity" of the moment. And yet this mood of profundity is irresistibly ironized by the fact that what they strain to read is a confectionary advertisement. This satirizes misreading or over-reading: misreading that leaves you with the senselessness of A-C-E-L, letters that remain stubbornly separate, refusing to render any meaning (and thereby demonstrating how meaning inheres in relationality: between letters, between minds); or over-reading that lets you think that you've discovered a K-E-Y where there is none. The transience of the letters mimes the resistance of texts to reading: "Only for a moment did they lie still; then they moved and melted and were rubbed out." Even in a printed text one might find that its message refuses to stay still for long.

This un-pin-downable-ness is not something we should lament, however. Ambiguity, uncertainty, even equivocation, maintains a space of openness and possibility, which is again counterposed by Septimus's pathologically closed mode of reading signs. He interprets the airplane, like the commotion around the car, as a message directed only at him: "So, thought Septimus, looking up, they are signalling to me" (18). This form of reading eschews ambiguity for certainties and absolutes, so that meaning is saturated and non-negotiable; it is a reading that goes by way of madness and ends in death. For Septimus, the pattern of "sparrows fluttering, rising, and falling" conspires with the sound of a child's cry and a horn to create a special significance—"All taken together meant the birth of a new religion" (19)—while his wife's removal of her wedding ring (really because "she had grown so thin"), is read by him not only as the end of their marriage but also as a sign of his new role: "it was decreed that he, Septimus, the lord of men, should be free; alone (since his wife had thrown away her wedding ring; since she had left him), he, Septimus, was alone, called forth in advance of the mass of men to hear the truth, to learn the meaning, which now at last [. . .] was to be given whole" (57).

In *Pip Pip: A Sideways Look at Time*, Jay Griffiths (2000) writes that the past, present, and future all have a different symbolic location:

> The past is underground; it is the place of burial, of geological history, of archeology. The present is at ground-level, those who walk the earth today. And the future is off-ground, its site is the sky, its castles are in the air. In terms of the human mind, if the past is the place of memory and the present is the place of perception, the future is the place of imagination, of thought, of dreams. (202)

We look to the sky and see possibility written there. To find absolute and certain meaning, as Septimus does, is to cage the future, to shut off its space of possibility, and therefore to close down his own. When he tells Lucrezia that he will kill himself, he "explain[ed] how wicked people were; how he could see them making up lies [. . .]. He knew all their thoughts, he said; he knew everything. He knew the meaning of the world, he said" (56–7). Without the generative sky of ambiguity, polysemy, uncertainty, Septimus's future plummets, literally, down to earth.

Jacques Derrida (2005) remarks that "writing is *inaugural*, in the fresh sense of the word" (11). His qualification ("in the fresh sense of the word") points us in the direction of a particular meaning of "inaugural" as marking a beginning or commencement. Writing inaugurates worlds, bringing them into being: not just for the reader but for the writer.[3] But the very need for that qualification draws attention to the fact that there *are* other senses of the word: the freshness of such inauguration will always find itself contaminated by the rich ferment of other senses, which cannot be sterilized away. And so there are at least three other ways in which the statement "writing is *inaugural*" might be read. One might be that sense of increase or augmentation to which I just referred. Another, as Sarah Wood (2013) recognizes, has to do with how "this fresh sense of the word 'inaugural' might concern the revival of its ancient reference to birds"—to the ways in which texts take off, are airborne, their meaning eluding our grasp (29). And finally, to say that "writing is *inaugural*" is to recognize how writing, like augury, depends on reading. It is the *practice* of reading traces, and not the traces themselves, that gives rise to meaning. Writing "does not know where it is going, no knowledge can keep it from the essential precipitation toward the meaning that it constitutes and that is, primarily, its future" (Derrida 2005, 11). Again: "Who is to foretell the flight of a word?" (Woolf 1931, 76).

Woolf too, I think, recognizes writing as inaugural in all these ways, as the various scenes of reading in *Mrs Dalloway* dramatize a lively and birdlike freedom of meaning. The book sees the life of art and the art of life as avian, and encourages us to attend to signs in the same way that we watch birds: without gunshot or capture, without arresting flight. If Septimus's pathologically closed way of reading ends in death, watch how Clarissa revels in a mode of reading that remains asymptotic, drawing dangerously and excitingly close to the "verge" of "some inner meaning," "some astonishing significance," the capture of which is held at bay by an "almost" that leaves the space of reading open:

> It was a sudden revelation, a tinge like a blush which one tried to check and then, as it spread, one yielded to its expansion, and rushed to the farthest verge and there quivered and felt the world come closer, swollen with some astonishing significance, some pressure of rapture [. . .]. Then, for that moment, she had seen an illumination; a match burning in a crocus; an inner meaning *almost* expressed. (27, emphasis added)

THIRD WATCH: AWAKE TO DREAM

The word "watch" comes from the Old English "*wæcnan*," "to wake": to wake up, to be or remain awake. You must be awake to watch or to keep watch, to see what is going on. But when we engage in the watching of birds and words—in attentiveness to more-than-human forms of life and acts of augury—we might need to trouble this easy distinction between sleep and wakefulness. For when we oppose waking life to the world of sleep, we set up a false dichotomy between rationality and irrationality, between the stable "I" of a conscious self, and the shifting phantasmagoria of the unconscious. As Derrida (1976) asks, "The opposition of dream to wakefulness, is not that a representation of metaphysics as well?" (316). It is a dichotomy that fails to acknowledge the rich forms of watching necessary for dreams, and that denies the ways in which waking life is contaminated by the subterranean drifts of what moves beneath rational thought. Perhaps the watching of birds and words requires a form of attention not opposed to dreaming.

In an oneiric essay which meditates on the relations between reading dreams and reading texts, Wood (2013) "reason[s] on the dream and on what it gives us to think" (18):

> The dream beguiles the dreamer, who is at the same time everywhere in the dream. You might be anywhere, you might be water, shore, bird, the rhythm of an event, the relation of elements of a scene, a sentence or a word, a word away from a word, or the field of possibility this relation may open [. . .]. We do not know what is interpretable and what is not, what is psychic machine, what is mere remnant, what is precious. (20)

Dreaming turns you inside-out, so that self as subject or watcher unfolds into the environment of the dream. Everything could be significant, meaningful, readable, and your "self" is no longer what you thought it was. Every sign is a sign of self, which is thus subject to an irrevocable dispersal: "If I am everywhere, I dimly realise, not even half awake, where am I? What am I? Who?" (Wood 2013, 20). But having lost your "self" in or to the world of the dream, you lose the dream too. You realize that the text you are reading— the dream—will always have escaped you. As soon as the dream becomes a dream—that is, upon waking—it has already half flown, and the reading of dreams or texts is also always, and inevitably, an act of rewriting: "The text leaves me behind. It takes off without me, like a bird" (Wood 2013, 21–2).

There are two scenes of dreaming in *Mrs Dalloway* that complicate senses of identity and the identity of sense, and that call us to recognize the dream scene in which we find or lose ourselves whenever we read. One is the sedative-induced sleep of Lucrezia right after Septimus's suicide, and the other is when Peter Walsh, on a bench in Regent's Park, falls "down, down [. . .] into the plumes and feathers of sleep" (48). In that partially conscious state that often accompanies daytime naps, a figure from the waking scene—the "elderly grey nurse" next to whom Peter has sat, and who "resume[s] her knitting" as he falls asleep—accompanies him to the dream world, becoming "the champion of the rights of sleepers, like one of those spectral presences which rise in twilight in woods made of sky and branches" (47, 48). What follows is an enigmatic passage in which Peter is loosened into the general figure of "the solitary traveller" "advancing down the path with his eyes upon sky and branches" (48); in which the gray nurse is cast as both weaver and thread of the scene, "moving her hands indefatigably yet quietly" as she knits beside or inside him (48); and in which the narrative voice is neither identifiable as the dream itself nor as a reading of it. The "plumes and feathers of sleep" spread in a soft succession of images over two pages, culminating in these final paragraphs:

> Such are the visions. The solitary traveller is soon beyond the wood; and there, coming to the door with shaded eyes, possibly to look for his return, with hands raised, with white apron blowing, is an elderly woman who seems [. . .] to seek, over the desert, a lost son; to search for a rider destroyed; to be the figure of the mother whose sons have been killed in the battles of the world. So, as the solitary traveller advances down the village street where the women stand knitting and the men dig in the garden, the evening seems ominous [. . .].
>
> Indoors among ordinary things, the cupboard, the table, the window-sill with its geraniums, suddenly the outline of the landlady, bending to remove the cloth, becomes soft with light, an adorable emblem which only the recollection of cold human contacts forbids us to embrace. She takes the marmalade; she shuts it in the cupboard.
>
> "There is nothing more tonight, sir?"
>
> But to whom does the solitary traveller make reply? (49–50)

The phrase "such are the visions," repeated here for the second time, takes us beyond the singular occurrence of Peter's dream, as if this stands in for some ur-dream: the shared experience of traveling a world beyond waking life. Are the readings of the dream—the fact that the elderly woman "seems [. . .] to be the figure of the mother," that the "evening seems ominous," and that the landlady is cast as an "adorable emblem"—are these readings to be taken as emanating from the dream itself or from Peter's waking recollection of it? Or does this reading only happen through the spectral perspective of the narrative, the dream-hide in which we readers find or lose ourselves? In what placeless locus "where the women stand knitting" does the weaving and reading of dreams occur? The closing question ("to whom does the solitary traveller make reply?"), which again issues from a source not clearly identifiable with either dream or "external" narrative, foregrounds this uncertainty: the source of the dream, and therefore the source of the question, remains unidentifiable: it is neither self nor world.

As a reader, when you drop into "the plumes and feathers" of *Mrs Dalloway*, when you journey as a solitary traveler through the question posed by the text, you must accept that you do not and cannot know "to whom"—or to what—you make your reply. As Cixous (1993) writes, "texts escape us as the dream escapes us on waking" (98). Dreams and texts will have always already flown, but this is what makes them worth chasing. It is why the work of reading is never finished, for to capture the text is to put it to death: "We must know how to treat the dream as a dream, to leave it free, and to distrust all the exterior and interior demons that destroy dreams" (Cixous 1993, 107). The avian aesthetics of *Mrs Dalloway*, in its flights of birds and auguries and dreams, asks us to leave the text free, to watch it escape without pinning or penning it down. Its closing line—"For there she was" (165)—stages an appearance that is also a disappearance. It describes a moment or place from which the woman Clarissa Dalloway or the novel *Mrs Dalloway* has already flown: she *was* there, but where or who or what she *is* remains out of sight. I watch as the text traces a message on my mind's sky, that, appearing to disappear, might have said that our acts of reading-augury will have been birds or dreams.

NOTES

1. "To probe whether birds might be capable of making distinctions based on human concepts of beauty, [Shigeru] Watanabe trained pigeons to distinguish between 'good' and 'bad' paintings, as defined by human critics. He found that the birds could indeed pick out the beautiful from the ugly using cues of color, pattern, and texture" (Ackerman 2016, 189).

2. In *The Uncanny*, Royle (2003) explores why the term "omniscient" narration fails to account for what goes on in literary texts:

> The continuing use of the term "omniscience" serves to promote and protect the thinking of the world of narrative fiction as holistic, unified and closed. It colludes with a thinking of the experience of reading as asserting or presupposing a fixed and totalising interpretation. It thus helps to ward off the transformative possibilities of reading, to limit and close down in advance what is incalculable and unprogrammable in the experience of a text. (259)

3. I have written at more length on the indistinction between the writer and reader elsewhere (Deer 2020, 78, 171).

REFERENCES

Abram, David. 2010. *Becoming Animal: An Earthly Cosmology*. New York: Pantheon.

Ackerman, Jennifer. 2016. *The Genius of Birds*. New York: Penguin.

Arnold, Matthew. 1877. "Philomela." *Poems by Matthew Arnold*. London: Macmillan.

Auerbach, Erich. 2013. *Mimesis: The Representation of Reality in Western Literature*, translated by Willard R. Trask. Princeton: Princeton University Press.

Bradshaw, David. 2000. "Introduction." In Virginia Woolf. *Mrs Dalloway*. Oxford: Oxford University Press.

Cixous, Hélène. 1993. *Three Steps on the Ladder of Writing*, translated by Sarah Cornell and Susan Sellers. New York: Columbia University Press.

———. 1998. *Stigmata*. London: Routledge.

Crawford, Jackson. 2015. *The Poetic Edda: Stories of the Norse Gods and Heroes*. Indianapolis: Hackett.

de Man, Paul. 1979. *Allegories of Reading: Figural Language in Rousseau, Nietzsche, Rilke, and Proust*. New Haven: Yale University Press.

Deer, Jemma. 2020. *Radical Animism: Reading for the End of the World*. London: Bloomsbury.

Derrida, Jacques. 1976. *Of Grammatology*, translated by Gayatri Chakravorty Spivak. Baltimore: Johns Hopkins University Press.

———. 2005. *Writing and Difference*, translated by Alan Bass. London: Routledge.

Griffiths, Jay. 2000. *Pip Pip: A Sideways Look at Time*. London: Flamingo.

James, William. 1892. Rep. 1997. "The Stream of Consciousness." In *The Nature of Consciousness: Philosophical Debates*, edited by Frank H. Tainter, Owen Flanagan, and Güven Güzeldere. Cambridge: MIT.

Lee, Hermione. 1997. *Virginia Woolf*. London: Vintage.

Moore, George. 1919. Rep. 1936. *Avowals*. London: William Heinemann.

Pendell, Dale. 2009. *The Language of Birds: Some Notes on Chance and Divination*. Three Hands Press.

Royle, Nicholas. 2003. *The Uncanny*. Manchester: Manchester University Press.

———. 2017. *An English Guide to Birdwatching*. Brighton: Myriad.

Wood, Sarah. 2013. "Swans of Life (External Provocations and Autobiographical Flights That Teach Us How to Read)." In *The Animal Question in Deconstruction*, edited by Lynn Turner. Edinburgh: Edinburgh University Press.

Woolf, Virginia. 1925. Rep. 2000. *Mrs Dalloway*. Oxford: Oxford University Press.

———. 1931. Rep. 1990. *The Waves*. London: Hogarth.

———. 1941. *Between the Acts*. London: Penguin.

———. 1953. *A Writer's Diary*, edited by Leonard Woolf. London: Harcourt.

———. 2009. *Selected Essays*, edited by David Bradshaw. Oxford: Oxford University Press.

———. 2021. *Love Letters: Vita and Virginia*, edited by Alison Bechdel. London: Random House.

Chapter 2

Birds as Character, Motif, Allusion, and Symbol in Meir Shalev's *A Pigeon and a Boy*

Laura Major

As evidenced by its title, birds, specifically homing pigeons, play a central role in Meir Shalev's 2006 prizewinning novel *A Pigeon and a Boy* (*Yona Ve'naar*). Not only do pigeons drive the plot, they also function symbolically. In addition, they serve as vehicles into the fantastical in an otherwise realistic novel, and the fantastical elements destabilize the realistic narrative, posing questions about myth in the national story.

The novel is about conception (of a child) and inception (of a nation), about love (parental and romantic) and war (the 1948 Israeli War of Independence), about birth (of nation and child) and death (of the boy/father and of the mother), and about what a home is, nationally and personally. Narrated by Yair Mendelsohn, who is an Israeli tour guide specializing in birdwatching tours, the novel intertwines his contemporary love story with the dramatic love story of Yair's mother and "the Baby," as the pigeon handler in the novel is known. Both the Baby and Yair's mother, or "the Girl," as she is called, are pigeon handlers for the Palmach (a clandestine military force working against the British in 1948), who train homing pigeons to carry vital communications from the battlefield. The Baby is mortally wounded in the war, and his final act is to dispatch his sperm by pigeon to the Girl, who conceives Yair by inserting the sperm in a sexless and rather miraculous conception.

This chapter focuses on the multiple functions of pigeons in the novel, employing the insights of narrative theory to analyze the telling of this remarkable tale, and showing the connection between ideology and narrative technique—with its shifts in focalization and temporality. The narrative framework, presenting a detour from the discussion of pigeons in the novel, in fact lays the foundation for this discussion by establishing a paradigm for reading. In addition, this essay examines how symbolism in the text functions to express national desire, not naïvely, but sometimes ambivalently, sometimes hesitantly, in conversation with ancient and modern texts. Finally, the interplay between the national and the personal will be explored through the tropes of home represented by pigeons.

Shalev introduces the pigeon of his novel directly in the first sentence, and this bird will return as a character, motif, symbol, fantastical creature, and biblical allusion. Pigeons are the most prosaic and ubiquitous of birds, neither particularly beautiful nor colorful. In fact, they are often considered vexing. Although the pigeon is really the same species as the dove (in fact pigeon is simply the French translation of dove, and in the Hebrew original of Shalev's novel, the same word—*yona*—describes both), this bird is often considered inferior to its whiter and more diminutive sibling. But the homing, or messenger, pigeon possesses a unique ability to find its way home over considerable distance, making it an important war communications instrument prior to the technological age. Andrew Blechman claims that no animal "has developed as unique and continuous a relationship with humans as the common pigeon" (Blechman 2007, 3–4), and it is on this history between the human and the pigeon that Shalev draws in this novel.

The paradoxical nature of the pigeon, both commonly plain and exceptional, is embedded in the first real description thereof in the novel:

> A plain looking pigeon: bluish gray with scarlet legs and two dark stripes like those of a prayer shawl adorning the wings. A pigeon like a thousand others, like any other pigeon. Only an expert's ears could pick up on the power of those beating wings, double that of normal pigeons; only an expert's eyes could discern the width and depth of the bird's breast [. . .]. Only the heart of the pigeon fancier could grasp and contain the longing that has collected inside such a bird and determined its course and forged its strength. (Shalev 2007, 4–5)[1]

The pigeon is "plain," "like any other pigeon," yet concealed within is its unique ability—its wing power, its increased breast span, and its "yearning for home" (5). Even the simile describing this "plain" bird is taken from the spiritual realm, compared as it is to the traditional Jewish prayer shawl, or *tallit*, with its dark stripes. The very use of this spiritual symbolism, together with the description of the pigeon's hidden abilities, contests the pigeon's external appearance as prosaic and common.

Furthermore, the "yearning for home" that characterizes the pigeon also characterizes the narrator-protagonist, Yair Mendelsohn. Yair takes the money his mother left him for this purpose: "go find yourself a home [. . .] A place of your very own" (18), and embarks on a quest for such a home. He announces explicitly, several times: "I went / set out to find myself a home" (18, 103). And in this novel, home is personified: the mother teaches her sons to address their home, always pronouncing "Hello house" (31, 32, 42, 103, 105) before entering. She also attributes emotions to a home: "the house was happy" (32). Yair knows that he has found the right home when "the house breathed and answered" (105).

Moreover, the ongoing desire for home characterizes the Jewish people. In fact, the land of Israel has been imagined for centuries of exile through the metaphor of home, so much so that the idea of the land, or homeland, is almost synonymous with the idea of home, a trope reinforced in prayers and Jewish poetry through the ages. Dr. Laufer, the veterinarian in the book, will ask later in the novel, somewhat in reverse: "Who but the Jewish people returning to their homeland can better appreciate the tremendous yearning of the pigeon for the home and homeland" (66). The pigeon embodies the desire for home.

Much of the delight of this novel is found in its narrative structure. Gérard Genette introduces some significant terminology that breaks with the age-old descriptors of narrators. He differentiates between homodiegetic narrative, otherwise known as first-person, and heterodiegetic narrative, otherwise known as third-person, when the narrator is not a character in the story. Yair Mendelsohn is both a homodiegetic and heterodiegetic narrator. He tells his own contemporary story, as an experiencing-I (Jahn 2021, 5). He also tells his mother's story, which is embedded in the contemporary story, but is not an experiencing-I during this narration. Rather, he is almost entirely outside the story even though it is the tale of his inception.

This mixed narration is curious. When Yair Mendelsohn tells his own story as homodiegetic narrator, the reader knows that he is limited by his human subjectivity. But when he relates the back story of his mother and the Baby, or the pigeon handler, as a heterodiegetic narrator, "somebody who is not [. . .] a character in the world of the story" (Jahn 2021, 8), the reader must accept his omniscience despite his absence. The first-person narrator, given human limitations, cannot know what is going on in another character's mind. By making Yair Mendelsohn the narrator of his mother's story, Shalev transgresses certain narrative norms, in that the narrator tells more than the character could possibly know. Genette identifies this kind of transgression of norm established by the focalization of a text as paralepsis (Genette 1972, 211). To enable the reader to believe his narration, the heterodiegetic narrator, while known to the reader as Yair Mendelsohn, makes himself much more covert than in the homodiegetic narration. However, the embedded narrative (the mother's story) and the primary narrative (Yair's story) merge through the vehicle of the pigeon. Yair's narratorial presence grows more and more overt as he moves back to the position of homodiegetic narrator.

As the narrative progresses, Yair addresses his homodiegetic narration to his mother. In fact, in the brief and highly reflective twenty-first chapter, Yair tells his mother: "You are not the central character of this story. I am. Not you, but your son" (273). That Yair feels the need to differentiate himself and his story from his mother and her story, intertwined as it is with his own, reveals his ongoing difficulty in extricating himself from her. In his attempt to separate himself from her, he takes possession of her story and tells it as his: "I shorten it and lengthen it, I fabricate and I confess" (272). We might even say that he undermines himself as heterodiegetic narrator, reminding readers that he, who is not a character in the world of his mother's story, is not a reliable narrator.

Shalev here adopts focalization, a term that Genette uses to replace point of view or perspective (Niederhoff 2011). Burkhard Niederhoff (2011) explains that for Genette focalization is about the amount of knowledge and information a narrator has, a topic identified in classic literary analysis as omniscience. What was wrong with the popular terms first-person narration, omniscience, and point of view? Genette claims that using the term "focalization" dismisses the confusion of "the question who sees? and the question who speaks?" (Genette 1988, 186) and clarifies "the question who is the character whose point of view orients the narrative perspective" (Niederhoff 2011). In the heterodiegetic narration of Yair Mendelsohn's mother's story, the internal focalization shifts as various characters (e.g., the mother, the father, the pigeon handler) orient the narrative perspective. For example, in this description of the Baby dispatching a pigeon, Yair cannot possibly know the content of his narration; thus, the focalization shifts to the Baby: "His gaze escorted her as she grew distant, his lips wishing her a safe and swift journey. There is joy and newness in every dispatch, he thought to himself" (Shalev, 63).

Manfred Jahn (2021) claims that readers of fiction, or "prose narratives," "establish their narrative situation quickly [. . .] and then stick to it throughout the whole text" (10). He warns, however, "that there are texts that switch narrative situation from one chapter to the next" (2021, 10). In *A Pigeon and a Boy* Shalev moves between the homodiegetic and heterodiegetic narrator (who is the same character in the novel) from chapter to chapter, and Jahn's warning establishes that this multiplicity of perspectives is unusual and that there is thematic and ideological significance in this narrative choice.

Finally, the issue of temporality, or sequentiality, is significant when discussing narration in this novel. Sequentiality refers to the accord or lack thereof between the order in which events are narrated vís-a-vís the order in which the events in the story occur. Genette discusses distinct types of discordance between the order of narrative and that of the story resulting mostly from analepses (flashbacks) and prolepses (flashforwards) (Genette 1972, 84). The absence of a clear-cut temporal order produces a more engrossing and denser plot:

As in straightforward narrative, we wonder what will happen next, but, since important facts are being concealed from us for the moment, we also wonder what has happened. That is, curiosity is the reader's main passion here, or curiosity combined with suspense. We wonder about the nature of the past in order to explain the present, but we also wonder about the way in which the past will be revealed, the revelation of its full hold on the present. (Angel 1990, 4)

In *A Pigeon and a Boy*, the narrative constantly shifts between the homodiegetic telling of the narrator's past (as a child and as an adult) and heterodiegetic telling of the narrator's mother's past. However, at each of these points in the narrative, the symbols and motifs of pigeon, home (national and personal), yearning, and family are repeated, and in these recurrences the distance and discord shrink. For example, in the magical realism of the novel, talking pigeons utter the same words in both Yair's and his mother's stories. Or, in the contemporary story, Yair's lover Tirzah destroys the pigeons' nests in the roof of the home she is renovating for Yair, calling them "filthy birds" (Shalev, 188) and ironically stating "that's all you need: pigeons on your head" (Shalev, 188). In fact, Yair does have pigeons on his head, or mind, and destroying those living in the roof does not eliminate their presence in his psyche. That pigeons are at the same time "filthy," bothersome, and magical once again drives home their paradoxical nature.

At two points in this otherwise realistic novel, fantastical events occur involving pigeons. The first is when the Baby, mortally wounded in the battle of San Simon, dispatches the Girl's pigeon (which the Baby had taken with him in order to communicate with her) with a vial of his sperm. The pigeon, on arriving with this unique parcel, the contents of which the Girl inserts by syringe into her body, thus conceiving Yair, in a fantastical sexless conception, begins to speak to the Girl. The Girl asks questions about the journey and the Baby, whose very nickname becomes highly significant at this moment of conception. The pigeon recalls the Baby's last actions: "the trickle, the pouring, the closing and affixing of the capsule to my leg. He took hold of me, crawled, dispatched and expired" (245). The pigeon further declares: "I am the flesh and the soul, I am the breeze of the body and the burden of love, I am wind and strength" (245). The chief pigeon handler, Dr. Laufer, sensing drama at the zoo, rushes to the Girl, who informs him of the Baby's death, announced to her by both the Baby and the pigeon. Dr. Laufer asks: "How can a person announce his own death? How can pigeons converse? This cannot be!" (247). In asking, he returns the novel to its realism, not before declaring the event "a miraculous new story" to be reported at "our next convention for pigeon handlers" (247). Miracles aside, the violent underpinnings of the narrator's conception, with the bloody death of his biological father, parallel the violence inherent in the inception of the nation.

In the second instance of talking pigeons, Yair sleeps in his new home, the home his lover Tirzah has renovated for him, the home away from his wife Liora's apartment, and dreams about his mother, the narrative's addressee. As he awakes from his dream, he sees a pigeon on the floor, "a completely plain looking pigeon [. . .] like a thousand others" (299). Unlike the Girl, who welcomes her talking pigeon, Yair orders the pigeon away, saying "Not in this house. Not in my home. Not You" (300), pursuing and hitting it with a plank. But the pigeon declares the same words as did the Girl's pigeon: "I am the flesh and the soul [. . .]. I am the breeze of the body and the burden of love. I am wind and strength" (300). Unmoved, and in a violent and rash act, Yair decapitates the bird, rips out its organs, and then "roasted [. . .] and ate her" (301). He tries to wash away the violence but is haunted by "soft crowing" coming from "the highest heaven but from my deepest depths as well" (301).

According to Henrik Scov Nielsen, magical events such as these within the realistic narration "cue the reader to employ interpretational strategies that are different from those she employs in nonfictionalized, conversational storytelling situations" (Alber et al. 2016, 72). Nielsen continues:

> Such narratives may have temporalities, storyworlds, mind representations, or acts of narration that would have to be construed as physically, logically, mnemonically, or psychologically impossible or implausible in real-world storytelling situations, but that allow the reader to interpret them instead as reliable, possible, and/or authoritative by cueing her to change her interpretational strategies. (Alber et al. 2016, 72)

Applying such alternative interpretational strategies, Efraim Sicher and Shuly Eilat (2013) suggest that Yair "is trapped in the cycle of historical violence not only in the story of his birth, but also in his relationships with domineering women, and he cannot free himself from these ties except by eliminating the figure of the father in an Oedipal love-hate relationship with the mother and the nation" (110). The figure of the father is accordingly symbolized by the pigeon, who is proxy for the Baby, Yair's father. The Oedipal killing of the father is then, according to Sicher and Eilat, "acted out in Yair's ritualistic killing of the dove and cannibalistic eating of the Christological symbol of divine conception" (110). In this act, Yair attempts to release himself from the burden of his national and personal story, from the burden of violence, bloodshed, and death that has dictated his life, his personal relationships, and his home/homeland. He tries to break free in his own "War of Independence" from everything paralyzing him and holding him back.

While Sicher and Eilat see the slaying of the pigeon as an Oedipal destruction of the father, it might be argued equally that it represents a symbolic slaying of the mother. As discussed above, Yair's story and indeed his whole life is inextricably linked to that of his mother—the Girl—and the pigeon handler. Indeed, as early as "six months old his mother brought him to a pigeon handler's conference" (248). And later, his life is attended by her story with pigeons at its center: "the wounded pigeon [. . .] and of the pigeon loft in the Tel Aviv zoo and of Dr. Laufer [. . .] and of Miriam the pigeon handler and of the Belgian pigeon" (273). Of course, Yair himself was, so to speak, dispatched by the Baby to his mother by pigeon. His mother is almost synonymous with pigeons. That Yair chooses to guide birdwatching tours, focusing on cranes, pelicans, storks, and vultures, might also show his complicated relationship with his mother. He is solidly involved with the avian world but stays far away from pigeons. In his impulsive and violent decapitation and destruction of the pigeon, Yair might also be symbolically battling the weight of his mother's story upon him and his life.

Smadar Shiffman (1993) argues that magical realism in Shalev serves to "reconsider the possibility of things we have automatically classified as impossible" (266), for example the very creation of a Zionist state. Shiffman draws on Tzvetan Todorov's conceptions of the magical, describing how in Shalev, "the extraordinary events occur in a natural and familiar environment" and "no natural explanation is forthcoming for the 'supernatural' occurrences" (258). Shiffman argues that Shalev's brand of the fantastic blurs the line we typically draw "between the possible and the impossible, natural and unnatural, object(ive) and subject(ive)" and that this blurring "is immanent to the represented world" (Shiffman 1993, 260). Robert Alter (1996) dissents, claiming that the antirealist moments "serve to throw the realistically represented world into sharper focus" (158). According to Alter, the use of magical realism is the author's way of coping "imaginatively with the constrictions of Israeli existence" (166).

Both Shiffman and Alter, though in disparate ways, connect magical realism to nationhood—Shiffman, drawing attention to the possible impossibility of the Zionist project, and Alter, focusing on the fantastical working "within, and against" the Israeli reality of "constriction and intractability" (166). Joyce Wexler (2002) expands on the connections between magical realism and nationhood, focusing on symbolism: "But realism cannot establish commonality or create a distinct identity. National identity requires some unifying principle that transcends empirical experience, some conviction that events are related to one another, some constant to establish a pattern among events" (138). Thus, Wexler continues, various postcolonial novelists "have discovered that magic realism promotes national identity because it represents the empirical reality of the historical past and present while also expressing longings that transcend the flux of events" (139). Notwithstanding the debate between postcolonial scholars regarding the legitimacy of magical realism in national narratives, with one side arguing that it effaces history and the other that it "makes the contingencies of history resonate with meanings" (Wexler 2002, 151), the symbolic function of the pigeon in its magical manifestation clearly expresses a national desire and collective identity.

Wexler argues that "paradoxically, realism can make nations appear surprisingly similar, while the unrealistic aspects of magic realism can make them distinctive by expressing desire in original ways" (142). In two magical-real scenes, Shalev expresses this national desire (interweaved with the personal) through the pigeon, such a contradictory yet resonant symbol in Hebrew literature from the Bible onward. That the pigeon in both instances of its magical speech announces itself to be the "burden of love" highlights its paradoxical symbolism: it is the symbol of peace yet carries messages in war; it is the symbol of love, yet Yair slaughters it in hatred; it brings about Yair's life yet heralds the Baby's death.

To really understand Yair's slaying of the pigeon, its deeper symbolic or even mythical resonance should be further explored. Shalev has said: "I believe myself to be part of a very long dynasty of Hebrew writers that started 3,000 years ago" (Cooper 2019). As such, he is in dialogue with a continuum of texts, from formative biblical to modern works, that accompanied the establishment of the Zionist state. And many of these texts draw on the multifaceted symbolism of the *yona*—the dove or pigeon. The dove is first mentioned in Genesis, when Noah, following the deluge, dispatches the bird in search of dry land. When it returns, "in her mouth was an olive leaf plucked off; so Noah knew that the waters were abated from off the earth" (Genesis 8:11). From this point, the dove becomes a symbol of peace, heralding the end of God's wrath. Dr. Laufer, in his unique ability to view everything through the lens of the homing pigeons, sees something further in this biblical tale, as inspiration for his dream to train two-directional pigeons: "Even the dove that returned to Noah's ark," he says, "could be seen as a homing pigeon returning to a portable dovecoat" (Shalev, 196).

In Leviticus 1:14 only one type of bird is permitted for ritual sacrifice, and that is the pigeon or turtledove. The pigeon was considered the sacrifice of the poor (Leviticus 14:21), of those who could not afford a bullock or lamb, and this reinforces the image of the pigeon or dove as common. Nahmanides, the biblical commentator, explains that the turtledove and young pigeon were chosen to symbolize the attribute of cleaving, loyalty, and steadfastness.[2] This symbolism is carried through also in the Song of Songs, which metaphorically describes the love between the Israelites and their God through the dove, with the eyes of doves standing for the faithful, faultless,[3] and beloved nation.[4] Indeed Dr. Laufer quotes the Song of Songs, referring to "*yonati tamati*, my undefiled dove of innocence" (Shalev, 66). In Talmudic literature, the dove takes on further meaning and is compared to the spirit of God, known in Hebrew as the *shechina*[5]: "And the spirit of God hovered over the face of the waters—like a dove which hovers over her young without touching [them]" (Talmud, Tractate Moed, Hagigah, 15a). Once again, the paradoxical nature of the pigeon or dove, on one hand the cheapest sacrifice in the temple and on the other a metaphor for the very presence of God, is manifest in biblical and Talmudic symbolism.

Hayyim Nachman Bialik, the national poet of the Jewish people, who happened to also be a biblical scholar, taps into this latter symbolism in his poem "Behind the Fence," from which the title of Shalev's book is taken. Incidentally, the mother's apartment in Tel Aviv is located on Bialik Street. Dr. Laufer explains to the Girl how homing pigeons "belong to a place" and not to people. He explains "that is why they are called *home*-ing pigeons in English" (Shalev, 77). The Girl cleverly suggests that this English name is actually "from the Hebrew word *homiya* [trans. longing]" (77), to which Dr. Laufer quotes Bialik: "light colored pigeon of my longing, my dove / Wings of the ship she does guide from above" (77). In Bialik's poem, the speaker expresses a deep longing to enter "the promised land," but "my key is broken and the door is locked."[6] The personal, spiritual, and national longing are all interweaved in Bialik's poem: the "pigeon of my longing" is the very desire of the *shechina* to dwell in "the promised land," but is accompanied by the boy's desire to enter "the gate."

The poem's third and final eponymous stanza betrays a futility in this personal and national longing:

There is no voice and no answer.[7]
And a pigeon and a boy
Still knock
On the door of the gate.[8]

The eternal knocking, the absence of voice and answer, and the closed door and gate are all part of Yair's story, as he searches for himself, his independence, and his home. The conflation of home and homeland in the Jewish national narrative is a burden for Yair, just like the conflation of his mother's tale with his own. It is similar perhaps to the "burden of love" that the magic pigeon announces itself to be (Shalev, 300). There is after all a conflict between the collective sense of home and the private desire to have a space, a home, away from that burden. The pigeon, a paradoxical figure, embodies the conflict for the narrator.

NOTES

1. From this point, every time I reference the novel, I shall do so without the date.
2. "As long as the pigeon is young it is attached with greater love to the nest where it is reared than are all other fowls. Our Rabbis have mentioned *Shir Hashirim*

Rabbah 1:5 that if a person touches the nest of all other fowls to take therefrom the young ones or the eggs, they leave it and never nest therein again, but the pigeon never abandons it under any condition. And so is [the people of] Israel. They will never exchange their Creator and His Torah."

3. "Let me in, my own, My darling, my faultless dove!" Song of Songs 5:2
4. Song of Songs 1:15, 2:4, 4:1, 5:2, 5:12, 6:9.
5. The *shechina* in Jewish thought is different from the Christian Holy Spirit and refers to "the majestic presence or manifestation of God which has descended to 'dwell' among men." (JewishEncyclopedia.com, s.v. "Shekinah")
6. My translation.
7. 1 Kings 18:6.
8. My translation.

REFERENCES

Atler, Robert. 1996. "Magic Realism in the Israeli Novel." *Prooftexts* 16, no. 2: 151–68. Accessed April 19, 2021. http://www.jstor.org/stable/20689448

Blechman, Andrew D. 2007. *Pigeons: The Fascinating Saga of the World's Most Revered and Reviled Bird*. St. Lucia: University of Queensland Press.

Cooper, Marilyn. 2019. "Meir Shalev: Israel's Dictator-in-Writing." *Moment Magazine*, January 28. https://momentmag.com/meir-shalev-israels-dictator-writing/

Garcia Landa, Jose Angel. 1990. "Time Structure in the Story." *Narrative Theory*, no. 3. n.p. doi: 10.2139/ssrn.2723564

Genette, Gérard 1980. *Narrative Discourse: An Essay in Method*. Translated by Jane E. Lewin. Ithaca: Cornell University Press.

———. 1988. *Narrative Discourse Revisited*. Ithaca: Cornell University Press.

Jahn, Manfred. 2021. *Narratology 2.3: A Guide to the Theory of Narrative*. English Department, University of Cologne. http://www.uni-koeln.de/~ame02/pppn.pdf

"SHEKINAH." JewishEncyclopedia.com. Accessed May 12, 2021. https://jewishencyclopedia.com/articles/13537-shekinah

Nahmanides. "Ramban on Leviticus 1:14:1." *Sefaria*. Accessed May 27, 2021. https://www.sefaria.org/Ramban_on_Leviticus.1.14.1?lang=bi&with=all&lang2=en

Niederhoff, Burkhard. 2011. "The Living Handbook of Narratology." *Focalization: The Living Handbook of Narratology*. Hamburg University. http://www.lhn.uni-hamburg.de/node/18.html

Nielson, Henrik Skov. 2016. "Naturalizing and Unnaturalizing Reading Strategies: Focalization Revisited." In *A Poetics of Unnatural Narrative*. Edited by Jan Alber, Brian Richardson, and Henrik Skov Nielsen. Columbus: The Ohio State University Press.

Sicher, Efraim, and Shuly Eilat. 2013. "Inception of a Nation and the Birth of the Hero: Magic Realism in Meir Shalev's *A Pigeon and a Boy* and Salman Rushdie's *Midnight's Children*." *Symbolism* 12/13: 107–20. doi: 10.1515/9783110297201.107

Shalev, Meir. 2007. *A Pigeon and a Boy.* Translated by Evan Fallenberg. New York: Schocken.

Shiffman, Smadar. 1993. "On the Possibility of Impossible Worlds: Meir Shalev and the Fantastic in Israeli Literature." *Prooftexts* 13, no. 3: 253–67. http://www.jstor.org/stable/20689372

Talmud, Tractate Moed, Hagigah, 15a. Sefaria. Sefaria.org 2017. https://www.sefaria.org/Chagigah.15a.5?lang=he&with=Translations&lang2=he

Wexler, Joyce. 2002. "What Is a Nation? Magic Realism and National Identity in *Midnight's Children* and *Clear Light of Day.*" *The Journal of Commonwealth Literature* 37, no. 2, June: 137–55. doi: 10.1177/002198940203700209

Chapter 3

"With an Aviary Inside Its Head"
Surrealist Sensibilities and Avian Ontologies in the Work of J. G. Ballard and Ted Hughes

Declan Lloyd

This chapter looks to the great significance of birds within the literary imaginary of J. G. Ballard and Ted Hughes. Despite one being a lifelong poet and the other predominantly a prose writer of speculative fiction, their writing bears affinities. Biographical similarities include that both were born in 1930, attended Cambridge in the early 1950s, and lost their wives while at a relatively young age (both women were in their early thirties), which would have a meaningful impact on their writing. Above all, aesthetic and philosophical interests unify these two authors, presenting a central dimension to their works. Ballard and Hughes shared an obsession with the world of myth and the workings of the unconscious mind. Both authors saw their writing as a means to channel some deeper, more primal selfhood, a process intricately interwoven with their explorations of myth and mysticism. Their work often explores something of an upsurgence or reemergence of myth, a realm thinly veiled behind our modern, civilized world.

This chapter addresses some standout works mainly published within the same decade, and which center around birds and avian ontology. These texts also epitomize the idea of an eruption of myth and some lurking unconscious other self. Ballard's *Unlimited Dream Company* (1979) is distinct within his opus for offering a supremely surrealist vision of his hometown of Shepperton, within which any boundary between dream and reality is severed at the outset with the crash-landing and symbolic fall of the aptly named protagonist, Blake. Blake comes to view himself as something of a William Blakean spirit, a messiah driven by the desire to transform the people of Shepperton into gigantic birds, free from the worries of everyday life. Ted Hughes's poetry brims with birds of all kinds, perhaps most notably in his collections

Crow (1970) and *Cave Birds* (1975). The former is a work of similar mythic power and portentous drive, the eponymous corvid emerging out of grief for the loss of Hughes's wife, the poet Sylvia Plath. Crow is a creature of chaos and omens, a trickster spirit who assimilates myths across times and cultures. Many of his cave birds, inspired by the Surreal bird sketches of Leonard Baskin, are strange human-avian hybrids. Birds are situated at the very heart of these texts: as symbols, as metaphors, as new perspectives on reality. Birds are a means by which Hughes and Ballard re-perceive and recalibrate reality, whether by seeing through their eyes, inhabiting their ontology, or adopting their forms.

Surrealism, an important historical art movement, is intimately connected to many of the aforementioned preoccupations of these authors—their connections to mythology, the occult, mysticism, and their explorations of the unconscious in the wake of psychoanalysis. Both authors show deep ideological ties to the European Surrealists, epitomizing that central aim of the movement identified by André Breton in his first manifesto of Surrealism: the "resolution of these two states, dream and reality, which are seemingly so contradictory, into a kind of absolute reality, a *surreality*" (Breton 1972, 14). In a movement spawned of dreams, myths, and mysticism, it is no surprise that the artworks are saturated with birds. Salvador Dali's artworks teem with birds, often in fossilized, skeletal forms. Swans appear in a large number of his best-known works, often alluding to the Greek myth of Leda.[1] Rene Magritte's paintings often depict gigantic doves sailing across stormy seas or eagles adorned in suit jackets.[2] Leonora Carrington's birds and angelic creatures populate hypnagogic landscapes, as in her most famous work *The Giantess (The Guardian of the Egg)* (1942), in which the gargantuan figure of a woman is surrounded by flying geese, many of which are human-avian hybrids. Perhaps most notable, and most significant for Ballard, is the work of Max Ernst, which is inundated with avian imagery, most famously in the form of Loplop, Ernst's bird-man alter-ego, which he came to call the "superior of the birds" after an early 1928 painting. Two prominent works featuring Loplop include *The Robing of the Bride* (1940), which depicts the avian incarnation of Carrington (who was his wife at the time), and the collage novel *Une Semaine de Bonté*, or *A Week of Kindness* (1934), which repopulates a series of Victorian illustrations pilfered from penny dreadfuls and pulp French fiction with birdmen and birdwomen.

The pertinence of birds for the Surrealists is clear: as unifying symbols and images of the unconscious mind, birds occupy a unique and central position across cultures, religions, myths, and epochs. They are most commonly symbols of the ascension of souls, of transition, of release from the shackles and torments of waking life. Sometimes they symbolize dreams themselves. For Sigmund Freud, whose theories underpinned the Surrealist perspective, dreams of birds and flight were among the most common of all, often symbolizing longing and desire, while dreams of falling represented deep-seated fear and anxiety.[3] Birds, therefore, also represent a paradox: for if dreams really were a nightly process of wish fulfillment, as Freud proposed, an encoded narrative interwoven with reparations for all the trivial failings of the everyday, then birds represented a soaring longing in the midst of unconscious satiation and appeasement. This avian paradox fits within the idea of birds and avian hybrids so often depicted as the messengers between worlds, occupying the liminalities between the heavens and the earth. Their presence clearly weighed heavily on Freud's mind. Only recently has the overwhelming presence of birds in Freud's archeological collection come to light, far outweighing all of the other animal-human figures he had collected from a mélange of ancient cultures (Davies 2019). Bryony Davies (2019), who notes the prominence of Egyptian avian deities, such as Horus, Ra, and Thoth, also points to the personal significance of birds for Freud, who in *The Interpretation of Dreams* describes one of his own anxiety dreams from his youth:

> The dream was very vivid, and showed me my beloved mother, with peculiarly calm sleeping countenance, carried into the room and laid on the bed by two (or three) persons with bird's beaks. I awoke crying and screaming, and disturbed my parents. The very tall figures—draped in a peculiar manner—with beaks, I had taken from the illustrations of Philippson's bible; I believe they represented deities with heads of sparrowhawks from an Egyptian tomb relief. (Freud 1913, 460)

Freud reads the dream as emanating from a primal dread of his mother's death and believes the emergence of the birds to be linked with word association. He had only recently learned about sexual intercourse from a young friend who described it with a word closely related to the word *vogel*, German for bird (Freud 1913, 460). The interweaving of psychology and language—the manifest content preserving some latent trauma or truth—is crucial to both Ballard and Hughes. Their birds occupy a similarly central position when it comes to representing the more primal aspects of the psyche, the vessels of our most innate and instinctual drives. Freud used many Greek myths as the basis for his psychoanalytic models wherein birds are often depicted as "the epiphanies of deities" (Pollard 1977, 155). They are, as with Ballard's Blake and Hughes's Crow, creatures of revelation and inspiration. Emily Wilson (2017) goes so far as to say that

> birds in Homer are the ultimate image of speech and of freedom. Athena repeatedly transforms herself into a bird of prey, whooshing up to the rooftops or

surfing across the waves of the sea. The silenced slave girls are "like doves or thrushes," caught in a hunter's net. Penelope, meanwhile, is like a "pale gray nightingale" who "sits among the leaves / that crowd the trees."

Surrealism suffuses Ballard's writings to the extent that Jeanette Baxter (2009) has identified his work as "a radical Surrealist experiment in the rewriting of post-war history and culture" (2). Ballard's tie to the Surrealists is made evident in his speculative fiction, which explores inner as opposed to outer space. In an early essay for *New Worlds*, "Which Way to Inner Space" (1962), Ballard proclaims his desire for authors to explore new forms of science fiction which incorporate "more psycho-literary ideas [. . .] synthetic psychologies and space-times, more of the sombre half-worlds one glimpses in the paintings of schizophrenics" (Ballard 1997, 198). Many of Ballard's works, much like that of the Surrealists, immerse us within worlds as viewed by alternate psychologies, wherein the unconscious bleeds into the surrounding environment, offering new insights. His writing often veers into quasi-ekphrastic mode, recalling the landscapes of Dalí and Ernst, a means of conjuring painterly worlds or submerging us within the Surrealists' reality.

Ballard has noted the importance of flight within his writing (Ballard 2012, 242), and, much like space and aircraft, birds often play a similarly presiding, although altogether different, symbolic role. An early standout is "Storm Bird, Storm Dreamer" (1966), a Surrealist story of an apocalyptic future when birds have grown to an enormous size and prey on humans. Crispin, a bird hunter and ship's captain, watches over an enigmatic woman who lives alone on an isolated coastland after a giant white dove kills her husband and steals her son. The story ends like a Greek tragedy with Crispin shooting down the murderous dove and adorning himself with its feathers before the woman shoots him. The story resonates with Magritte's doves: at one point Crispin "caught a last glimpse against the moonlit night of a huge white bird flying away across the river" (Ballard 2006, 187).

Many other stories similarly merge dream-like worlds and avian flight, as in "Myths of the Near Future" (1982), in which a mysterious "space sickness," the symptoms of which are extreme introversion and delusions of space flight, sweeps the world (Ballard 2006, 606). At one point Sheppard, the protagonist, while ill, describes how "wings of light hung from his shoulders, feathered into a golden plumage drawn from the sun, the reborn ghosts of his once and future selves" (Ballard 2006, 621). In "Memories of the Space Age" (1982), Ballard describes how the character Mallory finds himself in a world where "the forest oaks were waiting for him to feed their roots [. . .] motionless trees [which] were as insane as anything in the visions of Max Ernst. There were the same insatiable birds, feeding on the vegetation that sprang from the corpses of trapped aircraft" (Ballard 2006, 576).

Ernst is significant for Ballard, whose avian figures pepper his stories, and his characters' dreams, as seen in *The Atrocity Exhibition* (1970), in which the central character often "dreams of Max Ernst, superior of the birds" (Ballard 2006, AE, 12).

The importance of birds is most pronounced, however, in his novel *The Unlimited Dream Company*, which opens with Blake retelling the key events in his life, leading to his theft of a Cessna plane from London airport, its subsequent crash, and his awakening into a dream-like Shepperton where all of his messianic dreams are realized. Through Blake, Ballard's mundane hometown metamorphosizes into something akin to William Blake's divine and epiphanic visions in painting. Ballard depicts Blake as an angelic figure whose transformation is a sacred, transcendental event. Ballard's Blake catches a glimpse of himself in a store window: "I see my skin glow like an archangel's" (Ballard 2008, 9). He often sees himself as a herald, a "savior," emphasized by eschatological imagery throughout. Blake is a fallen angel figure, who "died, then returned again" (Ballard 2008, 34), and who is haunted by apocalyptic visions (Ballard 2008, 32). Blake's final battle with the corpse of a drowned pilot (his human body perhaps) echoes Milton's battle with Satan in William Blake's *Milton*. The townspeople's transformation into gigantic birds emulates an avian rapture. Such allusivity situates us in some aesthetic liminality, within a *painterly* reality. This is a Surrealist Shepperton—Blake describing how it seemed as if he were "looking at an enormous illuminated painting [. . .] people were watching me, like figures posed by the artist in a formal landscape" (Ballard 2008, 17). Our immersion into the painterly imagery of the novel progresses with Blake's transformation and momentum toward transcendence. Eventually he becomes almost analogous with Loplop, described as "superior of the birds" (Ballard 2008, 62), an allusion to Ernst. Loplop was the painter's alter ego and liberated self.

Early on, following Blake's initial plummet, Ballard overwhelms us within an aesthetic collage of avian imagery. The title of the opening chapter plays on the name of a Surrealist painting by Colin Middleton, which depicts an angelic figure surrounded by birds: *The Coming of the Birds* (1943) now becomes *The Coming of the Helicopters*. Blake's megalomaniacal views are clear: he is plagued by obsessions with flight and freedom from mundane living. He relates how, even in childhood, his schoolmates used to mock his gait, which was the result of a car crash that killed his mother. His "shoulder developed a slight upward tilt that I soon exaggerated into a combative swagger [. . .] I thought of myself as a new species of winged man. I remembered Baudelaire's albatross, hooted at by the crowd, but unable to walk only because of his heavy wings" (Ballard 2008, 11). The reference to Baudelaire's poem "The Albatross," from his collection *Les Fleurs du mal*, or *The Flowers of Evil* (1861), influences the text more broadly. The poem draws upon Samuel Taylor Coleridge's *The Rime of the Ancient Mariner* (1798), where the titular sailor shoots down an albatross that the crew sees as a bad omen, leading to a curse being placed on their ship. Baudelaire's version intensifies the violence but stultifies the symbolic pertinence of the albatross: these sailors lure and capture albatrosses (or sometimes just shoot them down), often damaging and breaking their wings: "How droll is the poor floundering creature, how limp and weak / He, but a moment past so lordly, flying in state!" (Baudelaire 1936). The final stanza then compares the fallen bird to the poet: "that wild inheritor of the cloud / A rider of storms, above the range of arrows and slings; / Exiled on earth, at bay amid the jeering crowd, / He cannot walk for his unmanageable wings" (Baudelaire 1936). This tether between the bird and the poet (or the poetic sensibility) is a symbolic archetype. Avian transformation is the principal symbol of this escape.

Our view of Blake incessantly wavers between the delusional madman and the divine seer who transforms the hyper-mundane world and frees the imagination. Surrealism attempts to capture this liminality, that "place between states" as Breton identifies, where the conscious and the unconscious, the quotidian and the surreal, merge (Breton 1972, 14). The lens of Surrealism is adopted for aesthetic, subjective, and revelatory empowerment: to enable us to see significance in the everyday where it was once skewed or hidden. As Ballard expresses, "Surrealism is the first systematic investigation of the most unsuspected aspects of our lives [. . .] [and has] a particular relevance at this moment, when the fictional elements in the world around us are multiplying to the point where it is almost impossible to distinguish between the 'real' and the 'false'" (Ballard 1997, 88). Ballard explores this polarization through contrasting man-powered and natural flight. His opening allusion to Colin Middleton is also important in this regard, drawing attention to the stark contrast between mechanized, superficial means of aviation and birds within his writing more broadly. Aircraft are often depicted as apocalyptic and destructive symbols (as in works such as *Empire of the Sun*) or commercialized icons of the technological age (as in *Kingdom Come*). Downed aircraft are also something of a repeated, Dalínian symbol in the Ballardian imaginary. Birds on the other hand appear as symbols of freedom and transcendence, symbols of passage into the dream space, or of a return to some more primal and essential mode of being. Blake's initial fall in the Cessna, the *false flight* if you will, contrasts with the freedom and liberation of his eventual avian transformation. Blake often makes this primordial return explicit, expressing that birds, "these primitive creatures, together seemed altogether more real than this civilised and sun-filled room" (Ballard 2008, 61), and presenting avian flight as liberating and positive: "I knew that I was flying, not as a pilot in an aircraft, but as a condor, bird of good omen" (Ballard 2008, 56). Ballard makes this contrast evident, describing how unsettled by the helicopters, the birds are rising into the air [. . .] thousands of them surround me, from every corner of the globe, flamingos and frigate birds, falcons and deep-water albatross [. . .] the barbarous plumage of cockatoos, macaws and scarlet ibis covers the shopping mall [. . .] the centre of Shepperton has become a spectacular aviary, a huge aerial reserve ruled by the condors. (Ballard 2008, 8)

Blake's gradual liberation coincides with the emergence and eventual flight of the birds themselves. But this progression can be read in two ways: as a gradual transition toward his dreams becoming reality, or as a progression into a fully formed delusion and eventual dislocation from reality.

In reading Blake's transformation as a gradual exacerbation of delusion, one recalls another important Surrealist text, particularly in relation to the two primary works of focus here: André Breton and Paul Éluard's *The Immaculate Conception* (1930), an innovative poet-visual artist collaboration. In Dalí's illuminating preface insert, he claims

if the first and second manifestoes were a statement of the manifest content of the Surrealist dream, *The Immaculate Conception* is a statement of its latent content [. . .] [this text] will be the experimental source to which one will have to return in order to recognise the power thought has of adopting all the modes of madness. (Breton 1990, 25)

The text is broken into "possessions" and "meditations," the former a creative attempt to channel the experience of altered states such as mania, dementia, and delirium. The most notable is the simulation of delirium, in which the figure is overcome with images of birds, to the extent that language transforms in their presence:

the double eyelid of the sun rises and falls on life [. . .] the earth that is webfooted with deserts is itself subject to the laws of migration. The feather summer is not over yet [. . .] Horus, with a finger to his lips, is the avalanche [. . .] Phoenixes come bringing me my food of glow worms and their wings which ceaselessly dip into the gold of the earth are the sea and the sky which we only used to see aglow on stormy days. (Breton 1990, 65–66)

Delusions (and delusions of grandeur) recurrently associated with birds, or the adoption of an avian ontology, no doubt also connects to birds' presences and prevalences within myth and spiritual beliefs. The symbolic crux of birds within mythology is that they often represent transcendence. For both Ballard and Hughes, inhabiting an avian ontology is central to this process of transcendence and transformation. This connection to a higher state necessitates a deeper connection to truth, nature, and primal impulses. This is also perhaps why the divine language that bears the capacity of communicating *absolute truth* across many myths, religions, and sometimes occult practices is referred to as the *language of the birds*. And much like the language of the birds, the idea of inhabiting birds and looking through their eyes is a process of seeing truth—much like augury practiced by ancient Romans—essential within the poems of Ted Hughes.

Despite the great prevalence of animals across his stories and poetry, birds still dominate Hughes's writing. There is variation and versatility in his bird poems: incessant shifts in style, form, perspective, as well as a mutative complexity and intricacy of language, imagery, and poetics to capture the essence of any particular species. At times his language becomes synesthesiac, capturing their movements, shapes, calls, and colors in singular images; form, too, adapts and interweaves with the bird in question. The significance of birds for Hughes can be traced back to his first collection, *Hawk in the Rain* (1957), which secured his station as one of Britain's most important rising poets. "Hawk in the Rain" is the collection's first poem, and in many ways it encapsulates the driving core of Hughes's poetry more broadly: a poem at once of raw, physical, earthly, human struggle, and of deep longing and need for some higher purpose and connection with nature. He describes in the opening line of the poem, "I drown in the drumming ploughland, I drag up / Heel after heel from the swallowing of the earth's mouth" (Hughes 1972, 11) while looming high above him "the hawk / Effortlessly at height hangs his still eye / His wings hold all creation in a weightless quiet" (Hughes 1972, 11). He struggles through the wind and the mire "towards the master- / Fulcrum of violence where the hawk hangs still" (Hughes 1972, 11), where the hawk resides contently within the harshest part of the storm. There is a struggle to find stasis here, a sense of some latent darkness, one which haunts both Hughes's poetry and his wider life. The poem presciently ends with some hope in the hawk's fallibility: one day he too "suffers the air, hurled upside down [. . .] the ponderous shires crash on him [. . .] Smashed, mix his heart's blood with the mire of the land" (Hughes 1972, 11). Once again we recall Baudelaire's albatross, cursed to a similar "exile on earth," and notice a similar tether between the bird and the poet, perhaps even a shamanistic unification of spirit.

This moment of the hawk crashing into the earth, its blood mixing with the mire, captures Hughes's ongoing attempt to unify the higher, romantic essence of poetry, in which the poet is overcome by nature and pure experience, with the far harsher, darker, *truer* aspects of the environment. He relates this convolution with his own interests in shamanism, seeing resonances of shamanistic practices and poetic inspiration: "the shamanic flight, and the figures and adventures they encounter, are not a shaman monopoly: they are, in fact, the basic experience of the poetic temperament we call 'romantic' [. . .] shamans seem to undergo, at will and phenomenal intensity, and with practical results, one of the main regenerating dramas of the human psyche: the fundamental poetic event" (Hughes 1994, 58). Hughes's work engages birds and the process of animism and spirit walking, or seeing through the eyes of animals. Mircea Eliade explains such practices and how the shaman "drums, summons his spirit helpers, speaks a 'secret language' or the 'animal language', imitating the cries of beasts and especially the songs of birds [. . .] the purest poetic act seems to recreate language from an inner experience that, like the ecstasy or the religious inspiration of 'primitives', reveals the essence of things" (Eliade 1964, 510–11). It is hard not to see a kindred process in many of Hughes's bird poems, which seek out some deeper connection and synchronization, a "recreation" of language borne of "inner experience" somehow transfigured through this new lens for perceiving reality.

The hawk is similarly important within his second collection, *Lupercal* (1960), appearing in what is often determined as the most famous poem of the collection, "Hawk Roosting." The key difference between this poem and "The Hawk in the Rain" is that now the roles are reversed. Before, we were situated far below, looking up in admiration and envy at the effortless grace, power, and certainty of the hawk in flight; now, we see *through* its eyes, looking down with nothing but instinctual, predatory prowess. "Hawk Roosting" reads as an allegory of tyrannical powers and even fascism, the brutality of which radiates from the lines, "I kill where I please because it is all mine [. . .] the one path of my flight is direct / Through the bones of the living" (Hughes 1984, 43). As in "The Hawk in the Rain," we find a certain latent connection and interchangeability of viewpoints. The symbolic associations with the hawk or eagle also play a part here: with Nazi Germany more overtly, but also with birds of prey representing power, domination, and empire more widely—for example, the Holy Roman Empire, the association of the eagle with Genghis Khan, and the association of eagles with sacred kings more widely (Waida 1978). There are moments in "Hawk Roosting" when the purely animal viewpoint slips, and we briefly flit back to Hughes's own perspective and voice, looking up from below, admiring and revering the effortless power of the animal: "It took the whole of Creation / To produce my foot, my each feather: / Now I hold Creation in my foot" (Hughes 1984, 43). These lines recall the inner language of ecstasy identified by Eliade. In addressing the question of the poem's fascistic edge, Hughes later clarifies, "in this hawk Nature is thinking. Simply Nature" (Bate 2015, 165). This sense of absolute power, of seeing into the essence of things, shows Hughes's view of the harshness and moral emptiness of nature. There are evolutionary ideas here too, which emerge later in *Crow*, through this sense of interconnectedness. Through the hawk's eyes, through nature's eyes, everything is cohesive, everything that has ever happened, ever existed, played some part in the creation of this foot, this shape, which now grasps onto pure creation in the form of the tree.

Hughes's depiction of birds across texts might be split into two broader categories. In his first category of poems (which, for ease, are here categorized under the umbrella of *birdwatcher Hughes*), the author is as keen as any naturalist or ornithologist in his exactitude and capacity to capture a particular species in words. In his second category (which we might call the *mythmaker Hughes*), the poet often depicts birds to an anthropomorphized extent, at times rendering them revelatory vessels for some higher power. The latter style is epitomized by *Crow* and *Cave Birds*. The former style can be seen in "swifts," from his 1975 collection *Season Songs*, in which the swifts "materialize at the tip of a long scream / Of needle. 'Look! They're back! Look!' And they're gone [. . .] On a steep / Controlled scream of skid" (Hughes 1984, 146–47). Here Hughes captures the kinetic dynamism of birds in flight, so that the "scream of needle" screeches into the "controlled scream of skid" in the next stanza, giving a sense of great velocity and movement as if the birds themselves fly through the poem. The needle image approximates the swifts' speed and agility, and a sense of space and distance. He almost shows us the shape of sound, so that the needle itself represents a specific fine-tuned pitch, pulled out and elongated to such a degree it becomes "needle sharp." It is also crucial to note here—and this is another signature trait of birdwatcher Hughes—that this is a highly experiential poem, of immediacy and directness, heightened by the many wispy fragments of voices, spectators, and fellow observers who see the birds and then quickly lose sight. His depiction in "skylarks" bears a similarly breathtaking lucidity: "A whippet head, barbed like a hunting arrow, / But leaden / With muscle / For the struggle / Against / Earth's centre" (Hughes 1984, 102). In "Curlews Lift," Hughes describes how "they trail a long, dangling, falling aim / Across water / Lancing their voices / Through the skin of this light" (Hughes 1984, 171). Hughes focuses on the physicality and shape of the birds; on the larks' musculature; on the shape of curlews in flight, showing a "dangling falling aim" due to the downward arc of the beak. "Lancing their voices" once again gives a sense of space through physicality, a sense of sharpness, pitch, as if their cries could pierce "the skin of this light."

Such sublime visions of birds starkly contrast with those featured in *Cave Birds* and *Crow*. The cave birds evoke a sense of enclosure or entrapment; they are birds confined to a cavernous underworld, transformed and disfigured by their inability to soar free. *Cave Birds* is distinct in that it is, to a significant extent (*Crow* to a much lesser extent), a work of ekphrasis: poems spawned of Leonard Baskin's striking and at times haunting drawings of birds and bird-human chimeras.[4] Baskin's birds are grotesqueries, their anatomies twisted and contorted, grossly bloated and sexualized, at times redolent of the surreal and often darkly humorous illustrations of Rabelais's *Gargantua and Pantagruel*. "The Judge," for example, appears opposite a frogmouth-like bird by Baskin. Hughes describes a figure swelling with stupendous, glutinous power: "He receives and transmits / Cosmic equipoise / The garbage sack of everything that is not / the Absolute onto whose throne he lowers his buttocks" (Hughes 1978, 16). Along with its stupendous girth, the bird's wings are tiny and malformed, so that the bird becomes representative of a larger body politic; he "lowers his buttocks" onto the throne of "the Absolute" and becomes the voice and representative of the law, transformed and disfigured by its power. Baskin's imagery, like Hughes's, offers a shamanic aspect. In "The Guide," his drawing reminisces of a bird-wicker man, while other images emulate tribal totems, tribesmen dress (as with "The Gatekeeper" and "A Green Mother"), and religious staffs ("His Legs Ran About"). Others feature bone fragments and skeletons, depicting avian forms seemingly perched on the verge between life and death. "Bride and Groom Lie Hidden for Three Days" stands opposite a perfect exemplar of this eerie liminality, and is an image which might have been plucked straight from the sketchbooks of Ernst. These are cave birds, a clear play on cave men, suggesting that these are to be read as primal depictions, remnants of some otherworldly past, bearing some innately spiritual essence. (The link to Baskin is also clear: images potentially etched on ancient cave walls.) Following such, many of the poems appear focused on drawing out the symbolic associations of certain birds: owls, eagles, roosters, vultures, rooks, and ravens.

What sets *Cave Birds* apart above all is the duality of narrative within many of its poems. Hughes distorts language to fashion parallel bird and human images. "The Interrogator" (figure 3.1.), a Baskin original of a great black-caped vulture, accompanies Hughes's description: "The bird is the sun's key-hole / The sun spies through her / [. . .] He ransacks the camouflage of hunger" (Hughes 1978, 12). We can certainly read this as a depiction of a vulture looking for food, its shadow drifting over the "empty badlands." The keyhole metaphor conjures an image of the bird's shadow, moving over the surface, a "keyhole" in terms of the only place where the sun's glare does not reach. But many of these poems were inspired by Baskin's images as something of an avian Rorschach test: images drawn from the unconscious threads of Hughes's inner life. Read in this way, as another utilization of avian ontology, the images take on entirely new dimensions. The eye of the sun, looking through the keyhole, could be read as a woman peeking through a keyhole, perhaps at some unfaithful act: "He ransacks the camouflage of hunger," which may suggest a sexual hunger. In this reading, the interrogator "herself" can be viewed as Plath, who poses "angered righteous questions" and is transformed into a powerful

Figure 3.1 "The Interrogator" by Leonard Baskin, from *Cave Birds*, 1978. *Source*: By permission of the Estate of Leonard Baskin. © Estate of Leonard Baskin.

vulture-like image, one enhanced by his description of how she flies "into the courts of the afterlife" denoting her death. This sense of finding significance in the images is something *Cave Birds* seems to intensify; it draws out and exaggerates symbolic associations, using the birds almost as *summoning* spirits. This summoning practice is almost literalized in Hughes's "The Summoner" (figure 3.2.), showing a sexual encounter and a nocturnal bird picking through refuse. The titular summoner is a woman in bed who pulls back the covers and "Beholds his bronze image, grotesque on the bed. / You grow to recognize the identity / Of your protector" (Hughes 1978, 8). Baskin's accompanying image presents an eerie convocation of images, the human and the avian hauntingly interwoven. We see a powerful summoned spirit wrapped in a writhing plumage (as if just recently conjured), which almost seems strangely reminiscent of bed covers. Once again, Hughes's work resonates with the Surrealists's, not just through its heightened sense of symbolism empowering the reader to unique decipherment, but also through the dual-faceted, manifest-latent structure, in which the everyday and the metaphorical dream world coalesce.

Figure 3.2 "The Summoner" by Leonard Baskin, from *Cave Birds*, 1978. *Source*: By permission of the Estate of Leonard Baskin. © Estate of Leonard Baskin.

Crow was originally proposed by Baskin just weeks after Plath's suicide in the hope to transform Hughes's deep despair into a creative and cathartic combustion. The collection was originally to be set, as with the poem "Cave Birds," alongside Baskin's images. With *Crow*, Hughes detoured and the birdwatcher fades almost entirely. Instead, the eponymous corvid becomes a god-like entity, a vessel of myth. Hughes draws upon the representation of crows in Alaskan, Inuit, Norse, and South American myth and folklore, assimilating various depictions of the godly "Trickster" (Bate 2015, 289). *Crow* plunges us deep into the very darkest corners of the human psyche, and the poems themselves appear something of a mythic flight, a relinquishing and an unleashing of the burgeoning darkness within. Jonathan Bate (2015) emphasizes that "the violence was internal to Crow's psychology: the images are not of violence per se but serve as metaphors of breakthrough into self-knowledge. The poems are always grasping towards some dark mystery of the inner life" (Bate 2015, 291).

The collection opens in a highly exaggerated biblical vein, as if gesturing to a kind of inner, quasi-spiritual renewal (although of a very different and much darker kind). Crow is born from "an egg of blackness [. . .] To hatch a crow, a black rainbow / Bent in emptiness / Over emptiness / But flying" (Hughes 2006, 3). Here we are almost instantly reminded of Genesis, of the earth which "was formless and empty, [and] darkness was over the surface of the deep" (King James Bible). This continues in "Crow's Lineage," which gives a blackly humorous rendition of the Crow's ancestry. But then, with "Crow and Mama," the mythic-biblical narrative slips, exposing everyday reality. Hughes states how, when Crow erupts in a fit of rage, his mother "closed on him like a book / On a bookmark, he had to get going. / He jumped into the car the towrope" (Hughes 2006, 7). This image of the book closing on the bookmark can be read as the ultimate breach into reality—the severed moment whereby the narrative ends and the reader looks up from the page. This occurs repeatedly, so that even certain metaphors jar us back into reality, such as when Crow "looked in front of his feet at the little stream / Chugging on like an auxiliary motor" (Hughes 2006, 14). Such breaches most often occur in moments of extreme violence, as if these traumatic events almost tear us away from the safety of narrative: for example, during a violent suicide in "That Moment," or during an existential breakdown in "Crow Alights," in which he "shivered with the horror of Creation" (Hughes 2006, 12). This is a text spawned of trauma, and so these intermittent transitions are akin to a flitting between the latent and manifest dimensions of said trauma. As with Ballard, and his blurring of dream and reality, Hughes presents us with a constant shift between states from which only the birds seem exempt.

The metanarratives of *Crow* draw us back to this idea of birds as the occupiers of a space *between*: they reside in the liminalities between myth and mundane reality (again, much like Blake in *The Unlimited Dream Company*[5]), between the heavens and the earth, between dreams and waking, and between life and death. Crow resides in this purgatorial abyss as the trickster figure so often does. While Hughes was certainly not overtly influenced or ideologically tethered to the Surrealists as Ballard, he was influenced by psychoanalytic theory, particularly by Carl Jung (Bate 2015, 63–64).[6] Bate elucidates that Hughes found particular influence in the experience of what Jung termed "synchronicity" whereby "the boundary between different worlds dissolves [. . .] the individual psyche comes into constellation with a deeper reality that transcends time and place. For Hughes, the same thing happens in the moment of red-hot poetic creativity" (Bate 2015, 95). Crow embodies synchronicity in this regard, as a transgressive, transcendental figure borne out of some deeper, primal experience that Hughes sought to tap into. It makes sense, therefore, that Crow would choose the Bible as a place of attack, where so many go to find deeper meaning beyond the everyday world. Throughout the text Crow becomes a biblical interloper, gliding between verses, hijacking key moments, and even rewriting them. Early in the text, in "A Childish Prank," Crow appears at the moment of creation in the Garden of Eden. Later, in "Crow Blacker Than Ever," Crow describes the process in a much more morbid way (which seems to capture something of the central aim of the text itself): as "Nailing Heaven and earth together [. . .] Then Heaven and earth creaked at the joint / Which became gangrenous and stank [. . .] Crow / Grinned / Crying: 'This is my Creation'" (Hughes 2006, 63). In a sense, readers are located within this gangrenous wound, and Hughes's language and imagery are the carrion. This disease owes to disjuncture: everyday reality and the transcendental world of religion and myth cannot reside in harmony. Yet Crow dwells happily within this juncture. This is perhaps why Crow becomes the perfect cathartic outlet for Hughes. Ballard's Blake can reside here too, inhabiting a similarly mythic, Blakean liminality, which is just as revelatory and cathartic in purpose.

NOTES

1. See, for example, Dali's *The Rotting Bird* (1928), *Bacchanale* (1939), *Leda Atomica* (1949).

2. See, for example, Magritte's *The Large Family* (1963), *Man in a Bowler Hat* (1964), *The Present* (1939).

3. Freud explains that "the dream of flying [often] had the significance of a longing: 'If I were a little bird!' Others thus become angels at night because they have missed being called that by day. The intimate connection between flying and the idea of a bird makes it comprehensible that the dream of flying in the case of men usually has a significance of coarse sensuality" (Freud 1913, 239).

4. In *The Art of Ted Hughes*, Keith Sagar (1978) identifies these original pieces by Baskin which were later expanded so that the roles were reversed: the artist began drawing images for the poems. As such the collection is very much a collaboration (Sagar 1978, 171, 243).

5. There is also a striking resonance with Ballard's Blake—and this idea of natural and artificial flight, and more overarchingly the civilized and the primal—in the conception of *Crow*, which was sparked when Hughes saw a crow and a plane flying in opposite directions (Bate 2015, 285).

6. Bate elaborates that Hughes's "hope was that poetry would emerge directly from his unconscious [. . .]. For Ted, dreams would always be the taproot into the unconscious" (Bate 2015, 64).

REFERENCES

Ballard, J. G. 1997. *A User's Guide to the Millennium: Essays and Reviews*. London: Flamingo.

———. 2006. *The Complete Short Stories: Volume 2*. London: Harper Perennial.

———. 2006. *The Atrocity Exhibition*. London: Harper Perennial.

———. 2008. *The Unlimited Dream Company*. London: Harper Perennial.

Ballard, J. G., Simon Sellars, and Dan O'Hara, eds. 2012. *Extreme Metaphors: Selected Interviews with J. G. Ballard, 1967–2008.* London: Fourth Estate.
Bate, Jonathan. 2015. *Ted Hughes: The Unauthorised Life.* London: William Collins.
Baudelaire, Charles and George Dillon, trans. 1936. *The Flowers of Evil.* New York: Harper and Brothers.
Baxter, Jeanette. 2009. *J. G. Ballard's Surrealist Imagination: Spectacular Authorship.* London: Routledge.
Breton, André. 1972. *Manifestoes of Surrealism.* Ann Arbor: University of Michigan Press.
Breton, André, and Éluard, Paul. 1990. *The Immaculate Conception.* London: Atlas Press.
Davies, Bryony. "Exploring the Birds in Freud's Study," December 3, 2019. https://www.freud.org.uk/2019/03/12/discovering-birds-in-freuds-study/
Eliade, Mircea. 1964. *Shamanism.* London: Routledge. 510–11.
Freud, Sigmund and A. A. Brill, trans. 1913. *The Interpretation of Dreams.* New York: Macmillan.
Hughes, Ted. 1972. *The Hawk in the Rain.* London: Faber and Faber.
———. 1984. *Selected Poems: 1957–1981.* London: Faber and Faber.
———. 1994. *Winter Pollen: Occasional Prose.* London: Faber and Faber.
———. 2006. *Crow.* London: Faber and Faber.
Hughes, Ted and Leonard Baskin. 1978. *Cave Birds: An Alchemical Cave Drama.* London: Faber and Faber.
Pollard, John. *Birds in Greek Life and Myth.* London: Thames and Hudson.
Russell, John. 1967. *Max Ernst: Life and Work.* London: Thames and Hudson.
Sagar, Keith. 1978. *The Art of Ted Hughes.* 2nd ed. Cambridge: Cambridge University Press.
Waida, Manabu. 1978. "Birds in the Mythology of Sacred Kingship." *East and West* 28(1): 283–89.
Wilson, Emily. "A Translator's Reckoning with the Women of *The Odyssey*." *The New Yorker*, December 8, 2017. https://www.newyorker.com/books/page-turner/a-translators-reckoning-with-the-women-of-the-odyssey

Chapter 4

The Optimism of Flight
Magical Realism in Little Nemo in Slumberland

Mark O'Connor

On January 2, 1910, readers of the Sunday color comics in the *New York Herald Tribune* found the titular hero of Winsor McCay's *Little Nemo in Slumberland* in deep trouble. A gigantic King Morpheus, in agony from gout, with his foot propped on an overstuffed pillow, roars at Little Nemo, "Find me Dr. Pill or I'll make mince-meat of you all."[1] The king's daughter, continual *objet d'amour* of Nemo's affection, offers Nemo the palace airship to aid in his quest. This royal medical crisis inaugurates a series of adventures, using birds and other avian avatars to blur the strict boundary between the oneiric and real world that McCay had firmly established in the previous five years of the highly successful strip. The airship series is one of the first (and longest) narrative arcs in early newspaper comics, and features aspects of magical realism which can be read as McCay's efforts to offer a hagiography about great North American industrial cities at the expense of the natural world.

Little Nemo was one of the most lucrative newspaper comics in the nascent mass-media art form. McCay's success and ambition led him to extend his brand to include merchandising, a Broadway show, and a vaudeville tour (Canemaker 2018, 105). Using the skills he developed as an illustrator, he became a pioneer in the even newer field of cinema animation, giving theater performances where he interacted before a screen with a cartoon dinosaur he had drawn (Bendazzi 1994, 17). McCay's deployment of animals, from dinosaurs to giant turkeys, all rendered with an Audubon-like scrupulousness and beauty, are part of the appeal of the comic as well as in the airship series.

The first section of this chapter briefly glosses McCay's publishing history. The second section examines McCay's deployment of magical realist elements in the airship series, an ontological shift that fundamentally changed the structure of *Little Nemo* by a colonization of airspace, including his frequent uses of birds as avatars of the natural world. The third section draws out the implications of the airship series that celebrates American cities, an apotheosis wholly dependent on the subordination or erasure of all aspects of the environment—air, water, wildlife of any sort, including birds—in support of industry.

THE FLEDGLING COMICS ARTIST

Before arriving in New York in 1903, McCay spent a decade apprenticing in Cincinnati, drawing illustrations for dime museums and editorial cartoons for two newspapers ("Winsor McCay," n.p.). His work at *The Cincinnati Enquirer* intersects with the creation of *Little Nemo*. In Cincinnati he illustrated poems by George Randolph Chester in *A Tale of the Jungle Imps by Felix Fiddle*, a comic containing deeply problematic black characters.[2] The poems are doggerel, aimed at children with titles like "Why the Parrot Learned to Talk" and "How the Turtle Got His Shield," and steeped in nineteenth-century racial tropes, both on the textual and illustrative levels. The "jungle imps," naked except for grass skirts and moccasins, cannot speak English and spend their days tormenting animals and making mischief in a wild, unnamed landscape. The imaginary landscape furthers the pursuit of visual and narrative goals, a strategy used throughout *Little Nemo* until he draws real North American cities in the airship series. The racialized portrayals in *A Tale of the Jungle Imps* echo in later stereotypes of Native Americans in the airship series.[3] The ease with which McCay draws and redraws these problematic images portends his expeditious disregarding of social and environmental boundaries. Capitalism in McCay's airship series is simply the dream world writ large and drawn real, something to be celebrated, while the actual denizens of the air above these cities, like birds, and the workers below, live in dangerous, polluted cities like Chicago, Detroit, and Pittsburgh.

McCay's fame began with his creation of *Little Nemo in Slumberland* for the *New York Herald*. The setup of every Sunday comic (tabloid-sized, full-color) was always the same—Nemo falls asleep, enters Slumberland, usually in search of the Princess, and is abetted in his adventures by the miscreant Flip, a green-faced, cigar-smoking clown, and an unnamed "jungle imp" that McCay imported from his Cincinnati tenure. Newspaper comics like *Little Nemo, The Yellow Kid, The Katzenjammer Kid*s, and others were born in the mass readership newspapers enjoyed at the beginning of the twentieth century. Every Sunday the cast of *Little Nemo* adventured in the urban American psyche, as Katherine Roader notes (2014, 1–2). *Little Nemo* is a quintessentially urban comic, both in its site of production and in most of its narratives. McCay's appeal even now is how he *activates* each panel. Trains leap off their rails, cars defy gravity racing upside-down in thrilling loop-de-loops, elephants rush toward readers in frightening forced perspective, and in one oft-reprinted strip, Nemo's bed grows long legs and gallops through town as he grasps the footboard in terror (July 26, 1908) (Chavez). In every strip someone is flying, falling, stumbling, or leaping, a hyper-kinetic transcending of the quotidian worthy of a Chaplin film. The comic is a weekly visit to Coney Island, Steeplechase, and Luna Park, all within short distance of the McCay family home. Nemo's dream falling at the end of the galloping bed strip is almost always visually replicated in final panels—he reenters the waking world in an imitative visual and noisome tumble that earns him parental admonishment. In the end, Nemo is always back home, safe for another week.

The 1910 airship series occurs around the same time as McCay's growing discontentment with his employer. McCay wanted to take his live theatrical performance to Europe, a desire apparently quashed by his bosses at *The Herald Tribune*. McCay could hardly have been unaware of other cartoonists who had lucrative theatrical side gigs, both at home and abroad (Canemaker 2018, 139). John Canemaker (2018) writes, "though he toured in vaudeville on a regular basis until 1917, [McCay] never ventured west of the Mississippi with his act" (2018, 54). By this time, McCay had a family and large house to maintain. Within a year he decamped for the richer lands of William Randolph Hearst's syndicate, but, before he left, the strip took flight.

THE MAGIC OF SLUMBERLAND

Magical elements are the sine qua non of *Little Nemo in Slumberland*. The Sunday strips always begin with Nemo in bed, visually priming readers to expect an oneiric landscape. The first and last panels are identical, like a theatrical set, featuring his raised bed, pale back wall, and a heavy curtain stage left. The only difference between the first and last panels involves the question of consciousness. The similarity of the opening and closing panels in the first year is a visual feint. While the opening panel ostensibly takes place in Nemo's bedroom, it almost always features Slumberland characters invading its sanctity. These characters wake Nemo, often with a request involving the Princess, but always leading him away from sleep, from home, toward a visually compelling, supranatural adventure.

The domestic natural world readers know is rarely far from McCay's eye. In one early episode, Nemo is awakened by his cat: "Is that you snoring that way? Get out from under there!" (January 28, 1906) (Chavez). In a moment of dramatic irony, the readers encounter sounds emanating from a full-grown lion, invoking the enduring childhood terror of the space beneath the bed. Upon waking in panel two, Nemo tames the lion, jumps on its back, and rides it out of his house. The drawings are Muybridge-like in their evocation of movement. Like in almost every episode of *Little Nemo*, the strip relies upon a slow build-up to chaos. When suddenly the wild/wide-awake lion begins to run, Nemo is no longer in control. Nature takes over. They gallop to the lion's "home in the desert," where an enormous pride of lions encircles and menaces Nemo. At the last minute, before he is eaten, he is saved by the sudden appearance of another Slumberland character who shoos the massive cats away.

This comic ends as they all do, with the iron-clad finality of Nemo waking in the last panel. Order is restored. The magic is dissipated. Nemo is safe and Slumberland recedes until the next week. McCay plays with notions of surety and home for both lion and boy. Where did the lion go in the end? Perhaps it too has returned home (is Nemo dreaming the lion or is the lion dreaming Nemo? Alas, McCay inclines us toward the former), but in the early years of the strip the demarcation is clear—everything before the last panel is oneiric. In the last panel, Nemo's real-life kitten appears beneath the bed. Nemo was right all along. Nature is subsumed.

Despite this framing device, the comic *always* begins in dreamscape. In panel one, though visually identical to the last panel, the domestic space has already been breached. Only the border of the cold bracing slap of the last panel marks the space between the oneiric/magical worlds. In the prehistory of each Sunday comic, Nemo is already asleep.

In the comic's second year, McCay jettisons this framing. The most necessary part, the final denouement panel that brings Nemo back to consciousness, remains for the run of the comic. That is the crucial moment, always.[4] From then on, the strip begins *in medias res*. Perhaps, McCay realized he did not need the framing device.

The airship series violates this fundamental structure by immediately situating itself in the real-waking world. In one episode, Nemo and friends lasso a giant bird to propel the crew (and the comic) when the airship breaks down. The bird is the literal engine that allows them to cross from one world to another. This blurring of boundaries, between the oneiric and the real, between dream characters and real ones, between Slumberland and North America, marks McCay's ontological shift, transforming *Little Nemo*. In this new space containing both worlds McCay depicts the costs of the great American experiment, particularly as enacted through its growing industrial might at the expense of any concerns—avian, environmental, or otherwise.

OF BIRDS AND OTHER FLYING THINGS

Birds and other winged beings are among the most important characters McCay featured throughout *Little Nemo*. In a Thanksgiving strip (November 26, 1905), an enormous turkey, hundreds of feet tall, occupies the center of the comic in a roundel. The image easily occupies 25 percent of the page. As Catherine Labio (2015) notes, the uniqueness of comics and graphic novels is the necessary movement between viewing images and reading texts, "a perpetual zooming in and out of the various frames that make up the page" and the reading experience (326). Here the turkey persists as the necessary focus because of its size and placement. The much-smaller figures of Nemo and his parents enhance the terror as the monstrous turkey picks up the house in its beak, and all scramble onto the porch roof for safety. Nemo barely escapes engorgement, falling from his bedroom to certain death, "until he landed. Fortunately, [in] a lake of nice springy cranberry sauce" (Chavez). The fate of his parents is unknown. This is the only strip in which Nemo's seemingly *real* parents appear in Slumberland. Now, his grandfather enters his bedroom and "quiet[s] him," implying that Nemo is the only survivor. If Nemo's parents were truly ground up in the turkey's gizzard in Slumberland, they would be unable to wake him in the real world, with the death-of-parents marking another entry in the catalog of childhood nightmares.

The wild nature of McCay's marauding giant turkey is ironic because any turkeys at the Thanksgiving tables of McCay's readers would have been farmed by this point, or brought in from places that still had extant wild turkey populations (Kennamer et al., n.p.). By 1905 there were no wild turkeys in New York City. As the city grew, the surrounding woods and wetlands, home to wild fowl like turkeys, ducks, and geese, were cut down and filled in, falling to progress, a pattern repeated throughout the western expansion of the United States. This strip is a humorous/terrifying reversal of the food-chain hierarchy inherent in Thanksgiving, a theme repeated in other Thanksgiving strips. Though perhaps silly, the giant, all-consuming turkey is a foretaste of the airship series' blurring of boundaries.

In a subsequent Thanksgiving strip, the ravenous trio wander through an empty Slumberland and find the palace kitchen closed. Nemo moans, "Thanksgiving Day and us starving. Oh! I'm as weak as a cat" (November 24, 1907). As before, a giant turkey threatens, but this time it brought friends. In the huge penultimate panel that stretches the width of the tabloid page, the characters encounter an angry herd of oversized Thanksgiving protein—two turkeys, a duck, a rabbit, a pig, a goose, a lobster, a crab, and a half-dozen oysters. The inclusion of oysters at the dinner table, while perhaps odd by contemporary Thanksgiving standards, clearly nods to the ubiquitous presence of oyster houses in New York City at the time, though the oyster beds were heading toward collapse. There was even an oyster shop in Grand Central Station, evidence of the popularity, abundance, and low cost of this delicacy (Kurlansky 2006, 123). Mark Kurlansky (2006) writes: "Before the twentieth century, when people thought of New York, they thought of oysters. [. . .] New Yorkers ate them constantly. They also sold them by the millions," domestically and internationally (123). But this abundance was provisional, always dependent upon clean waterways and estuaries tenanted by birds and other wildlife in a complex, interdependent series of relationships. The more New York City's waterfront developed, the less viable the shoreline became for wildlife of any sort. Nemo survives his starvation, but in a one-time break from the established denouement panel, he is shown asleep at the dinner table. We overhear his parents: "You'd better carry Nemo into the other room. He has fallen asleep. Looks like he enjoyed his dinner!! [sic]." He is taken *to sleep* from the dinner table, presumably a site of overconsumption.

In the next year's Thanksgiving strip, a giant plucked turkey grabs Nemo from bed in the first panel, noting, "You're the lad who was going to eat me. Eh?" Running past another giant turkey carrying Flip, Nemo's captor adds, "Well I'm going to show you what a mistake you made!" After being chased in a circle, Nemo dreams that he gets dizzy and falls out of bed. Again, the effects of overconsumption are poor sleep, and maybe a nightmare, but the worlds remain separate. This form-breaking use of fauna previews what occurs throughout the airship series.

Flight and birds are crucial to the success of *Little Nemo*. Birds are a practical plot device McCay uses to transcend the quotidian, even if they are objects of terror. Much of *Little Nemo* is about leaving the ground, elevating the ordinary life of this boy (modeled on McCay's son, Robert). Besides birds, McCay occasionally uses balloons for the same purpose. In one strip Nemo and the princess are shot from a cannon, in a cannonball that transforms into a balloon. Nemo, as usual, is stricken with anxiety from his lack of agency. The loss of control is characteristic of passenger balloons, a common sight in this time period. Alexander Rose (2020) explains:

> There was no way, in short, to control free-flying balloons in terms of speed, direction, or altitude, rendering them useless as a reliable means of transport, either for passengers, mail, or cargo. [. . .] Balloons held the tantalizing possibility of revolutionizing travel, but their impracticality remained insuperable. It was as if humans had discovered fire but lacked any way to regulate the flame. (9)

Manned balloons were a popular novelty. Most amusement parks featured tethered balloon rides for their patrons but were limited to a few passengers and the operator. McCay needed something more reliable, something like a bird, capable of directed flight and that could travel long distances but also carry his entire cast, hence airships. Airships, like newspaper comics, were in their infancy, so McCay accelerated their industrial development for his own purposes, drawing an airship that would span continents and carry everything from an enormous school of silver fish caught in the Atlantic to the cases of chewing gum Flip buys in Cleveland (Chavez).

McCay's deployment of a continent-spanning airship is a swipe from popular culture. The McCays lived near Coney Island: "Luna Park by day and Dreamland at night, [were] two Coney Island amusement parks near Winsor McCay's home in Sheepshead Bay, Brooklyn" (Canemaker 2018, 110). At Luna Park, visitors would have seen "Alberto Santos-Dumont's Airship #9, a sixty-foot-long cigar shaped balloon with a 35-foot-long gondola suspended below" ("Airship," 2021). Primitive airships were being developed all over the United States and Europe, often by amateurs, and were frequently displayed at amusement parks. At Pittsburgh's Luna Park, a photograph of a small airship was captioned: "Suspended on a single chair below a small sausage-shaped balloon, famed aeronaut Lincoln Beachey performed at Luna in August 1906, at a time when few people had seen any flying machine" (Butko 2017, 78). Anyone, it seems, could take flight. Amusement parks, with their massive crowds, were perfect sites for displaying futuristic marvels.[5]

The airship series allows McCay to extend the geographic and narrative possibilities of *Little Nemo*. In one comic (August 28, 1910), the crew somehow travels from Africa to the United States in five panels marked by inexplicable gatherings of threatening animals. In panel one, a pride of lions roars from below; in panel two, a crash of rhinoceroses and a bloat of hippopotamuses strain toward the airship's deck; in three, a staggering streak of tigers, a leap of leopards, and a lone black panther chase the ship; and in four, a herd of elephants raise their trunks in anger.

Two panels later, the crew is in America, for, as Nemo explains, he "can tell by the trees." In the penultimate and seventh panel, Native American characters threaten the crew with raised tomahawks, the same poses McCay drew earlier in his confederation of angry animals (Chavez). Luckily, in the last panel Nemo awakes, but is warned by one of his parents, "If you do not get up to your breakfast Nemo, I'll come in there and scalp you!!! [*sic*]." Native Americans and wild animals alike are untamed, savage creatures, only scrutable from afar. Nature serves as a plot element to amplify the adventuring.

The next Sunday, in the opening panel, Flip demands: "How do you know we are in the western part of the country Nemo?" "Because I see those redskins!" Nemo answers as myriad Native Americans threaten the airship with tomahawks and spears. In the next panel, another group chases the airship on horseback. The bird's-eye view, absent the presence of birds, allows for perspective that is at several removes. Nemo, readers, and McCay glide above any concerns about social, economic, and environmental issues.

Even when human-bird hybrids appear, the encounters represent one more tick mark in adventuring, nothing more. In a New Year's Day strip from 1911, a very old man with enormous wings takes refuge on the airship's deck, like an exhausted gull alighting on an ocean liner. The bedraggled man confesses, "There is no place for me. Here comes my boss" as Father Time flies up, scythe in hand, advising, "Keep up with the times. Don't even ever think of old 1910! He will take care of himself" (January 1, 1911). The imperative to forget the past seems central to McCay's project in the airship series, an optimistic reading of the American urban landscape with little consideration of the environmental costs or the effects on workers.

With amusement parks and exhibitions like the 1893 Columbian Exposition inspiring McCay's illustrations, it makes sense that he would also import the optimism inherent in these images (Canemaker 2018, 153). Airships were an on-the-cusp emblem of a burgeoning new century.[6] Airships capable of carrying a large number of passengers or traveling across oceans like the one in *Little Nemo* were at least a decade and a half off. At the time McCay was publishing *Little Nemo*, airships in the United States were mostly a curiosity.

THE ROYAL PAIN AND WORD BALLOONS

The word balloons containing King Morpheus's pain inaugurate the airship series and help to constellate the flight imagery in *Little Nemo*. Unlike the dialogue in word balloons throughout the rest of *Nemo*, these merge images and text. The pain is almost unwritable and the expressions of it visually overwhelm the first panels (see figure 4.1).

They are not text, so much as free-floating signifiers of immeasurable pain. "Oh" and "ouch" occur over a dozen times in the penultimate panel bursting with a single imperative: "Doctor Pill. Bring him to me" (January 2, 1910). This moment offers a visual preview of the flight from Slumberland to early twentieth-century industrial America. This event precipitates the ontological shift in *Little Nemo* from the oneiric and fantastic to the realistic and hagiographic. Dr. Pill's curative powers/powders are neither magical nor oneiric. Dr. Pill is discovered in the real world, in the North Pole, setting up an ice-transportation scam. McCay emphasizes the role of scientific interventions like medicine or chemistry. Only the importation of real medicine into Slumberland can fix the body politic and cure the King's agony. It is an elevation of the primacy of science.

The Optimism of Flight 61

Figure 4.1 Winsor McCay. *Little Nemo in Slumberland*. 2 January 1910. *Source*: Courtesy of The Comic Strip Library, accessed 21 July 2021, https://www.comicstriplibrary.org/display/578.

In spite of McCay's widely acknowledged artistic status, the lettering in his word balloons proves bafflingly atrocious. Almost every *Little Nemo* comic contains at least one example where a word balloon is poorly drawn—with misshapen lines, clipped letters, inconsistent word heights, or words so crammed they crawl up the side of a balloon. And yet the poorly fitted dialogue in the word balloons is crucial to understanding McCay's efforts.[7]

This dialogue, in Scott McCloud's (2000) taxonomy of text-and-image synergy, relies almost entirely upon additive combinations "where words amplify or elaborate an image or vice versa" (145). Without the dialogue, these airship comics would simply be beautiful polyptychs stretching across Sunday tabloid pages, letting readers see important American cities from multiple vantage points. At times, the airship is seen from the ground, like one might have watched it at an amusement park or over a city. But within the same comic McCay often shifts the viewer's position over Nemo's shoulder, from a bird's-eye view, so the city is seen from a privileged, heretofore unattainable vantage. McCay appropriates the literal vantage point of birds as part of his project for elevating the status of American industrial cities. Without this artistic and rhetorical move, the airship series as a coda to the run of *Little Nemo* would not exist.

OF AIRSHIPS AND MAGICAL REALISM

Toward the end, *Little Nemo* was getting a bit staid.

In the last panel of every comic Nemo awoke, clearly at home, safe in the domestic space. Viewers are released from Slumberland until the next week. The last panels define a clear demarcation between Slumberland and Nemo's real, if uneventful, life.

Through the airship series McCay offers something fresh for his readers. The preceding years of exploring dreamscapes prepared the ground for the ontological shift to celebrating American capitalism through deft deployment of magical realism. Unlike the naïveté of the transformation scenes in the Shanty Town series (Canemaker 2018, 120), airships—optimistic and futuristic—glorify the emerging industrial might while eliding avian habitats.

Lois Parkinson Zamora and Wendy Faris (1995) define magical realism as "a mode to exploring—and transgressing—boundaries, whether the boundaries are ontological, political, geographical, or generic. Magical realism often facilitates the fusion, or coexistence, of possible worlds, spaces, systems that would be irreconcilable in other modes of fiction" (5–6). Airships are perfect vehicles for ontological border crossings—Slumberland to North America, interior to exterior, fictional to real, bird to flying machine, and the collapse of the last panel as the demarcation between night and day.

Several critics have read the airship series as McCay's marketing ploy, a print trailer for the cities in which *Little Nemo* would appear once McCay decamped for the Hearst syndicate. Alexander Braun (2017) argues:

McCay did not extend his contract with James Gordon Bennet's publishing house; [. . .] like many illustrators before him, he switched over to William Randolph Hearst. Hearst royally rewarded this decision [. . .] The journey in the airship is not only one of the longest narrative arcs in the early days of comics but also a creative bombshell with which McCay recommended himself for greater endeavors. (6–7)

While partly true, some details undercut this reading. The precipitating conflict in locating Dr. Pill is satisfied by week nine. Surely there were few Hearst subscribers at the North Pole and many of the other sites Nemo flies over (Yellowstone Park comes to mind). The journey to the North Pole, though, is the first time *Little Nemo* intersects with a real, named place. This boundary blurring between the oneiric and the real is the most important aspect of the airship series as it renegotiates the entire structure of *Little Nemo*. Once McCay focuses on actual American cities, he subverts his carefully constructed imaginative universe.

Before the full subversion of *Little Nemo*, McCay makes a somewhat lengthy detour into outer space. After the North Pole, they journey to the moon, where they are menaced once again, this time by moon giants. Nemo says, "There is no use in us of staying around that moon! Those giants want to sleep and wont let us near [*sic*]" (April 17, 1910), and they fly to Mars. The irony of Nemo disturbing another character's sleep is great fun to read, but his plan is interrupted when the captain states that "the engines have broken down." In an elegant solution, a swipe right out of *The Adventures of Baron Munchausen*, Flip lassos the neck of one of the enormous birds flocking on the moon and has it fly the airship to Mars (Canemaker 2018, 78–79) (see figure 4.2).

McCay often uses engine problems to propel drama. A working engine, like the wings of a bird, allows for agency—directed flight. Once they near Mars, the captain repairs the engines and they cut the bird loose. When they are in outer space week by week McCay steers his readers into unknown territory. For instance, on Mars they are met by winged emissaries working for "B. Gosh," a despot who runs the consortium that literally controls the breathable air: "You can buy all you want from B. Gosh and Company, if you've got the price!" (April 24, 1910). Critics have identified the five-month Mars sequence as a thinly veiled attack on McCay's employer. Peter Maresca (2005) remarks, "One of the most fascinating sequences in all of Little Nemo takes place during the extended stay on Mars," where the crew finds "a society suffering from pollution, overpopulation, and the evils of capitalism" (n.p.). McCay's critique is even more curious considering the various real cities McCay will have his characters visit in the subsequent

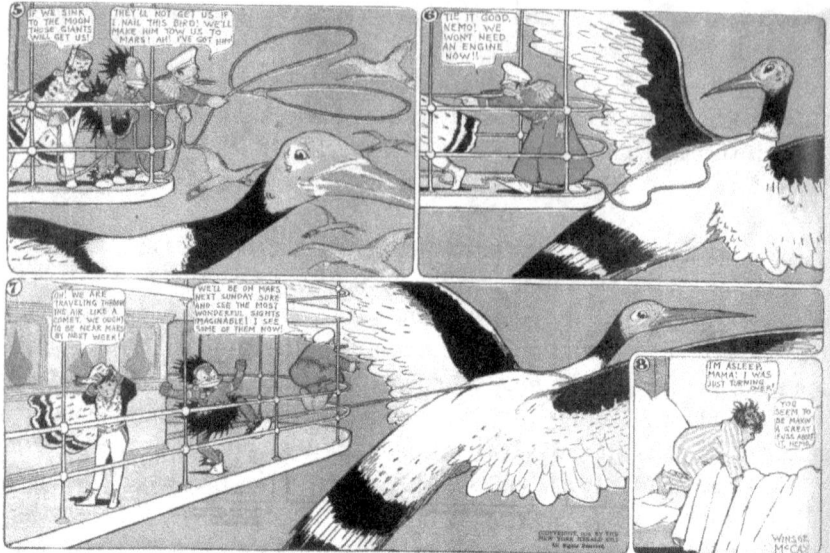

Figure 4.2 Winsor McCay. *Little Nemo in Slumberland.* 17 April 1910. *Source:* Courtesy of The Comic Strip Library, accessed 21 July 2021, https://www.comicstriplibrary.org/display/594.

Sundays, many of which are awash with poverty, environmental degradation, and racial inequity.

After Mars, Nemo instructs the captain: "Take us back to earth at once. I want to show Flip some of the wonders there," to which the captain replies, "I'll land you there next Sunday morning, Herald Square if you say!" (August 14, 1910). Herald Square in Manhattan, not uncoincidentally, is named for the newspaper for which McCay worked. When they land in Herald Square, the comic contains some of McCay's most intriguing intersections between the imaginary elements of *Little Nemo* and components of the real, extratextual world.

In spite of the captain's promise, thirteen weeks pass before they arrive in Herald Square, but these intervening weeks allow McCay to fly his readers through a dazzling display of geographic wonders. These side journeys are caused by the ever-malfunctioning airship. McCay is fond of using pseudo-engineering jargon to enhance this narrative trick. For example, as the airship glides over "Africa," the captain warns, "We must land here. Not only is our *commutator* out of whack, the gearing is causing a friction that is threatening the ignition of the *sparkulator*! The diaphragm on the *eccentric* is recipro-cating too [emphasis added]" (August 21, 1910). The problems are repaired quickly, usually by the end of the strip. They are just a way for McCay to introduce conflict.

Upon arriving in Manhattan, readers see a gorgeous six-panel polyptych that covers the top half and entire width of the page. The bird's-eye view is over the shoulder of the crew, and Nemo exclaims, "There is Luna Park, Dreamland, Steeple-Chase, Brighton and Manhattan Beaches. New York is beyond" (November 13, 1911). After this roll call of amusement parks the airship is met with another airship, marked with an American flag, and staffed by uniformed officials who turn out to be "inspectors of customs," demanding documentation. Moments later the sky fills with a flotilla of airships, a "Reception Committee [for] Little Nemo's Welcome."

Part of the magical realist appeal stems from the ordinary nature of this bureaucracy, the airship flotilla, and the exuberance of the citizenry in seeing Nemo. This combination of the ordinary and extraordinary seeds the ground for other magical realist intersections. As Rawdon Wilson (1995) argues, "The hybrid nature of this [magical realist] space becomes evident when you observe the ease, the purely natural way in which abnormal, experientially impossible and empirically unverifiable events take place. It is as if they had always already been there; their abnormality normalized" (220). The arrival in Herald Square is a good example of intersections with avian life.

In the first panel Nemo-cum-Winsor McCay speaks to the "art director" about "tour[ing] the big cities of this country" and requests supplies (November 27, 1910). Within the comic, the tour is already underway of course, but having Nemo ask for funding is particularly interesting. It is inviting to read McCay's dissatisfaction with the *Herald* here, but the more intriguing significance is the interpolation of worlds that happens two panels later when Flip, on the roof of the *Herald* building, speaks to one of the twenty-two stone owls that the owl-obsessed publisher had asked his architect to place.[8] The suddenly alive and gregarious owl promises, "If you'll come with me I'll show you one of the sights of the entire world that you'll never see from your airship." Flip agrees and the owl walks off its stone perch (see figure 4.3). The stone owl stands in for actual birds as their journey continues.

As Flip, the Imp, and the talking owl head down into a subway, the owl informs them that "this is an underground railway." In a magical realist text, the extraordinary and quotidian rub up against each other like crowded subway car passengers. As the three characters jostle with the other commuters to enter a packed subway car, the magic is the subway itself. (Perhaps this was true for readers who were not residents of New York City in 1910.) In the comic no one remarks upon a green-faced Flip, a nearly naked Imp, or a large talking owl. Everyone is simply advised by a conductor to "step lively." Flip gets separated from the other two, and in a series of slapstick mishaps, they continually swap places, and McCay shifts the points of view. At times, readers see a train car containing the Imp and the owl from Flip's perspective on the platform. Two panels later this is reversed. This constant shifting

Figure 4.3 Winsor McCay. *Little Nemo in Slumberland*. **27 November 1910.** *Source:* Courtesy of The Comic Strip Library, accessed 21 July 2021, https://www.comicstriplibrary.org/display/626.

between visual points of view is a narrative earmark of magical realist texts (Wilson 1995, 210). It foreshadows the rest of the series as McCay offers new perspectives, visually and narratively, about great industrial cities.

The crew remains in New York for three Sundays and then are off. Though Nemo has promised his readers to visit "Boston, Toronto, Buffalo, Pittsburg[9] [*sic*], Cleveland, Toledo, Detroit, Chicago, St. Louis, San Francisco returning by way of Los Angeles, Denver, Omaha, Kansas City, New Orleans, and Memphis, Atlanta, Baltimore, Washington, and Philadelphia" (November 20, 1911), they never make it west of Chicago or south of Wheeling.

The cities celebrate American industrial might, with few nods to the actual inhabitants. The crew is always met by a local guide, a boy who looks suspiciously the same in every city, as though he were racing ahead of the airship to meet them anew each Sunday. He is a prop for McCay to promulgate dry municipal highlights. For example, the Toledo guide informs viewers that, "Toledo has fifteen railroads entering the city besides every kind of lake craft, the biggest steam ships, and the smallest yachts making port here" (March 19, 1911). After gathering facts about the economic might of one city, the group dashes off to the next. They never remain very long. Nemo meets adoring crowds, Flip shops, and then they are gone. Like Theodore Roosevelt's 1900-whistle-stop tours, these excursions approximate a magical realist interpolation of worlds and are a neat marketing trick.

These strips transport readers into the real world through highly privileged vantage points. They are executive tourism devoid of any considerations of class and working conditions except for the most sanitized perspectives. The voyage-to-Pittsburg strip includes two panels that feature an amazing polyptych bird's-eye view of the city, and a discussion about its air quality. Flip says, "If that is Pittsburg let's side-step it! That's a bum looking town. Too much smoke and dismal looking for me! Let's not stop!" Nemo responds with, "There must be some mistake! Pittsburg is not smoky like it used to be or looks to us here! We'll land and see for ourselves!" (February 26, 1911). Despite Nemo's protestations, floating above Pittsburg/Pittsburgh in 1911 in the open-air gondola of an airship is the very last place any living creature, winged or otherwise, would ever want to have been (see figure 4.4). The same holds true for swimming in or eating fish from its fabled three rivers. As Joel Tarr (2005) explains, in early twentieth-century Pittsburgh:

> The by-product [of] coke works, then, along with the iron and steel mills, consumed huge amounts of land along the rivers, using the latter for purposes of cheap transportation and wastewater disposal as well as sources of process water. Their presence was indicated not only by the flaring of waste gases and columns of black smoke, but also by plumes of white steam that rose as the red-hot coke was cooled with process and river water. Since the plants worked

Figure 4.4 Winsor McCay. *Little Nemo in Slumberland.* 26 February 1911. *Source:* Courtesy of The Comic Strip Library, accessed 21 July 2021, https://www.comicstriplibrary.org/display/640.

twenty-four hours a day, these plumes constantly appeared in the visible landscape. (39)

The water was just as deadly, for "by 1910, the sewers drained over seven thousand acres of the city, discharging into the neighboring rivers. The outlets ranged in size from fifteen-inch terra cotta pipes to twelve-foot brick sewers. Forty-seven public sewer outlets flowed into the Monongahela River" (Tarr 2005, 39). Despite Nemo's reassurance in the end that Pittsburgh was not as dirty as it appeared in the picture, McCay's drawing was not of the city anyone experienced in 1910. Ironically, Flip purchases dozens of boxes of Pittsburgh "stogies" because he "heard so much about them." Perhaps McCay pokes fun at the air quality after all. The revision of Pittsburg/Pittsburgh may be the most extraordinary, supernatural aspect of this episode in the entire airship series. Unlike Slumberland, these cities exist beyond Nemo's dreams. Nemo awakens from adventuring in real places, beautifully illustrated, cities of possibility where readers may actually live or visit. This is the crucial difference, the one place where McCay's porous borders enable a celebration of America's industrial might, even if it comes at a pernicious cost to its wildlife, avian and otherwise, and citizenry. It is a flight to real cities, but also a flight from the reality of them.

McCay's final episode in the airship series is a three-Sunday visit to Chicago. This is significant for many reasons, including a startling drop in color quality in the last two strips. The final Chicago comics are red and black only. They still feature McCay's amazing line work and bountiful praise of industry, but the visual aspects of these comics are lacking. The last Chicago comic excludes much. The middle panel features a single drawing the width of the tabloid page showing the tiny airship floating over the Chicago Union Stock Yard. A word balloon informs readers that, "As far as the eye can see in all directions are these stock yards. 25000 pens, 75000 people employed in every minute, night and day, Sundays included of the 365 days" (April 23, 1911). That is the magical part of this episode: the infinite promise of America. Five years later Carl Sandburg's "Chicago" anoints the city as the "Hog butcher for the world"— shrieking and smells of the daily butchering of thousands of animals would have been ear-splitting and horrifying. Four months earlier, on December 22, 1910, a fire at the Stock Yards killed twenty-one firefighters, the largest loss of firefighter lives in United States history until September 11, 2001. McCay had to be aware of this, but he and his creation floated serenely above this very recent history, offering a point-of-view steeped in American exceptionalism.

This viewpoint literally and figuratively erases the presence of nonhuman worlds. At the end, the accompanying owl will presumably return to its perch as a stone emblem atop the *Herald Tribune* building in New York. Nemo will wake up and go about his day. Winsor McCay will leave this strip behind and head off to the Hearst Syndicate, ending the greatest early American newspaper comic strip with a limited color palette.

NOTES

1. For the sake of readability, I have changed the dialogue to sentence case, correcting for McCay's use of all capital letters.
2. Most crucially, McCay retains one of the "jungle imps" for *Little Nemo*.
3. See the attacking "redskins" in two strips from the airship series (August 28 and September 4, 1910) at Chavez <www.comicstriplibrary.org/display/613> and < www.comicstriplibrary.org/display/614>.
4. This moment is so integral to the structure of *Little Nemo* that Art Spiegelman (2004) swipes it in ironic homage in his graphic novel about 9/11, *In the Shadow of No Towers*.
5. Dumont's airship, like the Imp character, are, in Chris Ware's parlance, "a swipe," a visual referent from another source (Raeburn 2004, 54).
6. Airships flew across the literary landscape of America, in everything from children's books like *Uncle Wiggily's Airship* (1915) to novels in series like *Tom Swift and His Airship* (1910) and *The Airship Boys: or The Quest for the Aztec Treasure* (1910) aimed primarily at boys.

7. *Little Nemo* is almost entirely dialogue-driven. For a discussion of utterance and enunciation, see Phillip Lejeune (1989, 3–30).

8. Canemaker writes, "The architects had managed to persuade the building's owner, publisher James Gordon Bennett, Jr. (1841–1918), not to duplicate the Palace of the Doges in Venice. They were unsuccessful in dissuading the headstrong Bennett from his determination to place owls (his personal totem), their eyes wired with electric lights, as decorative" architectural embellishments (2018, 77).

9. McCay uses the old spelling of Pittsburgh. On July 19, 1911, the U.S. Board on Geographic Names officially added the letter "h" to the end of Pittsburgh.

REFERENCES

"Airship at Dreamland." *Glimpses of the New Coney Island Book*. www://coneyislandhistory.org. Accessed July 2021.

Bendazzi, Giannalberto. 1994. *One Hundred Years of Cartoon Animation*. Bloomington: Indiana. University Press.

Braun, Alexander. 2017. *The Airship Adventures of Little Nemo*. Cologne: TASCHEN.

Butko, Brian. 2017. *Luna: Pittsburgh's Original Lost Kennywood*. Pittsburgh: Heinz History Center.

Canemaker, John. 2018. *Winsor McCay: His Life and Art*. Boca Raton: CRC Press.

Chavez, Zachary. "Comic Strip Library—Digital Collection of Classic Comic Strips." *Comic Strip Library—Digital Collection of Classic Comic Strips*. www.comicstriplibrary.org/

Chute, Hillary and Patrick Jagoda, eds. 2014. *Comics & Media: A Special Issue of Critical Inquiry*. Chicago: University of Chicago Press.

Kennamer, J. E., M. C. Kennamer, and R. Brenneman. "History of the Wild Turkey in North America." *NWTF Wildlife Bulletin No. 15*. Edgefield: National Wild Turkey Federation.

Kurlansky, Mark. 2006. *The Big Oyster: History on the Half Shell*. New York: Random House.

Labio, Catherine. 2015. "The Architecture of Comics." *Critical Inquiry*, Vol. 41, No. 2, Winter: 312–43.

Lejeune, Phillip. 1989. *On Autobiography*. Translated by Katherine Leary. Minneapolis: University of Minnesota Press.

Maresca, Peter, ed. 2005. *Little Nemo in Slumberland: Splendid Sundays 1905–1910*. Palo Alto: Sunday Press Books.

McCloud, Scott. 1994. *Understanding Comics: The Invisible Art*. New York: William Morrow.

Parkinson Zamora, Lois and Wendy B. Faris, eds. 1995. *Magical Realism: Theory, History, Community*. Durham: Duke University Press.

Raeburn, Daniel. 2004. *Chris Ware (Monograph Series)*. New Haven: Yale University Press.

Roeder, Katherine. 2014. Wide Awake in Slumberland: Fantasy, Mass Culture, and Modernism in *the Art of Winsor McCay*. Jackson: University of Mississippi Press.

Rose, Alexander. 2020. Empires of the Sky: *Zeppelins, Airplanes, and Two Men's Epic Duel to Rule the World*. New York: Random House. Sandburg, Carl. "Chicago." https://www.poetryfoundation.org/poetrymagazine/poems/12840/chicago. Accessed July 11, 2021.

Spiegelman, Art. 2004. *In the Shadow of No Towers*. New York: Pantheon.

Tarr, Joel A. 2005. *Devastation and Renewal: An Environmental History of Pittsburgh and Its Region*. Pittsburgh: University of Pittsburgh Press.

Wilson, Rawdon. 1995. "Metamorphoses of Fictional Space." In *Magical Realism: Theory, History, Community*, edited by Lois Parkinson Zamora and Wendy B. Faris. Durham: Duke University Press, 209–33.

"Winsor McCay—A Tale of the Jungle Imps by Felix Fiddle." *Billy Ireland Cartoon Library and Museum*. https://cartoons.osu.edu/digitalalbums/winsormccay/imps.html. Accessed July 11, 2021.

Section 2

WRITING ABOUT/LIKE BIRDS

Chapter 5

The Fate of Birds in Anatole France's *Penguin Island*

Timothy Ruppert

While talking to the young biologist Nick early on in Edward Albee's *Who's Afraid of Virginia Woolf?* (1962; 1998), the cynical historian George mentions three places as literary analogues for the New England college town in which the two men work: Illyria, where William Shakespeare's *Twelfth Night* takes place; Gomorrah, a biblical city of the plain; and Penguin Island, the principal setting of Anatole's France's 1908 satire, *L'Île des Pingouins* [hereafter *Penguin Island*] (Act 1, 22). This reference to the novel proves appropriate to the professors' conversation insofar as the allusion evokes images of moral decay and political hypocrisy, positing these as the inheritance of history, a seemingly ineluctable legacy. George has *Penguin Island* in mind partly because the book has long stood as an especially erudite statement on the cyclical nature of human history. Consider H. R. Steeves's (1933) claim that *Penguin Island* reflects a sense of history that values a "positive dissent from every form of organized idolatry" (xiii) and so "questions persistently that cheerful and fallacious reading of history as a route-map of steady progress toward perfect human relations" (xiii). For an intellectual of George's generation, the story of Penguinia might well have epitomized a proper skepticism toward any ideals, even those born of youthful hopefulness, that contravene history's crueler lessons, supported by what Steeves calls "social evidence" (xiv).

The paucity of contemporary critical readings in English of *Penguin Island* suggests that this understanding of the novel has perhaps worked too well, militating against ongoing scholarly interest in the narrative's merits for the twenty-first century world. While authors such as Steven C. Ridgely (2013), Claire Rowden (2014), and Andrew Pigott (2017) have published, respectively, on the Bluebeard narrative in *Les Sept Femmes de Barbe et autres contes merveilleux*, on Jules Massenet's operatic adaptation of *Thaïs*, and on

Les Dieux ont soif, very little has been written in English on *Penguin Island* within the last decade and more. If indeed it has been overlooked in recent years, the cause may owe somewhat to the longstanding socio-historical take on the novel, the very notion underscoring George's comment to Nick in the Albee play. Applying a remark that Pigott makes of *Les Dieux ont soif*, perhaps "understanding too much too quickly" (1062) about *Penguin Island* has obscured the work's relevance for readers who today may see serious interpretation of the piece as a *fait accompli*. True, *Penguin Island* concerns social affairs and their interrelatedness with the recurring historical patterns of human time. But the book begins as a story of deep natural time, depicting a scheme of things to which the clock, the calendar, and the timeline are alien. We should not forget that the denizens of Penguinia are, in essence, birds—rendered human by heavenly fiat, yes, but birds all the same. And their shared fate, their obligatory inclusion in the history of people, registers the catastrophic outcomes of human intervention in the penguins' lives.

With this chapter, then, I want to explore the ways in which we may revisit *Penguin Island* in light of present-day questions regarding contact between humans and birds and the often-deleterious consequences for bird populations when humans interfere in ancient environments and ecosystems. My discussion focuses on the first of the novel's eight books, as it is here that the penguins' transformation into people takes place. Although my immediate goal is to spark new scholarly engagements with both *Penguin Island* and Anatole France (who a century ago won the Nobel Prize in literature), my overarching hope is that what follows will add in some modest way to our study of birds as the literary imagination has portrayed them, with special care given throughout the chapter to acknowledging the imperiled dignity and disregarded rights of these creatures—which injustices, regrettably, affect myriad species beyond the page-bound world.

For those unfamiliar with the work, the earliest incidents in *Penguin Island* take place at an unspecified point in Late Antiquity and result from the unfortunate tendency of a guileless monk to listen to the devil. The former, called Maël, oversees an abbey in Western Europe but also travels in a miraculous "trough of stone which floated like a boat upon the waters" (France 1933, 5) as he seeks out souls to Christianize. The latter frequently disguises himself as a holy man and tricks the abbot into making egregious choices, the most monumental of which involves, against the Lord's implicit wishes, equipping the stone vessel with a sail (10–13). The devil's recommendation leads Maël on a long phantasmagorical journey across the vicious waves of an icy sea, the home of serpents, sirens, and a polar bear who recites lines of Virgil's poetry (14–16). When the storm calms, Maël lands on a rainy island and finds "some yellow eggs, marked with black spots, and about as large as those of a swan. But he did not touch them, saying: 'Birds are the living praises of God.

I should not like a single one of these praises to be lacking through me'" (17). His noble feelings, though, prove insufficient guard against Maël soon making an immense mistake that affects the island's birds forever. His sight and hearing diminished by the terrible voyage, the abbot comes upon a group of beings whom he believes are kindly pagans convened in a sort of Parliament but are in fact a colony of penguins (17–18). Because these creatures listen patiently and trustfully to Maël, the only human they have ever seen, he welcomes the penguins into the Church: "for three days and three nights he baptized the birds" (19). Maël's error occasions a summit in Heaven, at which the most learned among the blessed discuss what should now be done (20–32). Despite St. Cornelius' warning that "the Christian state [. . .] is not without serious inconveniences for a penguin" (25), God ultimately favors St. Hermas's exhortation—"Change these penguins to men" (31–32)—and sends the Archangel Raphael to Maël with a sacred mandate (32). Acquiescing in the divine will, Maël transforms the birds into people (33–34).

Maël's presence on the island almost at once has irrevocable consequences for its avian denizens. Their ensoulment necessitates a complete physical alteration of the penguins, whose future, as God himself concedes, "will be far less enviable than if they had been without this baptism and this incorporation into the family of Abraham" (32). His delightfully illogical promise "to be ignorant of what I know [. . .] and in my blind clear-sightedness I will let myself be surprised by what I have foreseen" (32) indicates that the penguins now belong to a different order of time and must live within history as humans understand and experience it. Even if this were all, it would be devastating. But within moments of the penguins' translation into people, Maël steepens the price that the birds will pay for their souls. Fearing what might happen to the penguins after his departure, the monk resolves on "the idea of transporting their island to Armorica" (34). Attaching "a very fine cord about forty feet long [fashioned] out of the flax of his stole" to an escarpment on the shore, Maël makes course for home: "The trough glided over the sea and towed Penguin Island behind it; after nine days' sailing it approached the Breton coast, bringing the island with it" (34). Their bodies changed, their island relocated, the birds begin to live as humans: with clothing comes sexual violence; with labor comes suppression; and with property comes the first murder.

At times charmingly whimsical, at times shamelessly preposterous, the first book of *Penguin Island* readies us for France's seriocomic critique of the virtues and vices, the desires and despairs at the core of the human story. Indeed, as their generations pass, the penguins succumb to the eminently recognizable paradigms of history, and in Penguinia's chronicles we meet bloody monarchs, brutal imperialists, heartless capitalists, racist peacekeepers, and nihilistic terrorists, until, at last, Penguinia vanishes altogether: "The territory that had supported so many millions of men became nothing more than a desert. On the hill of Fort St. Michel wild horses cropped the coarse grass" (294). In a sense the novel ends as it began, at the point where a vast and peopleless timescape—"Days flowed by like water from the fountains, and the centuries passed like drops falling from the ends of stalactites" (294)—intersects with history as human beings, over the ages, gradually return (France 294–95). It is in this convergence of temporalities that the birds' story gets told.

Not surprisingly, the account of Maël's turbulent sea-crossing skirts any number of details that would decisively place the holy man's adventure on a map. Despite the novel's title, the text does not make plain whether Maël goes southward, toward the penguins (in French, *manchots*) of Antarctica, or northward, toward the auks (*pingouins*) of the arctic regions. While the birds' wings and markings (France 18) make the latter all but certain, the former nevertheless presents fascinating possibilities, especially given what Gillen D'Arcy Wood (2020) notes of Jules Dumont D'Urville's 1840 expedition to the South Pole: "Because they were becalmed, D'Urville allowed the men to present a pantomime on deck, titled 'Father Antarctica.' In the mock ceremony, a man dressed as a penguin announced the founding of a polar academy, Penguinopolis, which D'Urville duly approved" (163). That Wood records as well the shooting (161), dissecting (160), and consumption (163) of penguins by D'Urville's crew casts some doubt whether the distinction between the two groups of birds matters much when human beings intervene heedlessly in nonhuman lives.

Lucifer's ruse, then, has led Maël to a great auk colony in the north Atlantic at a remote time when these birds, the relatives of puffins, razorbills, and murres, thrived across the Atlantic. Likely the island Maël chances upon resembles Funk Island, a place off the Newfoundland coast that, for Franklin Russell, was "a midden of slain creatures [. . .] as significant to an ornithologist as Ashurbanipal's palace would be to an archaeologist" (Finch and Elder 2002, 612) because of its ancient connections to the now-extinct great auks. The last known great auks died in 1844, the year of France's birth. Like the moa and the dodo before it and the passenger pigeon and the huia after it, the great auk suffered a fate principally, if not exclusively, brought on by human predation and interference. In her Pulitzer-Prize winning book *The Sixth Extinction: An Unnatural History*, Elizabeth Kolbert (2015) tells a story that poignantly captures the nature of relations between great auks and humans. While conducting research at a Reykjavik museum, Kolbert finds a great auk exhibit that includes auk bones (58) and a filmed dramatization: "In the video, a shadowy figure crept along the rocky shore toward a shadowy auk. When he drew close enough, the figure pulled out a stick and clubbed the animal over the head. The auk responded with a cry somewhere between a honk and a grunt" (58). The spectacle compels Kolbert to view this video "half a dozen times" (58): "Creep, clobber, squawk. Repeat" (58). She lists some of the uses to which people put the birds; beyond eating auks, inhabitants and outsiders alike "used [the birds] as fish bait, as a source of feathers for stuffing mattresses, and as fuel" (60), this last meaning that fires were kindled with the bodies of auks (60).

The eventual loss of the great auks thus reflects a process that began in medieval Iceland (58) and ended on the miniscule island of Eldey in the mid-1800s, following a quick decline hastened by the "new threat [of their] own rarity" (62) as the birds' "skins and eggs were avidly sought" (62)—chilling proof of Helen Macdonald's (2014) contention that, as animal species dwindle, "rarity is all that they are made of" (181). We may see in the great auks' fate a parallel with the decimation of birdlife in the Hawaiian Islands, where, as Barry Lopez (1986) writes, the presence of expansionist Europeans sharply worsened the danger to a bird population already reduced by half before James Cook landed at Kaua'i (50). Like its distant relations the O'ahu nukupu'u, the O'ahu 'ō 'ō, and the kioea, all gone by the middle decades of the nineteenth century, the great auk now lives in our imaginations only, to "the diminution of the world," as Macdonald says of animals forever lost through extinction (2014, 181).

Of course, extinction as a general phenomenon has always been a fact of deep time; for example, creatures of the Late Cretaceous epoch, like the triceratops and the last titanosaurs, were not the victims of human beings. The great auks were, though. In 1990's *Last Chance to See*, Douglas Adams and Mark Carwardine (1990) lament the astonishing velocity and scope of extinction events during the Anthropocene: "Most of the extinctions since prehistoric times have occurred in the last three hundred years. And most of the extinctions that have occurred in the last three hundred years have occurred in the last fifty. And most of the extinctions that have occurred in the last fifty have occurred in the last ten" (212). The grim mathematics that Adams and Carwardine present indict humankind for expediting a horrifically fast lessening in biodiversity across the globe, and the great auk persists as an especially unsettling emblem of human destructiveness and irresponsibility.

Maël's arrival inaugurates the slow apocalypse of the great auks who inhabit the tiny island; the birds in effect are a dead clade walking, surviving their baptism and transformation without ever really recovering from them. The brilliance of the devil's trick includes using Maël's innocence to sinister advantage. When Maël finds the bird eggs, we feel that we can trust the sincerity of his pledge to harm neither the children nor their parents (17). But the storm has left Maël with difficulties in seeing and hearing clearly. The monk evangelizes the birds because he misperceives what they are, and without realizing it his promise falls apart. Here Maël's encounter with the auks hovers in shadows, somewhere between darkness and light. What David

Perkins (2003) shows regarding the British Romantics' use of songbirds in their poetry may help us to better understand Maël at this point in *Penguin Island*. In Percy Bysshe Shelley's "To a Skylark" (1820) and John Keats's "Ode to a Nightingale" (1819), for instance, "the birds are wild and at a safe distance from the poet [. . .] not pets, not caged, and not catchable" (Perkins 2003, 142). Such pieces give us birds who "are just voices" (142), bodiless, unreal: "Hence the bird may be endowed with spontaneity, unity of being, unconsciousness of death, immortality, and immediacy to the divine" (142). "Thus exalted," Perkins asserts, "an animal cannot be viewed with fellow feeling, much less with compassion" (147). Unlike Shelley's skylark or Keats's nightingale, Maël's auks are not invisible; the monk sees and hears them but never suspects that these indistinct shapes, bipedal and songless, made the nests that he found along the shore. By taking the birds for people, Maël unwittingly sets invalid grounds for his encounter with the avian other, with ruinous consequences. As in Samuel Taylor Coleridge's *The Rime of the Ancient Mariner* (1798), the misapprehension of the animal other engenders death (Morton 2010, 45–48), whether in an instant—the lot of the albatross— or after millennia—the fate of the auks who greet the saintly Maël.

When Coleridge's Mariner murders the albatross, God does not directly prosecute the crime; this task falls to the polar spirits and other supernatural creatures, such as Death and Life-in-Death, who live in or have access to the places where the Mariner travels. These otherworldly beings seem decidedly terrestrial, existing alongside the world of people and possessing the right and power to intervene at will in the human realm. When France's abbot gives a Christian sacrament to the auk colony, though, God adjudicates the matter personally, soliciting ideas from the great thinkers who reside in Paradise, beginning with a terse St. Patrick flatly denying the legitimacy of the baptism (France 1933, 20). Although Maël's earthly mentor, St. Gal, champions the birds (20–21; 26), most of the assembled initially dismiss any claim that the auks might have to the Christian afterlife: St. Guénolé proclaims that baptism, a sacrament freighted with scriptural and metaphysical significance, "is not a gift to bestow upon birds" (21). Yet the sacrament has indeed been properly administered, meaning that it is incumbent upon the birds to act as responsible Christians irrespective of their supposed soullessness. St. Augustine, a salient voice in the anti-bird faction, unpromisingly concludes that "the penguins will go to hell" (26). Saint Catherine of Alexandria (27) implores God both to refashion the auks as hybrids of birds and people and to vouchsafe these recreated creatures "an immortal soul—but one of small size" (29). Her recommendation receives support from Lactantius, who asks his colleagues "to bear in mind that the angels, who proceed from man and bird, are purity itself" (31). That such thinking influences God's decision and for now saves the birds scarcely proves comforting, as the auks continue to reap what they did not sow. The angels that Lactantius mentions were never beings of the earth, nor were their bodies forced on them as a doctrinal necessity. Heaven's intervention ensures that the auks belong to a history not their own.

Notwithstanding a few exceptions, the blessed conferees view the plight of Maël's birds with a blend of pity, indifference, and vague distaste; the auks, to their lasting misfortune, have no true advocate in Heaven to speak on their behalf. Because France takes care to avoid anachronism in this scene, he does not include among the delegates any major theological figure, such as Saint Thomas Aquinas or Saint Francis of Assisi, who lived after the very earliest years of the Christian era. It is expressly intriguing to imagine if the presence of the latter would have affected the fate of the birds in *Penguin Island* for the better. This saint, as Gilbert Simondon (2011) notes in *Two Lessons on Animal and Man*, held that "animal reality is not at all something vulgar and sordid" (68) but rather belongs intrinsically to "the universal order" (68), so much so that, Simondon claims, it became possible during the Renaissance to conceive of "animal saintliness" (69):

> The Renaissance discovered a relationship between man and things, between man and the Universe. Instead of considering human reality as a special creation by God for which the rest of the Universal order was finalized and to which it is subordinate in an absolute manner, it is actually rather according to an aesthetic order that the relationship of the human to the animal is thought. (69)

Accordingly, for Simondon, "the entirety of Creation is harmonious; the place of man is complementary to plants and animals" (69). None of these innovations in thought benefit the auks of France's novel. In a fashion all too familiar to us today, the birds become a subject of formal governance, and their home and bodies no longer have a future independent of human judgments. What happens to the auks owes more to political expediency than to a sincere regard for their dignity as living creatures. If René Descartes, who saw animals as automatons (Simondon 73), and Nicolas Malebranche, who asserted that "animals cannot suffer" (Simondon 77), had resolved the matter of Maël's auks, the outcome could scarcely have been worse.

With respect to the actual letter of God's edict, as shaped by an inscrutable legislative process and conveyed by an angelic intermediary, Maël's one duty is to transform the birds into people. Nevertheless, with greater tenderness than foresight, the abbot fears for the birds' spiritual survival and so expedites a strange dispossession: the bearing away of Penguin Island to a new home off the Brittany Peninsula, within the European sphere of influence (France 1933, 34). For all its comical improbabilities, this scene certainly invites us to consider the ways in which France's satire formulates ethical questions expressly relevant to environmentalist discourse and ecological studies today. However benign his motives appear to his own heart, Maël here initiates a translocation of the birds; to preserve their souls, Maël facilitates a vast migration that intentionally introduces the birds into the human wilderness (Schwartz et al. 2012, 733). Plainly, what Maël does goes well beyond contemporary relocations of flora, such as *Torreya taxifolia*, and of fauna, such as endangered butterflies (Schwartz et al. 2012, 734), yet his actions, their hyperbole aside, indeed resemble the irresponsibly managed or assisted translocations that seem to be a hallmark of the Anthropocene era. Consider what Kolbert writes of the role of *Batrachochytrium dendrobatidis* [Bd] (13) in the worldwide decimation and extinction of amphibian species such as the Panamanian golden frog: "Without being loaded by someone onto a boat or a plane, it would have been impossible for a frog carrying Bd to get from Africa to Australia or from North America to Europe. This sort of intercontinental reshuffling [. . .] is probably unprecedented in the three-and-a-half-billion-year history of life" (18–19). By giving the birds a new home in the European Atlantic, Maël completes the pattern of their destiny and ensures their eventual disappearance. While the birds did not develop in a coevolutionary manner with people, Maël's intervention ensures that the two groups have now become coincident in history, sharing in kind the thousand unnatural shocks that flesh is heir to.

Soon after Maël performs this questionable miracle, the devil reappears at his side to help in properly assimilating Penguinia into the chronicle of human affairs. As always, Satan shows a keen understanding of the world, and he is not content to foster the simple violence characteristic of so many encounters between birds and people. Satan takes pains to prevent what happened (or shall happen) at Honolulu International Airport when "the first wild snowy owl ever to have appeared in Hawaii," as Noah Strycker (2014) recounts, was "promptly shot [. . .] in the name of aircraft safety" (71). The devil envisions a more gradual and sophisticated fate for the auks. In the guise of a monk called Magis, he coaxes Maël to clothe a female penguin, Orberosia (later the patron saint of Penguinia), ostensibly for the sake of empowering the island's women because clothes will provide the females with an irresistible mystique and a lasting advantage over the males (France 38). "Wait for a thousand years," Satan says, "and you will see, father, with what powerful weapons you have endowed the daughters of Alca" (38). Maël acquiesces, and Orberosia immediately becomes the focus of fierce sexual competition, much to the devil's delight: her naked body now covered, the males must "represent it to themselves in their minds" (41). This deception means that Maël has occasioned a significant cognitive change in the birds, who begin to see themselves and their world in terms of possession, conflict, and power. The auks have taken their first step into human history.

As Penguinia marches on to nationhood, its earliest residents inevitably start to arrange their lives according to institutionalized codes and values, most of which have their nascence in brutality and fraud. A particularly important foundational story in this vein involves the dire days of the Dragon of Alca, a sinister beast that nightly terrorizes the island's farms and villages. By the time the citizens petition Maël for help, the creature has consumed several children, including a boy called Elo, and "mangled the maiden Orberosia, the fairest of the Penguins, with his teeth" (57). Maël deliberates with his colleagues—including Brother Regimental, the devil's most-recent impersonation—and concludes that only a pure virgin can overcome the monster (61). The monks quest across the island, but no virgin comes forward until Orberosia herself reappears (72–74). She tells of how she escaped the dragon and agrees to lure the animal to the Coast of Shadows, where Kraken, a wrongly banished hero, will kill it (74). As the frightened Penguins look on, the serene Orberosia places one of her garments around the raging creature, rendering it docile, and leads it to Kraken, who slices it open with his sword (75). Through the wound, "with curling hair and folded hands, little Elo and the five other children whom the monster had devoured" emerge unharmed (75). The Penguins honor their deliverer as Orberosia, instructed by Heaven, advises: "the Penguin people will pay to the knight Kraken an annual tribute" of harvest and livestock and allow the rescued children to wait on him in perpetuity, thus preventing the danger that "a new dragon will come upon the island more terrible than the first" (74). So profound is the general joy that neither the Penguins nor the monks ever realize that Orberosia and Kraken are married, that Elo is their houseboy, or that the Dragon of Alca is a contrivance of sealskins, bull's horns, and bird beaks created and operated by Kraken (69). With peace restored in Penguinia, "Kraken levied the tribute and became the richest and most powerful of the Penguins. As a sign of his victory and so as to inspire a salutary terror, he wore a dragon's crest upon his head and he had a habit of saying to the people: 'Now that the monster is dead I am the dragon'" (76). Kraken and Orberosia's son, Draco, will become "the founder of the first royal dynasty of the Penguins" (77). And so, monarchy and the rule of force come to Penguin Island, ushered in by fear, lies, and showmanship.

The long flight to apocalypse commences here, with the ironies and enmities of a singularly unusual past. Although Maël soon vanishes from the narrative, along with all the blessed and the damned, his legacy stays with the Penguins across the centuries until, at last, the birds exit human history through a collective self-destruction. As a genetic engineer acting on Heaven's behalf, Maël regrets his mistakes but never questions the expansionist Christianity that drives his evangelical campaigns. We may here recall Bill McKibben's (2006) warning that all biotechnology supports a particular idea of human hegemony over other species: "Man is at the center of creation and it is therefore right for him to do whatever pleases him" (128). And if we imagine, with Richard Powers (2018) in his novel *The Overstory*, the life of Earth taking place over a single twenty-four-hour period, during which time "modern man shows up four seconds before midnight" (475), we may better appreciate that Penguin Island receives mere milliseconds within human history before the clock runs out.

Just as St. Maël erred when he guided the birds into human history, so the Penguins misstep in their later attempts to efface the account of their origin. In his "Annals of Penguinia," Ovidius Capito rejects the story of Maël as "a tissue of puerile fables and popular tales" that gives an unduly mystical cast to "the ancient migrations of the Penguins" (France 1933, 118). In striving after scientific objectivity, Capito endorses a narrative in which Penguinia, "to-day the queen" of the "heaven-favoured seas" (118), achieved its international dominance naturally, as a matter of evolutionary course. Lopez (1986) identifies this sort of revisionism as typical of how humans tell the story of ecological crisis: "We lament the passing of the Eskimo curlew, the sea mink, the Labrador duck, Pallas' cormorant, and Steller's sea cow," but we shy away from blaming ourselves for their fates because of our shared "belief that there is nothing innately wrong with us as a species" (52). And because we are so seldom the villains of our own story, we forget that we too belong to "a universe of impersonal chemical, physical, and biological laws" (52). By discounting the memory of how the abbot forever changed life on the island, Capito suppresses a tale of human encroachment and sanctioned intervention from which Penguinia may have profited. Without those lessons, the birds go the way of all flesh.

With his picture of the Penguins' history and fate, France sketches an image of an accidental people trudging toward nothingness. In our twenty-first century, we stride as a world toward oblivion. Like France's Penguins, we seem to have learned precious little—or perhaps what we *have* learned came too late. Certainly, meaningful illustrations of responsible interactions with nonhuman beings deserve mention: for instance, while working in Port Lockroy, Pittsburgh filmmaker Keith Reimink photographed penguins only if the birds ventured willingly across the tundra toward his camera (see figure 5.1 and figure 5.2). Yet such conscientiousness and care seem all too rare as humans persist in committing unconscionable acts of interference against myriad species. Consider what Bill Fraser says of the human threat to the Adélie penguins of Antarctica: "Here you have this unbelievably tough little animal, able to deal with anything, succumbing to the large-scale effects of [human] activities. And that's the one thing they can't deal with, and they're dying because of it" (Montaigne 2010, 250). Interventions less global in scope render similarly deleterious outcomes, as was the case in 2012 when the

Figure 5.1 Image of Penguins at Port Lockroy, Antarctica. *Source*: Photo by Keith Reimink, used by permission.

Figure 5.2 Image of Penguins at Port Lockroy, Antarctica. *Source*: Photo by Keith Reimink, used by permission.

Tasmanian Department of Primary Industries, Parks, Water and Environment introduced Tasmanian devils, an endangered species, to Maria Island: within a decade, the marsupials "wiped out 3,000 breeding pairs of little penguins (*Eudyptula minor*) living on the island" (Baker 2021, *Live Science*). As we strive not simply to come to terms with recurring ecological tragedy but to end to it, the revaluation of texts like *Penguin Island* may make clearer the path to a living future.

REFERENCES

Adams, Douglas, and Mark Carwardine. 1990. *Last Chance to See*. New York: Ballantine Books.

Albee, Edward. 1998. *Who's Afraid of Virginia Woolf*. New York: Dramatists Play Services.

Baker, Harry. June 24, 2021. "Tasmanian Devils Wipe Out Colony of Little Penguins in Major Conservation Backfire." *Live Science*. https://www.livescience.com/tasmanian-devils-wipe--little-penguins.html

France, Anatole. 1933. *Penguin Island*. Trans. A. W. Evans. New York: Modern Library.

Kolbert, Elizabeth. 2015. *The Sixth Extinction: An Unnatural History*. City: Picador.

Lopez, Barry. 1986. *Arctic Dreams: Imagination and Desire in a Northern Landscape*. New York: Vintage.

Macdonald, Helen. 2014. *H is for Hawk*. New York: Grove Press.

McKibben, Bill. 2006. *The End of Nature*. New York: Random House Trade Paperbacks.

Montaigne, Fen. 2010. *Fraser's Penguins: Warning Signs from Antarctica*. New York: St. Martin's Griffin.

Morton, Timothy. 2010. *The Ecological Thought*. Cambridge, MA: Harvard UP.

Perkins, David. 2003. *Romanticism and Animal Rights*. Cambridge, UK: Cambridge UP.

Pigott, Andrew. 2017. "Rites of Holy Terror: Sadean Governmentality in France's *Les Dieux ont Soif*." *MLN*, vol. 132, 1062–89.

Powers, Richard. 2018. *The Overstory: A Novel*. New York: W. W. Norton.

Ridgely, Steven C. 2013. "Terayama Shūji and Bluebeard." *Marvels & Tales: Journal of Fairy-Tale Studies*, vol. 27, no. 2, 290–300.

Rowden, Clair. 2014. "*Thaïs*: Adaptation, Degeneration, and Intermediality." *Dix-Neuf*, vol. 18, no. 2, 134–49.

Russell, Franklin. 2002. "The Island of Auks." In *The Norton Book of Nature Writing*, ed. Robert Finch and John Elder. New York: W. W. Norton, 605–13.

Schwartz, Mark W., et al. 2012. "Managed Relocation: Integrating the Scientific, Regulatory, and Ethical Challenges." *BioScience*, vol. 62. no. 8, 732–43.

Simondon, Gilbert. 2011. *Two Lessons on Animal and Man*. Trans. Drew S. Burk. Minneapolis: Univocal.

Steeves, H. R. 1933. "Introduction." In *Penguin Island*, ed. Anatole France. New York: Modern Library, ix–xvi.

Strycker, Noah. 2014. *The Thing with Feathers: The Surprising Lives of Birds and What They Reveal about Being Human.* New York: Riverhead Books.

Wood, Gillen D'Arcy. 2020. *Land of Wondrous Cold: The Race to Discover Antarctica and Unlock the Secrets of its Ice.* Princeton: Princeton UP.

Chapter 6

Of Curlews and Crows

Representations of Avian Cognition in North American Animal Stories

Jennifer Schell

At the turn of the nineteenth century, many North American readers embraced animal stories, realistic but sentimental tales that described the lives of nonhuman animals often from the animals' points of view.[1] John Burroughs was not one of them. In 1903, the famous naturalist published an essay in *The Atlantic Monthly* entitled "Real and Sham Natural History" in which he instructed authors of North American animal stories to "not put upon our human credulity a greater burden than it can bear" insofar as their descriptions of behavior and cognition were concerned (Burroughs 1903, 303). Highlighting examples from Charles G. D. Roberts's *Kindred of the Wild*, Ernest Thompson Seton's *Wild Animals I Have Known*, and William J. Long's *School of the Woods*, Burroughs demanded from his contemporaries more "real observation" and less "deliberate trifling with natural history" (306). Partly because of the widespread popularity of the stories and partly because of the caustic tone of the essay, Burroughs launched a heated debate that lasted for several years. Only after Theodore Roosevelt (1907, 427) denounced Roberts, Seton, and Long as "nature fakers" in an essay published in *Everybody's Magazine* did the controversy begin to subside.

As I would emphasize, this dispute—often relegated to a curious footnote in the annals of literary history—altered the generic trajectory of North American animal stories because it prompted subsequent authors to rely more heavily on scientific ideas in their representations of nonhuman animals. To examine this shift and its impact, I describe the historical and scientific contexts of the "nature fakers" debate. Then, I trace developments in the fields of comparative psychology and cognitive ethology between 1950 and 2020 and examine the interplay of formal and scientific elements in some of the animal stories from this period. Because of dramatic advances in the scientific study of avian cognition in the twentieth century and beyond, I focus specifically on two texts that attempt to portray the emotional and intellectual lives of birds, Fred Bodsworth's *Last of the Curlews* and Kira Buxton's *Hollow Kingdom*. Published in 1955, Bodsworth's novella describes a single curlew and his doomed search for a mate.[2] Against all odds, he finds a suitable female, but she is shot and killed by a North American farmer just as they attempt to consummate their relationship. Published in 2019, Buxton's novel revolves around the exploits of a domesticated crow named S.T. (short for Shit Turd) as he attempts to navigate a zombie apocalypse without Big Jim, his human caretaker. Over the course of the book, S.T. learns to appreciate not just his own animality but that of the other organisms around him.

Though generically and stylistically different, these texts showcase the degree to which scientific theories about avian cognition have changed over time and the degree to which authors have incorporated them into their stories. They also indicate that the formal and scientific elements of avian animal stories do not always cohere. Influenced by the studies of graylag geese published by Konrad Lorenz in the 1930s, Bodsworth characterizes the curlews as instinct-driven machines who are incapable of thought and devoid of agency.[3] All of their actions represent ingrained, predetermined responses to external environmental stimuli. Insofar as they serve to depict the events of the novella—and the eventual extinction of the species—as inevitable, these scientific details threaten to derail the book's preservationist themes.

Informed by ideas advanced by avian ethologists in the 2010s, Buxton endows S.T. with intelligence, emotions, empathy, and agency. Over the course of the novel, S.T. uses tools, solves problems, experiences grief, and contemplates extinction. Not insignificantly, though, S.T. advances certain claims about the balance of nature that reflect outdated ideas regarding ecosystem processes. His decision to "change and evolve" to the conditions of a human-less world conflates behavioral-cultural responsiveness with biological evolution (Buxton 2019, 186). In the end, these portions of the book undermine both Buxton's careful characterization of her nonhuman protagonist and her warnings about anthropogenic environmental destruction.

THE NATURE FAKERS: EMOTIONS, INSTINCT, AND REASON IN THE ANIMAL KINGDOM

Although it grew more complex and convoluted as it progressed, the nature-fakers controversy stemmed from a fairly simple scientific question: are nonhuman animals conscious beings who operate according to reason, or unconscious beings who operate according to instinct (Lutts 1990, 72)? The participants sometimes raised questions about emotions, but they tended not to dwell on this issue, probably because many members of the scientific community—professional and amateur alike—endorsed the idea that at least some nonhuman animals possessed emotions. In *The Expression of the Emotions in Man and the Animals*, Charles Darwin (1872, 97–99, 116–46) describes the complex and varied emotional states of such mammals as dogs, cats, horses, and monkeys, and such birds as swans, owls, finches, and parrots. Other prominent experts of the period—including E. P. Evans, Allen Pringle, and Samuel Lockwood—offered similar claims about the emotional capacities of nonhuman animals. Not coincidentally, proponents of animal rights took advantage of these views to sway public opinion in favor of anticruelty statutes (Beers 2006, 31–32).

If questions of emotion were settled for many turn-of-the-century authors, activists, and scientists, questions of consciousness and reason were not. According to Margaret Washburn (1908), author of the groundbreaking comparative psychology textbook *The Animal Mind*, individuals interested in the study of nonhuman animals and their mental processes could be divided into three categories:

> Those who believe that consciousness should be ascribed to all animals; those who hold that it should be ascribed only to those animals whose behavior presents certain peculiarities regarded as evidence of mind; and those who hold that we have no trustworthy evidence of mind in any animal and should therefore [. . .] use only physiological terms. (17)

A naturalist and nonfiction writer by trade, Burroughs fell into the last group. In "Real and Sham Natural History," he insists that the idea that nonhuman animals possess "reasoning processes like our own, except in very rudimentary form, admits of grave doubt" (Burroughs 1903, 299–300). Instead, he makes the case for instinct, arguing "The young of all wild creatures do instinctively what their parents do and did. They do not have to be taught" (305). A year later, in an essay in *Century Illustrated Magazine*, he advances a more definitive statement on the matter: "Instinct, natural prompting, is the main matter after all. It makes up at least nine tenths of the lives of our wild neighbors" (Burroughs 1904, 514). Though Roosevelt (1955, 511) cautioned Burroughs about taking such an extreme stance—he referred to it as "stating a universal negative"—the naturalist never moderated his opinion about the primacy of instinct in the lives of nonhuman animals.

Perhaps not surprisingly, most of the authors targeted by Burroughs—Roberts, Seton, and Long—possessed very different views of nonhuman animals and their capacity for consciousness and reason. They fell into the first two categories outlined by Washburn. In *Kindred of the Wild*, Roberts (1902) notes that instinct and coincidence cannot account for the ingenuity behind the behaviors of certain nonhuman animals, and he argues for evolutionary continuity among species: "As far, at least, as the mental intelligence is concerned, the gulf dividing the lowest of the human species from the highest of the animals has in these latter days been reduced to a very narrow psychological fissure" (23). He concludes that "within their varying limitations, animals can and do reason" (23). Meanwhile, in *Wild Animals I Have Known*, Seton (1898) expresses a similar view, contending, "Man has nothing that the animals have not at least a vestige of, the animals have nothing that man does not in some degree share" (12).

Like Roberts and Seton, Long (1902) downplayed the significance of instinct in the lives of nonhuman animals. Thus, in his discussion of birds in *School of the Woods*, he maintains:

> The instinct to migrate is a mere impulse. [. . .] Left to themselves, the young birds would never find their northern or southern homes; but with the impulse to move is another and stronger impulse, to go with the crowd. So the young birds join the migrating hosts, and from their wiser elders, not from instinct, learn the sure way. (13–14)

To reinforce his theories about avian reasoning abilities, Long lists numerous other instances—drawn from his observations in the forests of eastern Canada—of birds teaching their offspring special survival skills. These include his suggestion that crow parents instruct their fledglings to fly by encouraging them to imitate their elders, and that osprey train their offspring to hunt by dropping injured fish into the water for them to catch (11, 101).[4]

Though he did not publish a statement on the controversy until 1907, Roosevelt wrote numerous letters to Burroughs expressing his distaste for the popular animal stories of the period. As this correspondence makes clear, Roosevelt (1955, 442) believed in the preeminence of instinct, but he allowed for the possibility of consciousness and learning, especially in those species whose experiences had taught them to fear humans. Thus, he was not necessarily bothered by the assertions about avian reason or evolutionary continuity that Roberts, Seton, and Long advanced in their books. What rankled the president was the so-called observations from the field that these men employed to buttress their claims. When he finally addressed the matter in his essay "Nature Fakers," Roosevelt (1907) dubbed them "yellow journalists of the woods" and took them to task for their irresponsible representations of North American wildlife:

> Their most striking stories are not merely distortions of facts, but pure inventions; and not only are they inventions, but they are inventions by men who

know so little of the subject concerning which they write, and who to ignorance add such utter recklessness, that they are not even able to distinguish between what is possible, however wildly improbable, and mechanical impossibilities. (428)

After describing and refuting a number of examples from specific texts, Roosevelt concluded his remarks, condemning Roberts, Seton, and Long for the "grave wrong[s]" they committed against natural history by filling their books with what he regarded as "deliberate or reckless untruth[s]" (430).

Taken together, Burroughs's and Roosevelt's insistence that authors privilege scientific accuracy over literary concerns—plot, character, and theme—testifies to the importance of realism in North American animal stories at the start of the twentieth century. At this point, though, I would emphasize that the scientific community had not yet established standards for field work or settled upon a particular view of nonhuman animal minds. Thus, I would argue that Roberts, Seton, and Long did not reject science so much as they elected to embrace a different version of it from Burroughs and Roosevelt, one that aligned better with their philosophical views of the natural world and their thematic goals for their writing. In subsequent decades, biologists and psychologists achieved greater consensus on issues of nonhuman animal cognition, first endorsing ideas advanced by behaviorists and then by ethologists. As they did so, they created certain difficulties for authors of North American animal stories who were invested in scientific discovery, artistic coherence, and thematic consistency.

FRED BODSWORTH: INSTINCT AND EMOTION IN CURLEWS

As the twentieth century progressed, the popularity of North American animal stories began to wane. Consumed by the horrors of two world wars and the cycles of privation and prosperity that attended them, writers focused their attention on political and social issues both at home and abroad. Perhaps the most famous collection of animal stories from this period, Rachel Carson's *Under the Sea Wind*, sold a scant two thousand copies and faded into obscurity (Lear 2007, xviii). At the end of World War II, however, North American authors became increasingly concerned with the ecological destruction caused by human military and industrial activities, and they began composing scientifically informed environmentally oriented animal stories as a means of protesting against it. These tales were not as popular as their turn-of-the-century predecessors, but they revived the genre and helped to perpetuate it into the future. An attempt to call attention to the plight of endangered birds,

Bodsworth's *Last of the Curlews* represents one of the first examples of this variant of postwar ecological writing.[5]

Though not the subject of protracted and intense controversy like its predecessors, *Last of the Curlews* has been criticized for its seemingly paradoxical depiction of avian cognition, its characterization of the curlews as mechanistic creatures—driven by instincts and hormones—and as emotional animals, motivated by fear and loneliness. Both Maija-Liisa Haru (2006, 176) and Janice Fiamengo (2007, 1) highlight this apparent inconsistency, attributing it to Bodsworth's inability to avoid the temptations of anthropomorphization. At first glance, this conclusion might seem plausible, but I would suggest that it discounts the degree to which *Last of the Curlews* adheres to the theories about the avian mind advanced by Lorenz in the 1930s. Insofar as its representations of instinct and emotion are concerned, I would argue that the novella presents ideas that are remarkably consistent with those endorsed by at least some contemporary scientists.

According to Richard J. Herrnstein (1998, 1), scientific interest in instinct declined sharply in the 1920s as behaviorism gained credence among comparative psychologists. Proponents of this mechanistic school of thought insisted that scientists restrict their claims about nonhuman animals to observable behaviors—some reflexive and some learned—prompted by external stimuli. In terms of their methodology, they conducted laboratory experiments designed to study behavioral plasticity, defined as the degree to which an organism's behavior patterns changed in response to environment or conditioning. They preferred not to consider such subjects as emotion, reason, and consciousness because doing so involved drawing unsubstantiated conclusions about subjective mental states (Griffin 1992, 20). As the behaviorists put it, they had no way of communicating with nonhuman animals; thus, they had no way of ascertaining whether these organisms generated thoughts or experienced emotions.

Despite its dominance, behaviorism had detractors, one of whom was Lorenz. He insisted that scientists pay less attention to learned behaviors and more attention to innate behaviors, including instinct. After spending several years observing the imprinting process in the graylag geese that he kept at his home in Altenberg, Austria, he published "The Companion in the Bird's World," in which he argued that instincts stem from physiological causes and remain fixed over the lifetime of the organism (Brigandt 2005, 571–72). No amount of learning or conditioning could change them. A landmark article that helped to establish ethology as an academic discipline, this piece reintroduced the concept of instinct to the scientific community and raised it to a position of prominence. Note that, at this early stage of his career, Lorenz possessed a view of nonhuman animal cognition that was just as mechanistic as that endorsed by his behaviorist contemporaries. As time passed, however, he came to accept the idea that some nonhuman animals—including geese and jackdaws—experienced subjective emotional states. In his various later publications, he offered descriptions of a wide array of avian emotions, such as fear, courage, despair, and grief, among others (Gorokhovskaya 2005, S34, S40).

With respect to *Last of the Curlews*, Lorenz's influence is readily apparent, for the words *instinct* or *instinctive* appear at least fourteen times in just the first two chapters. These portions of the book are especially important to scrutinize because they articulate the birds' *umwelt*, dictate the rising action, and foreground certain themes. According to the narrator, the curlew is not a bird of thought, for "his instinctive behavior code, planted deep in his brain by the genes of countless generations, told him only what to do, without telling him why. His behavior was controlled not by mental decisions but by instinctive responses to the stimuli around him" (Bodsworth 1963, 36). Like Lorenz before him, the narrator attributes avian behavior patterns to certain fixed and innate instincts, and, in so doing, he establishes his protagonist as a mechanistic organism who lives in a deterministic universe.

Over the course of *Last of the Curlews*, the narrator describes these instincts as falling into one of two categories—those that have to do with mating and those that have to do with migration—and attributes them both to the periodic release of hormones:

> As days shortened the decreasing sunlight reduced the activity of the bird's pituitary gland. The pituitary secretion was the trigger that kept the reproductive glands pouring sex hormones into the blood stream, and as the production of sex hormones decreased, the bird's aggressive mating urge disappeared and the migratory urge replaced it. It was entirely a physiological process. (Bodsworth 1963, 34–35)

Here, the narrator emphasizes the coordination of seasonal and anatomical cycles and their pronounced impact on his avian protagonist. This strategy provides further support for the characterization of the curlew as an individual whose every move is determined for him by internal instincts and external stimuli.

Following Lorenz, the narrator also endows the curlew with at least a rudimentary capacity for subjective emotional states. Though he is hampered by his limited memory—he tends to forget events as soon as they transpire—he experiences amorphous feelings of loneliness, fear, hope, and joy over the course of the novella. Not surprisingly, the narrator represents these emotions in instinctive terms. Thus, after the curlew joins a multispecies flock of migratory birds in search of others of his kind, the narrator explains, "A tenuous hope, part instinctive reaction and part a shadowy form of reasoning, formed nebulously in the curlew's brain" (Bodsworth 1963, 42). A bit later he adds another emotion to the mix, noting, "There was a vague, remote feeling of loneliness deep within him still, but the curlew was no longer alone" (43). While the use of the word "reasoning" in the first quotation threatens to render the book's depiction of nonhuman animal minds inconsistent, I would stress that the type of reason described above is qualified as "shadowy." As such, it does not necessarily represent conscious, intelligent thought in any meaningful sense.

After the male curlew encounters a female of his species deep in the wilds of Patagonia, he experiences another powerful blend of instincts and emotions. Again, though, the emphasis is on the former as opposed to the latter. Just the sight of the female prompts an immediate, visceral response, and the male begins to seethe "with the sudden release of a mating urge that had waxed and waned without fulfillment for a lifetime" (Bodsworth 1963, 85). As pent-up hormones course through his veins, the curlew feels "reborn"—as if he is "starting another life"—and he begins to forget "the torture of being alone" (86–87). According to the narrator, the "high body temperatures and rapid metabolism[s]" of the birds cause "an intensification of emotional development" and inspire them to "court and love with a fervor and passion that matches the intensity of all their other life processes" (118–19). Not insignificantly, these passages focus primarily on innate sexual urges as opposed to subjective emotional states.

When the female curlew is shot by the North American farmer, the male responds by obeying the dictates of his rudimentary emotions: "Terrified and bewildered at a foe that could strike without visible form, he took wing" (Bodsworth 1963, 123). Once he recovers his composure, he returns to the female, who eventually succumbs to her injuries and dies. For the next twelve hours, the male experiences competing biological imperatives, namely his desire to stay with his reproductive partner and his urge to continue his migration: "When the night came the lure of the tundra became a stubborn, compelling call, for the time of the nesting was almost upon them. He flew repeatedly, whistling back to her, then returning, but the female wouldn't fly with him. Finally he slept close by her" (124). In the end, overwhelmed by the directive to travel northward, he leaves the female behind and resumes his journey to the Arctic. At this point, the novella hastily concludes with a paragraph describing the bird sitting alone on the tundra, holding his territory "in readiness for the female his instinct told him soon would come" (125).

All told, the narrator's scientifically informed characterization of the curlews as machines—driven by instinctive urges and primal emotions—supports the book's deterministic themes. His descriptions of the environment serve a similar function. As he explains, the curlews experience a staggering array of dangers in their annual passages between the northern and southern hemispheres:

> For nine months of migration each year the curlews were the pawns on a great two-continent chessboard and the players that decided the moves were the cosmic forces of nature and geography—the winds, tides, and weather. Winds determined the direction the birds would fly. Tides and rainfall, by controlling the availability of flood, determined each flight's goal. Now another player, an ocean current entered the game. (Bodsworth 1963, 98)

Though clichéd, the chess metaphor serves to emphasize further the powerlessness of the birds as they struggle to survive the migration and propagate their species in a deterministic universe.

Just as the curlews are pawns of the environment, they are victims of evolution as well. According to the narrator, the birds fall prey to the North American farmer because they do not possess a sense of fear: "Far back in the species' evolutionary history they had learned that, for them, a highly developed fear was unnecessary. Their wings were strong and their flight so rapid that they could ignore danger until the last moment, escaping fox or hawk in a last-second flight. So their fear sense had disappeared, as all unused faculties must" (Bodsworth 1963, 117–18). Without fear to warn them of the imminent threat to their lives posed by the farmer and his shotgun, the curlews are doomed by their genetic heritage from the moment they land in the field.

All of this determinism threatens to undermine any arguments about the preservation of endangered species that *Last of the Curlews* advances. Significantly, the narrator establishes these claims from the beginning, prefacing the book with an epigraph drawn from William Beebe's *The Bird: Its Form and Function*, lamenting that "when the last individual of a race of living beings breathes no more, another heaven and another earth must pass before such a one can be again" (Bodsworth 1963, xvii). Throughout the remainder of the novella, the narrator attempts to raise awareness about and inspire compassion for the plight of the curlews by including extracts from a number of historical sources—some dating to the eighteenth century—that describe plummeting population numbers and overzealous human hunters. While these strategies are emotionally compelling because they emphasize the finality of species extinction and the cruelty of human beings, they lack logic. Expending effort to save a species whose extinction has been preordained by biology, environment, and evolution does not, after all, make much sense.

KIRA BUXTON: EVOLUTION AND ADAPTATION IN CROWS

In the waning decades of the twentieth century, some of North America's environmental problems seemed to improve, ameliorated by the passage of environmental legislation in the United States and Canada. Across the continent, pollution in waterways dissipated, air quality in cities improved, and populations of bald eagles increased. Elsewhere in the world, the situation remained dire as destructive anthropogenic activities continued to drive numerous species—whales, elephants, rhinos, tigers, and orangutans, among others—to the brink of extinction. Inspired by their affection for nonhuman animals, authors of North American animal stories tried to raise awareness by producing such books as Robert Siegel's *Whalesong*, Barbara Gowdy's *The White Bone*, and Alison Baird's *White as Waves*.

By the 1990s and 2000s, scientists began to recognize the dangers posed by the accumulated effects of anthropogenic climate change, and they started to issue warnings about protracted droughts, extended heat waves, and widespread wildfires, as well as sea-level rise, ocean acidification, and mass extinction. For some reason, most authors of contemporary North American animal stories did not follow their lead; instead, they elected to focus their attention on small-scale threats to biodiversity, such as wildlife poaching and habitat destruction. To date, Kira Buxton's *Hollow Kingdom* represents one of the only texts of its kind to tackle larger concerns such as global ecological collapse. Much like its predecessors, it relies on recent developments in the scientific study of nonhuman animal minds in order to characterize its protagonists and convey its themes about evolution and adaptation in the face of environmental catastrophe.

Although behaviorist doctrines and instinct theories maintained their dominance through the 1970s, they began to fall out of favor in the 1980s and 1990s with the publication of Jane Goodall's studies of chimpanzees, Donald Griffin's studies of bats, Marc Bekoff's studies of coyotes, and Frans de Waal's studies of bonobos. All of this research provided evidence for and lent credence to the idea that some nonhuman animals engage in complex thought processes and experience subjective emotional states (Bekoff 2006, 50–63; de Waal 2016, 7–28). It also prompted scientists to inquire into the cognitive capacities of various other species, including dogs, octopuses, sharks, and bowerbirds. And it inspired popular science writers to produce myriad books, including Carl Safina's *Beyond Words: What Animals Think and Feel*, Jonathan Balcombe's *What a Fish Knows: The Inner Lives of Our Underwater Cousins*, and Peter Godfrey-Smith's *Other Minds: The Octopus, the Sea, and the Deep Origins of Consciousness*.

Although much of this research addresses mammals, some of it focuses on birds, especially those in the corvid family (ravens, rooks, jackdaws, magpies, and crows). The list includes numerous studies conducted by John Marzluff, Thomas Bugnyar, Mathias Osvath, and their teams of scientific investigators.[6] Taking advantage of this research and its insights into the avian mind, *Hollow Kingdom* characterizes S.T. as a bird who possesses intelligence, emotion, agency, and self-awareness. Although he often represents himself as a hybrid organism—part crow and part human—he is still very much a bird, behaving just like the corvids described in Thom van Dooren's *The Wake of Crows* (2019, 67, 131–32). Like them, he uses tools to achieve certain desired ends, caches objects so as to save them for future use, and maintains physical health by rubbing ants on his feathers to rid himself of parasites (Buxton 2019, 151–53, 125, 74). Note that some of these behaviors—especially tool use—require reason and intelligence. As such, they attest to S.T.'s considerable cognitive capacities.

Insofar as perception is concerned, *Hollow Kingdom* also follows the science, depicting S.T. as possessing extraordinary visual acuity and navigational intelligence. Early in the novel, he explains that his eyes can see ultraviolet light, which enables him to detect "sexual dichromatism" and "paints a kaleidoscope of patterns and signals that MoFos [humans] appear to be blind to" (Buxton 2019, 46). He also reveals his ability to generate "mind maps" as he travels around Seattle, informing readers that:

> The sky is a bird's nature, home, an extension of the soul. They know it and remember it better than earthly dimensions. Feathered ones, except penguins and turkeys because they're fucking morons, have wonderful memories—not sure why elephants get all the damn credit. They travel by tips heard through Aura (sort of like GPS) and by their relationship to the sun and stars who engage them in a sensory conversation. (46)

Though different in tone, these descriptions of avian vision and navigation jibe remarkably well with those offered by Jennifer Ackerman in *The Genius of Birds* and *The Bird Way*. With respect to the former, she asserts that birds "see hues beyond our imagining," and, with respect to the latter, she posits that "Bird navigation involves sensing, learning, and above all, a remarkable ability to build a map in the mind, one far bigger than we ever imagined and made of strange and still mysterious cartography" (2016, 196; 2020, 94).

If Buxton's descriptions of her narrator's behavioral and sensory abilities are scientifically informed, so are the author's representations of S.T.'s emotional capacities. After losing Big Jim to the zombie plague, S.T. describes his initial feelings in a series of vivid similes: "A sadness crept under my skin like an army of termites, nibbling away at my resolve. At times, my heart felt like the fruit that shriveled and grew fur on the kitchen counter, bruised and rotting, fodder for flies. It made my legs feel heavy, made flight a chore" (Buxton 2019, 27). Toward the end of the novel, he grieves this loss—and that of his bloodhound friend Dennis—at a ceremony organized by a group of zoo elephants who have escaped from their enclosure. Adopting a more poignant tone and less disgusting language, S.T. observes:

> They formed a circle around our Dennis, facing outward. And the sun shone because that is her impassioned duty, to keep us from being swallowed by the dark. And I swear I felt the warmth lifting off nearby stones and an ancient song of sorrow that the evergreens shook from their leaves. The elephants swayed to this music, protecting him, honoring him. And we grieved like this in harmony, calling on the ocean with our breath. (272)

In their emphasis on avian grief, these passages draw on several of the anecdotes about crow mourning reported by John Marzluff and included in such popular books as *In the Company of Crows and Ravens* and *How Animals Grieve* (Marzluff and Angell 2005, 190–95; King 2013, 93–96).

As this evidence indicates, *Hollow Kingdom* is committed to scientific accuracy in its descriptions of S.T. and his behavioral, perceptual, and emotional capabilities. Significantly, though, the book advances outdated scientific theories about ecosystems and how they function. Although the zombie outbreak stems from a biotech virus whose vector is electronic screens, S.T. and his companions—Onida, a giant Pacific octopus; Kraai, an American crow; and Ghubari, an African gray parrot—attribute it to the fact that humans have "upset the natural order of balance" (Buxton 2019, 181). According to Kraai, humans were "a plague on the earth. They were not able to control their numbers or their consumption of the land, and so Nature did it for them" (181). While this idea coheres nicely with notions of cosmic justice, it does not accord with current scientific theories about the operations of ecosystems, which tend to emphasize disequilibrium, instability, impermanence, and stochasticity (van Dooren 2019, 43–45).

In *Hollow Kingdom*, ideas about natural balance are closely connected to ideas about evolutionary change. After talking with Kraai about the various factors contributing to the zombie apocalypse, S.T. thinks, "Perhaps Nature was balancing. And if you cannot evolve, you cannot survive—that is Nature's way" (Buxton 2019, 186). He concludes that he needs to "change and evolve" lest he "become extinct," and he spends the remainder of the book attempting to adjust to life without humans (186). At the end of the book, S.T. again sutures the concepts of balance and adaptation, explaining:

> Mother Nature is not kind, but she is balanced. Every single one of us, from amoeba to blue whale to the tenacious bloom that dares to dream of tomorrow, have their own destiny-fulfilling journey as long as their minds and hearts are open. And how we are all connected by a web that looks gossamer but is stronger than a chain-link fence. And though Nature is tough, she is always conspiring for your success, encouraging you to evolve. (304)

Here, S.T. mistakes biological evolution, a genetic process that takes place over the long term, for behavioral/cultural responsiveness, a learned process that takes place over the short term ("Misconceptions about Evolution," 2012). In so doing, he makes it seem as though evolution is a matter of will, not a matter of anatomy.

By presenting evolution in this way, *Hollow Kingdom* downplays the severity of many of the anthropogenic environmental issues that it attempts to address in its interchapter interludes. Narrated not by S.T., but by various other nonhuman animals, these portions of the book describe nuclear meltdown, invasive species, plastic pollution, and climate change. All of these real-world problems pose severe threats to the earth's biodiversity because they force species to adjust—biologically and otherwise—to dramatically altered ecosystems in very short periods of time. According to the novel's vision of evolution, though, the nonhuman animals attempting to survive these various challenges to their existences—the fairy pitta, armadillo, polar bear, and humpback whale—should be able to decide to adapt to their new circumstances, just as S.T. does. Insofar as it represents this feat as a possibility, *Hollow Kingdom* fails to convey the urgency of the current environmental crisis; therefore, it undermines its own environmental goals.

As North American animal stories, *Last of the Curlews* and *Hollow Kingdom* might seem very different. Driven by innate instincts and primal emotions, the curlew struggles to survive in a deterministic universe that has preordained his extinction. Motivated by intelligent thoughts and complex emotions, the crow in *Hollow Kingdom* overcomes adversity through the application of his free will and survives any number of existential threats. Despite their differences, these books share some important commonalities, insofar as they both characterize their avian protagonists according to contemporary scientific ideas about avian minds. In the process, they attempt to raise awareness about pressing environmental problems, including anthropogenic species extinction and climate change. As I have shown, they highlight some of the problems that occur when scientific accuracy interferes with artistic coherence, but I would add that they also demonstrate the remarkable staying power of the genre as authors like Buxton adapt it for twenty-first-century audiences.

NOTES

1. As a note of acknowledgment, I would like to express my gratitude to the students who took my *Intelligent Lifeforms* class in spring 2020, especially Alana Kilby and Annie Wenstrup. Our initial discussions of *Hollow Kingdom* inspired the idea for this chapter, and our subsequent conversations helped me develop and refine my argument. For this and more, I thank them.

2. Of the nine species of curlew, Bodsworth refers to *Numenius borealis* or the Eskimo curlew. Given that *Eskimo* is a pejorative, colonial expression, I refer to

the birds in the book as *curlews* throughout (Kaplan n.d.). Although the last confirmed sighting of this migratory shorebird in the United States occurred in 1962 on Galveston Island, it is categorized as "critically endangered" in the current edition of the IUCN Red Book (IUCN 2019).

3. An Austrian zoologist, Lorenz studied and wrote about imprinting in geese, describing it as an instinctive process. Together with Dutch researcher Nikolaas Tinbergen, he founded the discipline of ethology and received the Nobel Prize in 1973. Lorenz's legacy is complicated by the fact that he served as a scientist for the Third Reich during World War II (Burkhardt 2005, 231–32).

4. For the record, crows do not learn flight through imitation, but ospreys sometimes drop injured fish near their offspring (Basu 2012; Howard and Hoppitt 2017, 2–3).

5. Others include Allan Eckert's *The Great Auk* and *Silent Sky*, as well as Victor Scheffer's *The Year of the Whale* and *The Year of the Seal*.

6. A number of popular science books have made this research accessible to the general public, including Jennifer Ackerman's *The Genius of Birds* (2016) and its sequel *The Bird Way* (2020).

REFERENCES

Ackerman, Jennifer. 2016. *The Genius of Birds*. New York: Penguin.

———. 2020. *The Bird Way: A New Look at How Birds Talk, Work, Play, Parent, and Think*. New York: Penguin.

Basu, Neeraj. 2012. "Nature vs Nurture: How Do Baby Birds Learn How to Fly?" Last modified October 9, 2012. Accessed June 29, 2021. http://blogs.bu.edu/bioaerial2012/2012/10/09/nature-vs-nurture-how-do-baby-birds-learn-how-to-fly/

Beers, Diane L. 2006. *For the Prevention of Cruelty: The History and Legacy of Animal Rights Activism in the United States*. Athens: Ohio University Press.

Bekoff, Marc. 2006. *Animal Passions and Beastly Virtues: Reflections on Redecorating Nature*. Philadelphia: Temple University Press.

Bodsworth, Fred. 1963. *Last of the Curlews*. Toronto: McClelland and Stewart.

Burkhardt, Richard W., Jr. 2005. *Patterns of Behavior: Konrad Lorenz, Niko Tinbergen, and the Founding of Ethology*. Chicago: University of Chicago Press.

Burroughs, John. 1903. "Real and Sham Natural History." *Atlantic Monthly* 91 (545): 298–309.

———. 1904. "Current Misconceptions in Natural History." *Century Illustrated Magazine* 67 (4): 509–17.

Buxton, Kira. 2019. *Hollow Kingdom*. New York: Grand Central Publishing.

Darwin, Charles. 1872. *The Expression of the Emotions in Man and the Animals*. London: John Murray.

de Waal, Frans. 2016. *Are We Smart Enough to Know How Smart Animals Are?* New York: W. W. Norton.

Fiamengo, Janice. 2007. "The Animals in *This* Country: Animals in the Canadian Literary Imagination." In *Other Selves: Animals in the Canadian Literary*

Imagination, edited by Janice Fiamengo, 1–25. Ottawa: University of Ottawa Press.

Gorokhovskaya, Elena A. 2005. "Subjective Animal World and Konrad Lorenz's Objectivistic Ethology." *Entomological Review* 85 (S1): S34–S41.

Griffin, Donald R. 1992. *Animal Minds.* Chicago: University of Chicago Press.

Harju, Maija-Liisa. 2006. "Anthropomorphism and the Necessity of Animal Fantasy." In *Towards or Back to Human Values?: Spiritual and Moral Dimensions of Contemporary Fantasy,* edited by Justyna Deszcz-Tryhubczak and Marek Oziewicz, 173–84. Newcastle: Cambridge Scholars Press.

Herrnstein, Richard J. 1998. "Nature as Nurture: Behavior and the Instinct Doctrine." *Behavior and Philosophy* 26: 73–107.

Howard, Megan and Will Hoppitt. 2017. "Ospreys Do Not Teach Offspring to Kill Fish at the Nest." *Biology Letters* 13: 1–4.

IUCN. 2019. "Eskimo Curlew." Last modified July 26, 2019. Accessed June 27, 2021. https://www.iucnredlist.org/species/22693170/155293606

Kaplan, Lawrence. n.d. "Inuit or Eskimo: Which Name to Use?" Accessed June 27, 2021. https://www.uaf.edu/anlc/resources/inuit_or_eskimo.php

King, Barbara J. 2013. *How Animals Grieve.* Chicago: University of Chicago Press.

Lear, Linda. 2007. "Introduction." In *Under the Sea-Wind,* edited by Rachel Carson. New York: Penguin, ix–xx.

Long, William J. 1902. *School of the Woods: Some Life Studies of Animal Instincts and Animal Training.* Boston: Athenaeum.

Lutts, Ralph H. 1990. *The Nature Fakers: Wildlife, Science, and Sentiment.* Golden, CO: Fulcrum Publishing.

Marzluff, John and Tony Angell. 2005. *In the Company of Crows and Ravens.* New Haven: Yale University Press.

"Misconceptions about Evolution." 2012. *University of California Museum of Paleontology.* Accessed July 8, 2021. https://evolution.berkeley.edu/evolibrary/misconceptions_faq.php

Roberts, Charles G. D. 1902. *The Kindred of the Wild: A Book of Animal Life.* Boston: L. C. Page.

Roosevelt, Theodore. 1907. "Nature Fakers." *Everybody's Magazine* 17 (3): 427–30.

———. 1955. *The Letters of Theodore Roosevelt.* Volume 3. Edited by Elting E. Morison. Cambridge: Harvard University Press.

Thompson, Ernest Thompson. 1898. *Wild Animals I Have Known.* New York: Charles Scribner's Sons.

Van Dooren, Thom. 2019. *The Wake of Crows: Living and Dying in Shared Worlds.* New York: Columbia University Press.

Washburn, Margaret Floy. 1908. *The Animal Mind: A Textbook of Comparative Psychology.* New York: Macmillan.

Chapter 7

What Is It Like to Write (Like) a Bird?

Rethinking Literary Practice to Support Avian Subjectivity

Joshua Lobb

The question of whether humans can comprehend nonhuman consciousness has long been a matter of debate across a range of philosophical and scientific discourses. Perhaps the most famous articulation of this is Thomas Nagel's assertion in "What is it Like to be a Bat?" that a bat's perception is "beyond our ability to conceive [. . .]. If I try to imagine, I am restricted to the resources of my own mind" (1974, 439). Zoologists have uncovered extraordinarily different ways animals process their worlds: through visual spectra, sound, or sensitivities to magnetic waves (Wynne and Udell 2013; Radner 1994). There is also a divergence in animals' epistemological processes. Donald Griffin argues: "Should other species have feelings, hopes, beliefs, plans, or concepts of any sort [. . .] they would take a form so different from our own that we would not recognize them" (1981, 160).

These differences pose a challenge for writers who want to depict authentic experiences of nonhuman animals. Literature is full of examples that emphasize the impossibility of understanding other species. If we focus on one species—birds—we see several writers pointing up the perceptual differences. In his poem "Poor Matthias," Matthew Arnold reflects on the inner lives of birds: "Still, beneath their feather'd breast, / Stirs a history unexpress'd [. . .] / What they want, we cannot guess" (1945, 457). More recently, the filmmaker Ceri Levy comments that birds "are poetic creatures that almost work in an ethereal space to us. Inhabiting our world, but also inhabiting some other, unseen space, a place we can only glimpse [. . .] one that we can never exist in" (qtd. in Brower 2013, 60–61).

For writers, there is another, more significant problem: when we write about nonhuman animals, we express their perspectives through our own linguistic frames. The anthropologist Garry Marvin acknowledges:

> I am very wary about what I [. . .] can say about animals per se, outside of how they figure and are configured in the human imagination or in terms of human relationships with them [. . .]. How does one avoid anthropocentrism when the only languages available to write about animals are human languages? (qtd. in McHugh 2017, 14, 17)

This anthropocentrism can cause serious damage to the lives of the animals we want to portray. The writer and philosopher Thom van Dooren reminds us that "telling stories has consequences: one of which is that we will inevitably be drawn into [. . .] new accountabilities and obligations" (2014, 10). There is an inherent power relationship between writer and subject in many of the formal devices used by writers. Third-person focalizing narration, for instance, creates a hierarchy of power between one voice who is authorized to speak and others who are *spoken for*. As Dorrit Cohn notes, a character within a third-person context "is always more or less subordinate to the narrator," and our understanding of a character is controlled by what the narrator chooses to divulge (1978, 66). In the case of animal stories, because the writer is always human, the relationship is inevitably set up as *human speaks* and animal is *spoken for*. The nonhuman animal is, to use Donna Haraway's phrase, "subjected to human intent" (2003, 28). Haraway suggests that the representational act is a form of violence against animals: a kind of slavery or worse. She explains: "[we] 'hail' them into our constructs of nature and culture, with major consequences of life and death, health and illness, longevity and extinction" (17). This chapter, then, asks a question pertinent to writers, but perhaps also to all humans wishing to understand nonhuman lives: How can we represent the perspectives of animals without asserting mastery over them?

In response to the question, I draw upon an ethical model offered by Linda Alcoff in "The Problem of Speaking for Others" (1992). Alcoff's approach pivots on a series of principles, what she calls interrogatory practices. In this chapter, I focus on two of these practices. First, Alcoff asks us to consider our own position in the act of representation: the assumptions we bring and the powers we assert. Alcoff explains, "we must [. . .] interrogate the bearing of our location and context on what it is we are saying, and this should be an explicit part of every serious discursive practice we engage in" (25). Second, she asks us to consider the material impact of the act of representation: the ways our writing might position our readers to perceive animals in a particular fashion, and how this could change the way animals are treated in our daily lives. Alcoff declares: "[we] must [. . .] look at where the speech goes and what it does there" (26). Alcoff's approach, I believe, can be transposed to a discussion about the representation of nonhuman animals. Writers can adapt Alcoff's interrogatory practices to ask the following questions about our representational and aesthetic choices: *What are the discourses of power at work in our acts of representation of nonhuman animals?* and *How might speaking for animals affect real animals?*

In this chapter, my focus will be on the ways these questions can help us to interrogate the representation of birds' consciousness in fiction: the formal devices that might pose a threat to our treatment of real birds, and the tactics that may allow us to avoid mastery over our subjects. Using Alcoff's practices as a framework, I analyze two texts that explicitly speak for animals, but also overcome the dangers of such an activity. Philip Temple's *Beak of the Moon* (1981) advocates for birds through immersive sympathetic focalization. In other words, it provides opportunities for readers to get a bird's-eye view. But the novel also acknowledges the human presence in the act of representation. Readers are made aware of the human narrator as translator of the birds' thoughts, and so some of the discursive mastery of the narratorial position is attenuated. Daphne du Maurier's "The Birds" (1952) undermines the writer/subject power relationship through a subtle transformation of focalizing positions, from human to bird. The text enacts the struggle between human and birds' perspectives by creating lapses in the narration, moments when the narrator loses control of the account. In these slippages, a bird's consciousness might be glimpsed. I will also reflect on the attempts I have made in my own novel, *The Flight of Birds* (2019), to grapple with discourses of power present in my representations of birds.

Philip Temple's *Beak of the Moon*, set in the early stages of European settlement, tells the story of a flock of kea, a species of parrot native to the alpine regions of New Zealand's South Island. It concentrates on three adolescent birds, Strongbeak, Huff-Tuft, and Skreek, and their journey to find a nest and their return to find their home invaded by White farmers. Temple bases his account of the kea experience on historical research on the first contacts between humans and kea. The first recorded mention of a kea by European settlers is in Samuel Butler's *A First Year in Canterbury Settlement* (1860). Butler writes:

> there was a kind of dusky brownish-green parrot [. . .] two attended us on our ascent after leaving the bush. We threw many stones at them, and it was not their fault that they escaped unhurt. (qtd. in Temple 1994).

This event is replicated in *Beak of the Moon*, this time from the kea's point of view:

> Two large "birds" (for there had never been any other kind of animal in Kawee) climbed up the riverbed at the edge of the water. They had legs many times longer than a pukeko [. . .]. Their "wings" had no feathers, but they had long white claws . . . as Strongbeak and Skreek and Huff-Tuft all called out together, one of [the long-legs] picked up a stone and threw it at them. Skreek and Huff-Tuft flew up in surprise and Skreek cried, "he throws stones, like Highfeather when he's angry with the young ones."
>
> "But why should he be angry," cried Huff-Tuft, "when he's only just seen us?" (Temple 1981, 17–18)

In his reconstruction of the event, Temple's narratological decisions clearly ascribe agency to the kea, imparting not only a perspective but also a voice to the birds.

Further narrative strategies support the birds' agency. The narrative uses imagery and analogies that could come from the kea's own epistemology. Ripples on a lake look like "the passing glance of a wing" (172); winter's end is marked by the "moulting of the snow" (342); characters are asked to "swallow the bitter root" and dismiss arguments "that will never bear any berries" (23, 334). Most importantly, the narrative employs close focalization to present a kea's-eye view of the environment. The accounts of the kea moving in the air are among the most striking in the novel. Readers receive access to the physical sensation of the activity:

> Below them were the first gapes of crevasses, blue, matching the cold and empty sky [. . .] far behind lay Kawee, the forest diminished in size by distance and height so it appeared as nothing more than the swelling of black moss. The air felt like ice in their nostrils and it ran in slivers down their throats, even to their lungs, as they breathed deeper and harder, climbing until there seemed no end to climbing. Their shoulders began to burn with fatigue, the ache of tired muscles spreading along their wings until only willpower seemed to keep their wingtips flexing. The glare of snow-reflected sun began to dazzle their eyes. (124–25)

Such an evocative depiction gives readers the opportunity—almost—to experience what being a kea might feel like. In this, Temple's approach comes close to Nagel's notion of a sympathetic imagination. "To imagine something sympathetically," Nagel writes, "we put ourselves in a conscious state resembling the thing itself" (1974, 446). Through this approach, then, readers are aligned with the birds, inhabiting their world view.

One of the dangers of such an approach is that the (human) narrator is essentially speaking for the (avian) character, and, as such, has the potential to misunderstand and misrepresent kea experience, possibly with detrimental consequences. Alcoff states: "the practice of privileged people speaking for or on behalf of less privileged persons has [. . .] resulted (in many cases) in increasing or reinforcing the oppression of the group spoken for" (1992, 7). If we read Temple's narrative strategies through the framework of Alcoff's question *What are the discourses of power at work in* Beak of the Moon*'s act of representation?*, we may uncover a text that lessens the birds' agency. As noted earlier, third-person narration holds authority over the other perspectives in a text. Cohn affirms that "the narrator's superior knowledge of the character's inner life" implies a "superior ability to present and assess it" (1978, 29). Furthermore, in the process of speaking for a character, a narrator might misconstrue the intentions of their subject, or even impose their own values over the character.

It is possible to read the final section of *Beak of the Moon* in this way. The climax of the novel recounts the resistance undertaken by the birds against creatures who are taking over their habitat: animals they call pinkfaces (sheep). The response from the birds is violent. After generations of subsisting on a mainly herbivorous diet, some of the kea decide to attack and eat the pinkfaces. The narrator recounts that one of the kea:

> drove his beak into the sheep's side. Twisting its head in terror, the sheep dashed forward and in an effort to rid itself of its tormentor, ran beneath the thorny tangle of a tematakoura bush. [The kea] simply removed his grip, flew over the bush, and caught the sheep beyond, stabbing, stabbing, goading the sheep towards the creek. In a frenzy of pain, the sheep rushed over the edge of the steep bank and bounced heavily over boulders and clay [. . .] until it collapsed utterly exhausted in a pool. (351)

What is notable about this account is its stylistic difference from the representation of the first kea-human encounter. In the former, readers are aligned with the kea: the text uses their terminology for humans ("long-legs"). In contrast, here the narrator chooses "sheep" over "pinkface."

More urgently, the narrative frames the intention behind this act of violence within a human ethical framework. In the flock of kea, two groups emerge: those in favor of attacking the sheep and those against. Tellingly, the kea against the attacks are the characters whose perspectives the narrator has shared with readers, and who are therefore the characters with which readers are most aligned. Strongbeak makes his position clear, stating to the attacking birds that "you've violated the proper order of things, the real order of things [. . .]. *You have all been eating flesh* [. . .]. It is still not right!" (333). By presenting the argument through the voice of one of the protagonists, the narrative encourages readers to endorse Strongbeak's moral position. This encouragement is confirmed through the narrator's use of sympathetic focalization. Skreek is persuaded to take part in the killing of the pinkfaces but is uneasy about the action:

> Skreek hesitated, perplexed. It seemed such a violent, strenuous way to drive out the pinkfaces. Yet if this is what the bosses wanted, he had better try it [. . .]. Skreek took off and tried to use the same methods. But [. . .] Skreek could see the shine of fear in its eye. He could not bring himself to strike again. He had never been averse to settling arguments or maintaining his perch with a well-raked claw or well-aimed blow of the beak. But what argument was he settling? And this was no fight [. . .]
>
> "Keas don't kill," Skreek repeated stubbornly. (352)

The novel's depiction of the birds is that kea don't really want to kill; it is only the action of a few morally deviant birds.

In his writing on the novel, Temple points to the human belief that "not all kea directly attacked animals. Experience began to show that attacks on sheep were often led by one older male kea—a so-called 'rogue.' Remove that bird and the attacks ceased" (1994). This interpretation of kea behavior might have an adverse effect on actual kea: it could justify human intervention into kea flocks (removing the rogue kea is best for kea as well as humans), and it could implicitly endorse human invasion of kea habitat (the kea know that it is "not right" to resist the incursion). In this way, despite seeming to create a space for kea concerns to be voiced, the textual operations may work against Temple's intentions; imbuing kea with an agency also links them to a human voice and a human morality. Asking *How might speaking for kea in* Beak of the Moon *affect real kea?* could infer that this linking of kea-action to imagined kea-belief may have a damaging impact on readers' perceptions of the *real* behaviors of the birds.

However, I do not believe this is the ultimate response readers take away from *Beak of the Moon*. This owes partly to the care Temple takes to describe kea experience and to advocate for the lives of kea outside of his fictional creation. In his writing about *Beak of the Moon*, Temple makes it clear that he supports the rights of kea. He declares:

> for the last 130 years, high country farmers, with the support of sympathetic government agencies, have been "controlling" kea. Conservatively, 150,000 have been killed in the name of protecting sheep. . . . It could be that the real problem will be keeping this bird off the endangered, and ultimately, extinction list. It is estimated that fewer than 10,000 are left [. . .]. This is one of the worst cases of avicide in history. (Temple 1994)

The novel, he suggests, is a testament to and celebration of kea resilience. He continues:

> That the kea survived this massive slaughter, and the continuing pressures on its environment, seems little short of a miracle. [. . .] Its survival is a tribute to both its physical resilience and a level of intelligence that has enabled it to adapt to a radically altered ecology and to exploit whatever new opportunities have presented themselves for food gathering, chiefly through human agency. (1994)

If kea cannot speak out against the violence inflicted against them, perhaps *speaking for* is the most appropriate course of action. As Alcoff puts it: "If I don't speak for those less privileged than myself, am I abandoning my political responsibility to speak out against oppression?" (1992, 8). Alcoff's interrogatory practices allow writers to identify the discourses of power at work in their acts of representation, and, in doing so, acknowledge their own presence in the writing, what Alcoff calls "deconstruct[ing] my discourse" (1992, 8).

Temple circumvents the mastery of the human narrator over the kea characters by drawing attention to the narrator's presence in the writing. The novel begins with a preface by the narrator:

> it has taken many years to piece this story together and to translate it into a form that may be readily understood. [. . .] Although keas are generally fearless, friendly and forthcoming, they are very secretive. [. . .] Luckily I encountered Strongbeak [who] felt it important that the whole story should be told after I pointed out that not enough people knew the kea's side of it. (11)

The narrator makes explicit the authority inherent in his position as chronicler of kea experience. He comments, "I have taken some liberties in translation" and confesses "the narrative is my own" (11). This foregrounding of the narrator in the text continues as the story is recounted. The narrator makes comments like "When Strongbeak told me of the sight he saw next" (17); "Skreek said afterwards" (49); and "from the moulting feathers of kea memory, the following story can be put together" (34). In this act of making the chronicler visible in the text, and the sharing of information explicit, Temple's novel acknowledges the hierarchy between subject and subjected that is instituted in the act of representation. Moreover, by drawing attention to the narration, perhaps some of the power of the narrator diminishes. The narrator admits the limitations of his own human perceptions. He muses, "if it is true that what goes up must come down, should it not be equally true that what goes down must come up? It depends on one's point of view [. . .]. Would such a view readily occur to a bird?" (181). These interventions in the text may overthrow the hierarchy of power between narrator and character.

As the narrator notes, "many a human observer, wriggling surreptitiously through tangled mountain forest to study kea nest or habit has usually found that, on the contrary, he is observed, by keas who appear from nowhere and look down, suitably dumbfounded by his clumsy and antic behaviour" (149). In this way, *Beak of the Moon* overcomes some of the dangers of speaking for kea: it provides a space for a reader's sympathetic imagination, but also exposes the human construction of the space.

The approach undertaken in Daphne du Maurier's "The Birds" is almost opposite to Temple's novel. Readers of the story are not granted direct access to birds' perspectives, nor are birds given direct voices. The story is focalized through Nat Hocken, a farm laborer, who lives with his family outside an isolated Cornwall village. In her initial descriptions, du Maurier is careful to situate readers' vision of the birds through a human perspective, and, seemingly, to use this point of view to endorse a human interpretation of the birds' motives. The description begins: "sitting on the cliff's edge, [Nat] would watch the birds" (du Maurier 2004, 1). Immediately after, the narrator informs readers not only what the birds are doing but why they are doing it: "the birds flew inland, purposeful, intent; they knew where they were bound, the rhythm and ritual of their life brooked no delay" (1). This statement could be read at face value—that this is indeed what the birds themselves are thinking. But as the description continues, du Maurier slowly reveals that this is Nat's rendition of the birds' actions: "black and white, jackdaw and gull, mingled in strange partnership, seeking some sort of liberation, never satisfied, never still. Flocks of starlings, rustling like silk, flew to fresh pasture, driven by the same necessity of movement, and the smaller birds, the finches and the larks, scattered from tree to hedge as if compelled" (1–2). The qualifiers "some sort of" and "as if" uncover that Nat makes these statements about the birds, indicating that a human narrator muses on the birds' behavior from observation rather than through avian experience. Similarly, the analogy "rustling like silk" can only come from a human perspective. Du Maurier then exposes Nat's role in the interpretation of the birds even more explicitly. The description "crying, whistling, calling, they skimmed the placid sea and left the shore" precedes a direct inclusion of Nat's quoted ruminations: "perhaps, thought Nat [. . .] a message comes to the birds [. . .] like a warning" (2). Through this process, du Maurier's work demonstrates the discursive ways human narratives work to subjugate those who aren't permitted to speak.

Nevertheless, the story explores the possibilities of challenging this discursive control. As Richard Terdiman reminds us, "no dominant discourse is ever fully protected from contestation" (1985, 56). Indeed, even in the scene recounted above, it could be concluded that the presence of the birds in the text works to undermine the human-narrative domination. What began with a confident explanation of birds' behaviors ends with a voice unsure of his own interpretive skills: the inclusion of "perhaps" suggests that Nat's quoted thought is not exactly assertive. His movement from conclusiveness to uncertainty occurs elsewhere in the text. In one of the early depictions of the threat of the birds, the scene begins with Nat's assured comprehension of the world around him. Nat's thoughts and perceptions are presented directly:

> "The tide will take them when it turns," he said to himself. He looked out to sea and watched the crested breakers, combing green. They rose stiffly, curled, and broke again, and because it was ebb tide the roar was distant, more remote, lacking the sound and thunder of the flood. (11)

But this vision is then taken over by the birds. The text reveals that

> what he thought at first to be the white caps of the waves were gulls. Hundreds, thousands, tens of thousands. [. . .] They rose and fell in the trough of the seas, heads to the wind, like a mighty fleet at anchor, waiting on the tide. [. . .] Nat turned, and leaving the beach [,] [*sic*] climbed the steep path home. Someone should know of this. Someone should be told. Something was happening, because of the east wind and the weather, that he did not understand. (11)

In this moment, the incursion of the birds into Nat's view unsettles him, both physically and psychically. He can't comprehend the birds' intentions; moreover, he does not know what to do with the new information. Although he knows that "someone should be told," he can't articulate who that "someone" might be. The birds' presence has, as Terdiman might put it, caused a "a corrosive irony" to emerge from Nat's initial representation of the event (1985, 76).

Later, Nat's interpretative control over the events further deteriorates as the text gives access to what might be seen as the birds' authentic intentions. The scene begins through Nat's perspective:

> In the distance he could see the clay hills, white and clean, against the heavy pallor of the sky. Something black rose from behind them, like a smudge at first, then widening, becoming deeper, and then the smudge became a cloud, and the cloud divided again into five other clouds, spreading north, east, south and west, and they were not clouds at all; they were birds. (16)

As the birds reconfigure the image, Nat also becomes aware of their potential motives: "He knew from their speed, they were bound inland, up country, they had no business with the people here on the peninsula [. . .]. 'They've been given the towns,' thought Nat. 'They know what they have to do'" (16). The birds here may not have direct voices, but they have nonetheless communicated their intentions in the narrative. In this way, if we ask the question *What are the discourses of power at work in this text's act of representation?*, we can see that it not only exposes the relationship between narratorial voice and power, but also makes plain the ways in which silenced voices might find a position to be heard.

This reading of du Maurier's approach might also help answer the question, *How might speaking for birds in "The Birds" affect real birds?* Ostensibly, the text presents birds as a threatening, unstoppable force: "they kept coming at him from the air, silent save for the beating wings. The terrible, fluttering wings. He could feel blood on his hands, his wrists, his neck" (20). From this description, it is clear to see why the story is regarded as a prime exemplar of the animal horror form. However, I contend that du Maurier's text engages with birds in a different way from other texts in this genre. Peter Benchley, the author of the novel *Jaws*, declares that his principal activity in his narrative was "to demonize an animal" (qtd. in Rothfels 2002, viii). Although du Maurier's text may present birds as demonic beings, I believe that both the characters and readers of the story are not positioned simply to fight back against malevolent creatures, but in some ways also to sympathize with them, and even to acknowledge human complicity in causing the birds' actions. As Nat himself admits, "you can't help admiring the beggars [. . .] they've got persistence" (30). After the birds break into his children's bedroom and Nat has successfully defended his family, Nat sees the animals not as the enemy but with some sympathy for their deaths: he "gazed at the little corpses, shocked and horrified. They were all small birds, none of any size," leaving him "sickened" (5). His daughter, Jill, also takes an empathetic stance. She suggests: "perhaps if we put bread for them outside the window they will eat that and fly away" (7).

Elsewhere, Nat becomes aware of the indifference other humans have toward birds. He notices the tone in a radio announcer's report of the birds' actions and the way that it reveals a sense of human superiority over other species:

Nat had the impression that this man [. . .] treated the whole business as he would an elaborate joke. There would be others like him, hundreds of them. [. . .] There would be parties tonight in London, like the ones they gave on election nights. People standing about, shouting and laughing, getting drunk. "Come and watch the birds!" (13)

Similarly, when Nat tries to report the early attacks to a telephone operator, he realizes that she values the human experience above all others. Nat thinks: "she doesn't care. Maybe she'd had to answer calls all day. She hopes to go to the pictures tonight. She'll squeeze some fellow's hand, and point up at the sky and say 'Look at all them birds!' She doesn't care" (17).

Importantly, Nat begins to make the connection between this perceived superiority over birds and its link to more hostile behavior. Nat's neighbor, the farmer Trigg, demonstrates the direct line between the gleeful "look at all them birds!" and actions taken against birds:

> "It looks as though we're in for some fun," [Trigg] said. "Have you seen the gulls? Jim and I are going to take a crack at them. Everyone's gone bird crazy, talking of nothing else. I hear you were troubled in the night. Want a gun? [. . .] Why don't you stop behind and join the shooting match? We'll make the feathers fly." (18)

This aggressive behavior toward the birds does not go unpunished in the text. Trigg and Jim are the first humans whose deaths are described in the story. The day after Trigg threatens to "make the feathers fly," Nat discovers the corpses: "Jim's body lay in the yard [. . .] what was left of it"; "Trigg's body was close to the telephone. He must have been trying to get through to the exchange when the birds came for him. The receiver was hanging loose, the instrument torn from the wall" (34-35). Here du Maurier makes a connection not only to the direct attack on the birds, but also with the indifferent telephone operator.

In the end, though, it is not just the explicit aggressors who are targeted by the birds, but all human beings. Nat does not comprehend why he is included in the attacks until his subconscious reveals his culpability: "He dreamt uneasily, because through his dreams there was a thread of something forgotten. Some piece of work, neglected, that he should have done" (28). Upon waking, he reflects: "'I ought to be shot for this. It is all my fault'" (29). It is not explicitly stated in the story what Nat—or indeed all humans—might have done to deserve the birds' wrath, but it may have something to do with the human impact on the planet. It is implied that the Earth's changing climate is somehow related to the alteration in the birds' behavior. At the beginning of the story, Nat reflects that "never had he known such cold, not in all the bad winters he could remember" (10). This shift in the temperature is later linked to the birds' actions. A radio reporter states that "it is thought that the Arctic air stream, at present covering the British Isles, is causing birds to migrate south in immense numbers, and that intense hunger may drive these birds to attack human beings" (12). Later, Nat reflects that the actions of humans may have always had a negative effect on avian species. During the last assault on the family cottage, Nat "listened to the tearing sound of splintering wood, and wondered how many million years of memory were stored in those little brains, behind the stabbing beaks, the piercing eyes, now giving them this instinct to destroy mankind" (38). Du Maurier's decision to implicate humans in the actions of the birds destabilizes the opposition us/them and, as such, allows us to imagine experiences on the other side of the perceived binary. In this way, even though du Maurier's text does not provide the birds with direct voice or perspective, it does allow for a different kind of agency: one which is aware of the dangers of speaking for nonhuman animals, but nevertheless provides a space for readers to reflect on the motives of animals, without coloring these motives with the human perspective.

In *The Flight of Birds*, in which I contend with the ethics of representing birds, I have negotiated several representations of birds' agency. My novel does not present the direct voices of birds, as in Temple's novel; nevertheless, it does include birds' perspectives, albeit briefly and strategically. The novel is divided into twelve stories, each focusing on a different bird. The first story, "What He Heard," incorporates the experience of a lyrebird into a ghost story about a child lost in the Australian bush. A man walking with his dog hears the cry of a child in pain, only to discover that the sounds come from the beak of a lyrebird, one of a species of remarkable mimickers. Part of the point of the story is that it is extremely difficult to get away from our own perceptions and preconceptions of the world: in other words, our understanding of our environment is tied to our own hegemonic centrisms. The dog views the environment in the bush in terms of scent lines. The human transforms the bush to reflect his own anxieties: eucalypts become "talon-scratched," and rocks are "ossified" (Lobb 2019, 3). But the story is also about reckoning with other ways to engage with the world. After the human story is resolved, readers are presented with this epilogue:

> The lyrebird is scratching the dirt in the gravelly corner. He lifts his head. His larynx vibrates. Out of his beak come three short notes. The second is microtonally higher than the first and third. This is followed by a long high trill. The noise he is making is not full of sadness or pain. The lyrebird is not thinking about lost or abandoned children. His head pivots. The dwindling light points out a speck in the dirt. The lyrebird pecks and then he sings his song again. (7)

This is the only scene in the novel where a human is not present; even so, the influence of the human is still central to the account. What the lyrebird thinks is not actually represented here. Rather, readers are given the viewpoint in terms of negatives, presented by a human narrator: "the lyrebird is *not* thinking about lost or abandoned children"; his song "is *not* full of sadness or pain" [emphasis added]. Readers are kept on the outside of the lyrebird's pivoting head, but also asked to recognize the presence of the human story over the bird: the man's thoughts about lost children and his sadness frame the lyrebird's unrepresented thoughts.

In another story, "Do You Speak My Language?", I incorporate a moment when the narrator presents this imagined version of a kookaburra's thoughts:

"the kookaburra, round-chested and alert, will spy [a piece of bacon] from his vantage point on the branch of the old gum tree. He'll scissor through the air—a streak of azure in his gray-brown feathers—and back up to the branch. In the kookaburra's mind the bacon is a worm, maybe" (85). Like the account of the lyrebird, this is a human interpretation of a bird's thoughts rather than an unmediated presentation. The inclusion of an external description of the kookaburra ("a streak of azure"), as well as the use of future tense and the qualifier "maybe," indicate the depiction as a human version. Here I am following du Maurier's tactic to expose the human presence in any description of another species' life.

Du Maurier's influence over my writing is more explicit in the collection's final story, "The Flight of Birds." I include a description of seagulls focalized through the human character, but the birds' presence takes over the text:

And then it happens. As if they'd choreographed this moment, all the birds unfurl their wings. They lean to the left, they lean to the right. Then they all glide skyward. For a moment, the young man isn't certain if they levitated or if the rocks dropped from under him. They're all in the air above him, sharp against the blue sky. They form a synchronised circle that wheels above the young man's head. Even the one with the missing foot flies smoothly, turning this way and that, letting the sun catch his wings at different angles. Even the one with the gaping eyehole can drift and swoop through the air. In fact, it is impossible to tell which bird is which: they are all perfect, all elegant, all miraculous. The birds move as a group, concertinaing in and out like a lung. Sparkling in the light as they turn, flipping from black to blinding white. The young man watches in awe at this sight, as the birds soothe the sky, their white feathers glinting. Then they soar out to sea, swifting down to the water and up into the air again. (210–211)

This sequence is held tightly by the narrator. The description is located always in relation to the young man's vantage point, above him or flying away from him. There are also touches of the human configuring of the action. As with du Maurier's descriptions of her birds, analogies are made that could only be fashioned by a human: the movement of the birds is both a "concertina" and a "lung," the feathers "glint" like a mirror or glass. Despite this control, brief points in this description give birds access to the narration: the seagull with the missing foot receives agency to "let [. . .] the sun catch his wings"; the seagull with the gaping eyehole has permission to "drift and swoop." These are only fleeting moments—the birds are soon viewed from the human angle so that it is "impossible to tell which bird is which," and the birds will soon disappear into the horizon. Nevertheless, these moments give humans a new way to perceive the world, and this perspective may allow for birds to be accepted on their own terms. As the ecophilosopher Val Plumwood puts it, "our willingness and ability to recognise the other as a potentially intentional being tells us whether we are open to potentially rich forms of interaction and relationship which have an ethical dimension" (2002, 181). "Potentially intentional" is a central phrase for me. Like Nagel, I am aware of my own inability to think like a bird. So, when birds' perspectives are included in the work, they are, in some sense, empty: places where the birds' thoughts could be presented, if only we had access to them. Given this, the answer to the question *What discourses of power are at work in* The Flight of Birds' *act of representation?* is perhaps that the whole text is a demonstration of the ubiquity of human discourse, but also evinces a willingness to consider other species' perspectives, without speaking for them. In taking this approach I also hope to avoid doing any more harm to the birds in the text.

Alcoff identifies another interrogatory practice central to the act of ethically representing others. She declares that "speaking should always carry with it an accountability and responsibility for what one says" (1992, 25). By linking Alcoff's practices to the representation of birds, I hope to have shown the challenges of representing the perspectives of other species: the harm some formal devices might cause to the lives of real animals, but also the tactics used by writers to avoid discursive violence. This may lead to a reevaluation of some of the conventions of representation, even the strategies which we thought provided a positive account of animals' experiences. Alcoff stresses that anyone speaking for another group needs "a serious and sincere commitment to remain open to criticism and to attempt actively, attentively, and sensitively to 'hear' (understand) criticism" (1992, 26). If writers bear Alcoff in mind, then we may at least minimize the potential for misrepresentation. Haraway writes that "fiction is in process and still at stake, not finished" (2003, 19–20). If we keep experimenting with new representational forms, and always remain vigilant to the problem of speaking for other animals, then we may find forms that allow for animal perspectives on their own terms.

ACKNOWLEDGEMENTS

"The Birds." Quotation reproduced with permission of Curtis Brown Group Ltd, London, on behalf of the Chichester Partnership. Copyright © The Chichester Partnership, 1952.

Beak of the Moon. Quotation reproduced with kind permission from Philip Temple.

REFERENCES

Alcoff, Linda. 1992. "The Problem of Speaking for Others." *Cultural Critique* 20 (Winter): 5–32.
Arnold, Matthew. 1945 [1882]. *The Poetical Works of Matthew Arnold*. Oxford: Oxford University Press.
Cohn, Dorrit. 1978. *Transparent Minds: Narrative Modes for Presenting Consciousness in Fiction*. Princeton: Princeton University Press.
du Maurier, Daphne. 2004 [1952]. "The Birds." In *The Birds and Other Stories*, 1–39. London: Virago.
Griffin, Donald R. 1981. *The Question of Animal Awareness: Evolutionary Continuity of Mental Experience*. New York: Rockefeller University Press.
Haraway, Donna. 2003. *The Companion Species Manifesto: Dogs, People and Significant Otherness*. Chicago: Prickly Paradigm Press.
Lobb, Joshua. 2019. *The Flight of Birds*. Sydney: Sydney University Press.
Nagel, Thomas. 1974. "What is it Like to be a Bat?" *The Philosophical Review* 83, no. 4 (October): 435–50.
Plumwood, Val. 2002. *Environmental Culture: The Ecological Crisis of Reason*. London: Routledge.
Radner, Daisie. 1994. "Heterophenomenology: Learning about the Birds and the Bees." *The Journal of Philosophy* 91, no. 8 (August): 389–403.
Rothfels, Nigel. 2002. *Representing Animals*. Bloomington and Indianapolis: Indiana University Press.
Temple, Philip. 1981. *Beak of the Moon*. Auckland: William Collins.
———. 1994. "Kea–the Feisty Parrot." *New Zealand Geographic* 24 (October-December): n.p. https://www.nzgeo.com/stories/kea-the-feisty-parrot/
Terdiman, Richard. 1985. *Discourse/Counter-Discourse: The Theory and Practice of Symbolic Resistance in Nineteenth-Century France*. Ithaca: Cornell University Press. van Dooren, Thom. 2014. *Flight Ways: Life and Loss at the Edge of Extinction*. New York.
Wynne, Clive D. L. and Monique A. R. Udell. 2013. *Animal Cognition: Evolution, Behavior and Cognition*. Second Edition. Houndsmills: Palgrave Macmillan.

Chapter 8

Margaret Atwood's Bird Narratives

Danette DiMarco

Rita Felski (2008) imagines innovative ways for professionals engaging in twentieth-first-century literary critique to gain disciplinary ground. With a call to move beyond "theological" and "ideological" hermeneutics—the former unwilling to situate literature in its social world, and the latter guilty of feeding readers repetitious and suspicious critical interpretations—Felski engages in a much-needed rethinking of the uses of literature (Felski 2008, 9). But what if literature professionals extend the dilemma of the uses of literature, as Felski describes, to include critics *and* those producing the art? How do literary artists with activist interests render work with both pleasurable "aesthetic power" and "political functionalism" (Felski 2008, 9)? In other words, what approaches do literary artists use when they wish to produce pleasurable reading that purposively educates about politically salient issues? What might their texts look like when they position readers as armchair activists? How do these texts merge literary and aesthetic delight with epistemological and political designs?

    Literary writers with personal and artistic commitments to bird conservation negotiate this dilemma of providing narrative or poetic pleasure and knowledge about avian populations. Sometimes their anxieties over seamlessly synthesizing the two reveal themselves in a text's content. For instance, Steve Burrows (2016), creator of the Birder Murder Mystery series, divulges his authorial tentativeness over this creative problem. In a crucial scene from *A Cast of Falcons*, DCI Dominic Jejeune offers his expertise about bird deaths and glass windows. While entering a building important to a case, Jejeune observes that "the open space soared above him all the way to the roof. In the centre was an immense skylight that flooded the atrium with natural light" (Burrows 2016, 94). Where Jejeune's coworker, Danny Maik, sees only difficult human labor in this "impressive" architecture, commenting that he "wouldn't fancy being the window cleaner for this place," Jejeune sees danger: "Or a passing bird [. . .]. They don't see glass. They see a reflection of trees, or the sky, but otherwise, from a bird's perspective, glass is invisible. Collisions with glass buildings are considered the second leading cause of non-natural mortality among songbirds" (Burrows 2016, 94). Immediately after instructing Maik on this fact, however, Jejeune dispels his authoritative tone, shifting knowledge to some unknown and expert other: "I know somebody who studied it [the topic of birds flying into windows]" (Burrows 2016, 94). Could this backing away from personal and important bird knowledge also reflect Burrows's anxiety about how to effectively and fluidly fit the poetical and political into his own art? Is Jejeune's hesitancy also a nod to a reading public aware of the traps that authors face when they piece together environmental education and literary aesthetic? I would argue that Jejeune's response reflects the subtextual crisis of bird-interested literary writers as they follow conservationist desires and seek ways to provide readers with pleasure.

This chapter examines how literary superstar and bird activist Margaret Atwood has negotiated the tension, pushing younger readers to want to proactively shape environmentally sustainable futures. The essay discusses Atwood's personal and lifelong appreciation for and commitment to avian life in the context of her children's book *For the Birds* (1990) and her young adult graphic novel *The Complete Angel Catbird* (2018).[1] About *AC* Atwood has said, "I wanted to create a positive conversation around cats and birds that didn't just completely annoy cat people," so writing in this genre, for this audience, made sense: "there's nothing that influences families' behavior around their pets like agitated, involved 10-year olds" (Stephens 2017). The first part of this argument lays the groundwork for better understanding Atwood's activist involvement with birds. While Atwood has repeatedly said that she has been interested in birds since childhood, it is also likely that her participation in important avian-oriented organizations, like BirdLife International, has been made easier because of her acclaim as an author. *AC*'s *New York Times*-bestselling standing is no doubt linked with her post-1990 celebrity status. Well-known prior to the publication of *FB*, and recognized most for *The Handmaid's Tale*, her fame soared with the release of Hulu's TV adaptation of that same novel as well as the earlier dystopic *MaddAddam* trilogy.[2] Global acclaim facilitated her networking with like-minded conservationists so that she could speak more openly to a broader lay audience about environmental concerns.

FB's significance increases when revisited thirty years later through Atwood's conservation work. The second part of this chapter analyzes *FB* as an intratextual literary prototype for *AC*. The work instructs children on caring for the environment. Published within a year of Bill McKibben's *The*

End of Nature (1989)—often considered the first book on global warming written for general audiences—*FB* did not yet have recourse to a climate change narrative to support its educational messages. But the book serves as an important predecessor on environmental and avian topics also tended to in *AC*, a text published in the wake of climate change disaster. The former's focus includes consideration of the top causes of bird deaths: cat predation, toxicity, habitat loss, and—as Jejeune tells Maik—"flying into windows" (Burrows 2016, 94).

The final portion of this essay considers *AC*'s elaboration on such topics through Atwood's innovative turn to the graphic novel. Using this text-image form to help merge narrative content and paratextual design, *AC* evolves the epistemological and activist project started in *FB*. In the end, *AC* is successful and pleasurable popular literature with important ecological messaging critical to changing future human "accountabilities" and "obligations" (van Dooren 2014, 10) in worldbuilding.

BIRDS AND ATWOOD'S ACTIVISM

Atwood has been birdwatching since she was six (Sethi 2016). She has "always lived in the birdy world" (Atwood 2010). Growing up around biologists in the northern Canadian bush, she thought "it was simply a given that you knew what else might be in the forest with you. [. . .] Bird watching [. . .] was part of the daily fabric" (qtd. in Nicholson 2014). Anita Sethi (2016) explains that birds are prominent in Atwood's novels, "perfect accompaniment" to common themes like "freedom and imprisonment" repeatedly seen in her works. Sethi cites Atwood: "Prospero calls Ariel 'my bird' in *The Tempest* itself and also 'my chick', so that imagery is already there" (Sethi 2016). Atwood's allusions to birds appear in several works: "The jay and the heron in *Surfacing*, the raven in the story 'Death by Landscape,' the story 'Scarlet Ibis,' and the crows and vultures in the MaddAddam trilogy" (Nicholson 2014).

Leonard Lutwack's (1994) *Birds in Literature* is one of only a few late-twentieth-century monograph-length critical texts devoted to closely examining birds as mechanisms for exploring literary themes. In his final chapter, "Literature and The Future of Birds," Lutwack pushes past birds as symbols and/or metaphors for aesthetic reasons, and connects Atwood's uses of birds in literature with public environmental engagement. In Lutwack's opinion, Atwood recognizes "the new breed of nature lovers" who, like the heroine in her early novel *Surfacing* (1972), "is appalled by the 'cause-less undiluted' killing of a heron by two shooters she believes are Americans" (Lutwack 1994, 235). The protagonist in *Surfacing* fears that the Canadian future is the United States present: "they're [Americans] what's in store for us, what we are turning into [. . .] [and] I felt a sickening complicity" (qtd. in Lutwack 1994, 235). Lutwack also interprets Atwood's "Scarlet Ibis" (from *Bluebeard's Egg*, 1983) as a perceptible sketch of the "reprehensible" tourist "who has no special regard for wilderness but, out of boredom and a feeble desire to do the things recommended in the travel brochures, must have a wilderness experience" (Lutwack 1994, 235): witnessing the migratory return of the scarlet ibis to Trinidad where they can be viewed roosting at sunset.

Lutwack's reasons for invoking Atwood are tied to his book's bigger question, "Can literature be of help in" the "process" of "learning to deal with a diminished natural world?" (Lutwack 1994, 255). In other words, can a literary artist's use of bird knowledge in literature (here novels and short stories) be an instrument for better public education about our society's own entanglements with multiple other species? Lutwack's forward-looking question reflects the transition that literary scholars may need to make, and that Jessica Leber (2019) captures in an *Audubon* interview with Atwood, in best understanding Atwood's uses of birds in her art:

> I ask her [Atwood] about how birds are used as symbols in literature, a tactic that she deploys often. A cursory answer, then the pivot: "Why don't we talk about why birds are important," she says. Later, this time with a chuckle punctuating her trademark wry monotone, she turns a question I have posed around with this: "That's important from the point of view of people, but let's talk about it as being important from the point of view of birds." (Leber 2019, 2)

The "pivot" is to understand the birds as aesthetic (i.e., symbols in literature) *and* as living creatures within their own worlds. Having grown up with a keen awareness of ornithology, and with a continued commitment to activist work regarding avian life, Atwood has only ever known a literary career inside of her care and concern for birds.

Atwood's avian activism has flourished, especially in the last thirty years, mostly helped by her global success. As a literary celebrity, she has no doubt found it easier to speak out and do more for the birds. She and her late husband Graeme Gibson served as "joint honourary presidents of the Rare Bird Club within Birdlife International" (Atwood 2010). Both received this organization's President's Medals for being "conservation-minded biodiversity champions" (Nicholson 2014). They founded the Pelee Island Bird Observatory (PIBO). A major stopover for migratory birds (Munroe 2017; Stephens 2017), PIBO is "the confluence of the Atlantic and Mississippi migration routes," where "as many as half of Canada's more than 400 recognized bird species can be seen [. . .] each spring" (Munroe 2017). At the southern tip of the Canadian keys, Pelee Island is part of the Canadian Migration Monitoring Network that "gather[s] data on passing avifauna" (Munroe 2017) like completing nest censuses (Dundas 2017). Atwood explains, "We count birds because birds count" (Munroe 217). She also emphasizes that "birds, especially migratory birds, are like an early-warning radar system [. . .]. When things are going wrong with their habitats and their numbers are declining, that's a wake-up call" (Stephens 2017).

Atwood maintains a sense of humor and joy regarding bird life even while she is genuinely serious about PIBO and bird conservation. Both she and Gibson have "hosted the Botham Cup, a car-free birding contest and fundraiser each spring on Pelee Island" (Nicholson 2014; Dundas 2017) to benefit the island's heritage center. And, with Gibson's aid, Atwood partnered with Balzac's Coffee, a female-led company advocating for sustainability ("Balzac's Coffee" 2020) to support shade-grown coffee. This collaboration originated during Atwood's promotional work for *The Year of the Flood* when she asked audience members to take oaths to buy such coffee. The story goes that after the event, and with Gibson's mediation, Balzac's Coffee chain owner Diana Olsen "sent Atwood four options [of shade-grown coffee beans] [. . .] that were certified bird friendly by the Smithsonian Migratory Bird Center and roasted at Balzac's. Atwood brewed the coffees at home and picked her favourite" (Bain 2010). When *The Star* reported on the Balzac-Atwood alliance, its headline read "Atwood's coffee is (literally) *for the birds*" (Bain 2010, emphasis added).

The Cornell Lab of Ornithology indicates lack of awareness as the primary reason why people do not usually purchase shade-grown coffee ("Shade-Grown Coffee" 2021). Other factors include cost and availability. Survey research compiled by Williams et al. (2021) reveals that 49 percent of birdwatchers consider "bird habitat" when buying coffee, suggesting that much of this same population is not keeping habitat in mind. Atwood's arrangement with Balzac's is one sort of advertising push to educate coffee drinkers on the intersections between their own and avian worlds. To support the PIBO conservation project, for each one-pound purchase, one dollar goes to PIBO and twenty-five cents to the Smithsonian (Bain 2010). Although committed to funding PIBO, Atwood has also extended her reach beyond it to raise awareness about historical human-bird entanglements. As commentary about bird extinction and the need to protect migration paths has flourished, Atwood has also participated, via knitting, in Ceri Levy and Chris Aldhous's art exhibition *Ghosts of Gone Birds* ("Ghosts of Gone Birds" 2011).

Atwood's "Act Now to Save Our Birds" in *The Guardian* (2010) publicly calls attention to her understanding of biodiversity and the interconnectedness of life systems. In an interview with Deborah Dundas (2017), Atwood emphasizes this point: "Anybody interested in conservation knows that everything's connected and if you influence one part of it [. . .] you may find that all sorts of other things are being affected" (qtd. in Dundas 2017). A genuine understanding of systems will inevitably lead to why we should care about birds. Atwood connects marine algae and birds to illustrate her point: "We would be dead if the marine algae died," and "Seabirds poo into the water and fertilize it [marine algae]" (qtd. in Dundas 2017). Soil retains carbon, protecting the atmosphere as well as helping plants. When we engage in inorganic farming, we harm the soil, "along with the insects that birds usually eat" (qtd. in Dundas 2017). In "Act Now," she argues that bird deaths lead to human deaths: "It doesn't take a very smart augur to read that kind of bird omen" (Atwood 2010). In fact, Atwood and Gibson originally agreed to support the Rare Bird Club because they intimately understood that "the crisis in the life of birds" was really "about the connection between a healthy ecosystem and a healthy human population" (Atwood 2010). The message of "Act Now" resembles Thom van Dooren's (2014) discussion of "avian entanglements" (4).

As van Dooren (2014; 2019) pushes humans to realize their obligations to birds, so Atwood makes a case for us to act now. Her focus on systemic breakdowns in *FB* and *AC* are literary mirrors for human-bird entanglements. *FB* discusses several avian dangers that *AC* revisits years later in new form. Several jaw-dropping examples spelled out in "Act Now" further support her vigilant push to educate readers: "Cats polish off approximately 30 million birds in the state of Wisconsin"; over 67 million birds annually are killed from pesticides; "power lines kill 130–174 million birds" annually; somewhere between 60 and 80 million birds are killed by roadway vehicles; and "tall buildings—especially those that leave their lights on all night—are a major hazard for migrating birds, leading to between a hundred million and a billion bird deaths" per year (Atwood 2010). In 2018, nearly a decade after publishing "Act Now," Atwood spoke to the International Ornithological Congress to "bridge the gap between academic science and the way ordinary folks feel about birds" (Jackson-Houlston 2018). She did so while wearing plastic cat ears and bird wings, a tongue-in-cheek homage to her own art and its hero, Angel Catbird. But she started this cat-bird narrative nearly thirty years earlier, in the blueprint *FB*.

FOR THE BIRDS: A BLUEPRINT FOR ANGEL CATBIRD

Atwood is on record as saying it's important to write for children. She acknowledges the importance of stories in providing helpful lessons for how to act in our world. About *AC* particularly, but about children's narratives more generally, she has said, "What better way to influence your family's behaviour than through nine-to-12-year-olds. [. . .] You can teach much better through stories than numbers. It's a very old human technology" (Perkins 2018). In saying this, Atwood demonstrates her understanding of Lutwack's query about the role of literature in providing affective and rational knowledge regarding "a diminished natural world" (Lutwack 1994). Her experimental children's book *For the Birds*, published through the earth care books series, presents Samantha's fifty-four-page transformation from young girl uninformed on human contributions to diminishing bird populations to someone wanting to help birds. Changed into a scarlet tanager by her avian-like neighbor Phoebe Merganser, Samantha learns to see from a bird's perspective. *FB* combines fictional narrative and paratextual sidebars based on science to educate younger children on bird crises, care, and how to become environmental activists in their own backyards and local communities.

Phoebe Merganser leads Samantha on a magical bird migration journey. Her first name, Phoebe, alludes to a type of songbird, and her last name, Merganser, invokes a kind of duck. Phoebe looks like a bird "with white feathery hair, a long beaky nose, small friendly eyes, and tiny claw-like hands, wearing an odd wispy black cloak over her shoulders" (Atwood 1990, 8). She changes Samantha into a bird because of the latter's brattish disregard for nature, culminating in her name calling: Phoebe is a "nut-case" who "is *really* for the birds" (Atwood 1990, 8). Samantha's negativity derives from her own father's attitude about Samantha's cat, Furball. He says Furball is "useless" and "dim-witted," and claims that "All cats are *for the birds*" (Atwood 1990, 5). Samantha's attitude about wildlife and the environment generally, and birds more specifically, is what Atwood challenges and corrects in this story. The phrase "for the birds" suggests something silly, unimportant, or not logical. Learning to see the world from a bird's perspective, she eventually begins to advocate for them instead.[3]

FB takes up the narrative of cat predation from its start. Pete Marra, a population ecologist working for the Smithsonian Migratory Bird Center, states that "cats are by far [. . .] the direct cause of mortality" in birds ("Cat Wars" 2016). Atwood is also aware of this: "Cats are the major killer of migratory songbirds in North America" (Atwood 2010). A 2019 report published in *Science* claims as its thesis that the "cumulative loss of nearly three billion birds since 1970, across most North American biomes, signals a pervasive and ongoing avifaunal crisis" (Rosenberg et al., 2019). Although *FB* was published in 1990, nearly thirty years before this claim, it still harnesses the worry over bird deaths, particularly as it focuses on such deaths in the context of free-ranging cats. Samantha permits Furball to roam freely. She doesn't think about the dangers of this until she is herself a bird. In the second chapter, "Cats!", Samantha-as-tanager experiences Furball stalking and attempting to pounce on her: "Flying at her through the air was a monster! It had fiery yellow eyes, huge sharp claws, a mouthful of evil-fang-shaped teeth, and it was covered all over with horrible bristly fur! [. . .] The cat was Furball, her own warm and cuddly pussycat!" (Atwood 1990, 14). In response, Samantha "landed on a handy low branch and began to scold. 'Cat! Cat! Cat!' she yelled, warning any other birds within hearing distance" (14). Readers perusing the marginalia in the previous chapter intuit that this sort of chatter-as-warning, what Jennifer Ackerman has called "alarm communication" (2020, 44), indicates how birds might use their "voices [. . .] to tell other birds of food or danger" (*FB* 9). With her newly acquired bird cognition, Samantha can't understand why "they," meaning humans, "let those vicious killers roam around free" (Atwood 1990, 16). Phoebe loses no time in making this a lesson about changing one's personal behavior: "That's not how you felt when you were a human" (Atwood 1990, 16). Phoebe then frames Furball's predation as an opportunity to educate both Samantha and Atwood's readers about precautions humans should take to best protect birds from cats because birds, as she says, "don't usually get a second chance, with cats" (Atwood 1990, 16). She tells Samantha:

> Keep them inside at dawn and dusk, when birds feed on the ground and the light is dim; and especially at nesting time, migration time, and when young birds are leaving the nest and learning to fly. Put cat-proof collars around the trunks of trees, so cats can't get at the nests. Have your birdfeeder in the open, with perching trees around but without bushes nearby where cats can hide and sneak up. Try bells on their collars. If you're really ambitious, you can make a cat-proof fence. (Atwood 1990, 16)

Marra and Santella identify cats as "opportunist predators" (2016, 48) that do harm birds when given the liberty to go outdoors. If owners would curb their cats' abilities to roam, they would help to slow avian species decline. While cats are not yet heroic protagonists in *FB* as they will be in *AC*, Atwood's Furball is a mechanism for informing younger readers about how humans can support bird conservation and, ultimately, biodiversity by keeping their cats indoors. In addition to cat predation, subsequent chapters address other major dangers to birds and serve as precursors to *AC*—toxicity, habitat loss, and the dangers of lights at night and windows.

Science historian, bird specialist, and creative writer Helen Macdonald (2020) acknowledges humans have not considered "air space as habitat [. . .] until recently" (37). Because of this omission, humans have not historically recognized how cities at night take "a terrible toll on migrating songbirds: you can find them dead or exhausted at the foot of high-rise buildings all over America. Disoriented by light and reflections on glass, they crash into obstacles, fly into windows, spiral down to the ground" (Macdonald 2020, 38).

"The Deadly Glass Mountain" from *FB* calls attention to the dangers of glass and light to birds. Phoebe describes these dangers to Samantha who interprets the urban skyscrapers as "just high-rises [. . .]. Downtown office buildings" (Atwood 1990, 22). Phoebe instructs: "When the birds are migrating by night, and all the lights are left on, the birds get confused. They smash into the glass and get murdered. [. . .] If they were people you'd call it murder [. . .]. Criminal negligence, at the very least" (Atwood 1990, 22). Published before the awareness of twenty-first-century aero ecology in avian studies, *FB* does not offer the same solutions to the migration-glass problem that we might today, like switching off city lights on major migration nights, as is now proposed by the Cornell Lab of Ornithology or BirdCast. While *FB* includes images of silhouetted urban smokestacks burping pollution, and a dead bird on a sidewalk, a victim of having flown into a window, its paratextual solution is to alter the concrete jungle by writing to local politicians about adding more "wilderness areas" (Atwood 1990, 22).

Just as human architecture has affected bird habitats, so has toxicity. While Atwood includes several marginal items about bird habitats throughout *FB*, the chapter "The Dying Duck" pauses to focus on poisoning. A supplemental marginal text, "Bad News for Birds," precedes the chapter, educating readers on the dangers of road salt used to clear highways of snow and ice; it invites birds to "gather to feed on the salt and are killed by cars" (Atwood 1990, 24). The chapter then goes on to focus on other poisons, like lead shots from guns infiltrating water sources used by birds, which invokes follow-up commentary on "irresponsible hunting" of birds that has impacted the populations of "insect[s], rats, and mice" (Atwood 1990, 30). Without the birds, increases in such populations occur.

Additional dangers about human-bird entanglements are revealed when Phoebe leads Samantha over Point Pelee and Lake Erie, past an insect-infested vampire forest in Florida, to the Amazon. Phoebe explains that the Amazonian fires below them "were started by people," which enrages Samantha. A sidebar instructs that "Today there are rainforest protection programs" in various countries that "are saving thousands of acres of rainforest from being destroyed" (Atwood 1990, 47). To encourage support, the note ends with a push for readerly activism: "For more information, you can write to the nearest office of the World Wildlife Fund" (Atwood 1990, 47). As might be expected in a children's book, Samantha learns her lesson. None of the environmental problems are for the birds at all. She reinvents the meaning of the phrase by caring for them in her own backyard: she puts up a bird feeder. Her father wants to know why she has changed her mind, and she responds, "You did [. . .]. Remember how you're always saying, *That's for the birds*? Well, this is for the birds, But it's for the rest of us, too" (Atwood 1990, 53).

When Atwood's late husband Graeme Gibson first tried to publish *The Bedside Book of Birds* in the 1990s, publishers didn't think it would be successful because people simply weren't ready for it: "they could envisage no market for it, but its niche was more than ready when it came out in 2005" (Jackson-Houston 2018). *FB* was published even earlier than *Bedside*, and I would argue that people were also not as ready for it as they would be for *AC*: there was not yet a strongly supported climate change narrative because environmentalism was too often considered separate and parallel to social concerns, Atwood herself was not yet publicly recognized for her part in bird conservation, and the graphic novel had not yet reached acceptance as mainstream literature.

ANGEL CATBIRD: AN ITERATION OF BIRD CONSERVATION

Atwood acknowledges that her avian-activist text *AC* combines literary and political goals: "The latest iteration of it [bird conservation] is my book *Angel Catbird*, which is done with a parallel conservation programme run by Nature Canada about keeping your cat safe and saving bird lives" (qtd. in Sethi). Marra and Santella argue that saving birds means saving cats. Discussing how domestic cats and humans arrived at commensalism, and how cat predation is a leading cause of diminishing bird populations, they insist that human behavior matters to both cat and bird health. This human-cat-bird entanglement provides a lens through which to examine *AC*. Atwood, committed to protecting feline and avian lives, identifies her purpose and audience for the work: "to create a positive conversation around cats and birds that didn't just completely annoy cat people" (qtd. in Stephens 2017). This graphic novel's design is as hybrid as its hero, Angel Catbird, who is part human, cat, and bird. Like *FB*, it combines fiction with facts offset as marginalia, which compels readers to advocate for birds and cats. This hybrid design, first manifested in Atwood's children's book, allows Atwood to forge a literary-political message for readers to see human-bird-cat entanglements and to adopt behaviors in support of bird and feline care.

John Carey (2019), in a review of *AC* for *Audubon*, notes how this graphic novel doesn't hide its political take on the intermingling of avian and feline lives. He writes:

> The conservation message isn't exactly subtle. The pages are littered with factoids on birds and cats, discussing everything from felines' acute sense of smell to the urgency of keeping pets indoors. The first installment of *Angel Catbird* was released in tandem with Nature Canada's Keep Cats Safe and Save Bird

Lives program, which urges cat owners to take a pledge against letting their pets roam outdoors, and increases their knowledge of the strain it puts on wild bird populations.

The "factoids" that Carey invokes are visually punctuated with black-inked cat stamps throughout the text, hailing readers to pause and reflect. Angel Catbird as hero is also just as unsubtle and hybrid as the novel's form. Strig Feleedus—a human male researching a secret "super-splicer" (21) liquid technology—acquires cat and bird traits after a spill. Strig struggles to find cohesiveness with the merging of three species. Simple human acts like drinking coffee turn toxic: "Poison! What's the matter with me? I've always loved coffee!" (31). And what does a human do when he suddenly grows wings and sharp teeth? Landing appropriately, eating rats, helping birds, and negotiating a hypersexual desire are additional challenges.

Before Atwood demonstrates the dangers that birds face because of cat predation, she frames the narrative as an ethics of caring for cats. Strig is a cat owner. From the novel's inception, Strig recognizes, unlike Samantha his predecessor, the dangers that cats face if left outside unsupervised. He warns his cat, Ding, "You stay inside. You're an indoor kitty" (117), and when Ding instinctually runs out an open door to chase a rat, Strig pleads, "Ding! Come back! It's not safe" (23). Alongside this scene, located in the text's margins, is a factual and prescient warning informing readers about the dangers for roaming cats and Ding's future: "Outdoor cats live a fraction of the lifespan of indoor cats: as low as a third. They frequently get hit by cars" (23). Unlike Furball, who escapes danger, Ding represents what frequently happens to a cat permitted to roam. And, in fact, Ding succumbs to death by car. A sidebar printed a few pages later reminds readers that "cats aren't so streetwise," that "cars are a leading cause of sudden cat death," and that "in the UK, an estimated 230,000 cats are hit each year," while "in the US it's as high as 5.4 million," and "in Canada, about 200,000" (29). Set against these shocking facts is Strig's emotional cradling of a lifeless Ding. The roadkill crew, symbolizing the secrecy of cat deaths via automobile, remove feline cadavers in the dark of night. One of the crew comments, "If people knew how many cats were dead in the street every night, they'd be yelling" (29). In comparison to Strig's first embrace of Ding after he is hit, another frame depicts a road crew member standing in silence while holding the cat—a sort of mental pause to give readers reflection time.

In order to counter emotional evocation, however, additional facts fill the bottom margins of *AC* to remind readers of the cold, hard truth: cats are predators. Strig discovers that he now evokes catness, so much so that birds fear him. In one panel, a bird calls out to him, "Get out of here, you rotten predator" (31), which creates identity dysphoria: in Strig's human world, the bird is unseen, hidden in a treetop as Strig walks by on the sidewalk below; but in his feline world, he might himself hide during avian predation. And, because Strig is also a bird, he is potentially a cat victim. While on his way to work he questions, "I'm being stalked by cats?" (32). This confused sense of self—to follow the instincts of human or feline or bird—plays out in an alley scene where Strig tries to determine if he should return a fledgling to its nest or eat it instead. Strig counters the alley-cat urge to feast and renests the bird, unharmed, but the instinctual taunts of the cat collective haunt him: "Bite off its head," and "If you're not gonna eat it, at least play with it!" and "What a wuss! Predator fail!" (40). Against this conflict-filled scene, catsandbirds.org provides a useful message: "for cats, hunting is entertainment, providing stimulation and exercise" (40). And feral cats are not the only factors that contribute to bird deaths. Indoor cats left to roam also play a big role in avian mortality. Cats are an invasive species (Marra and Santella 2016), so humans thinking that cats are safe left outside is illogical. In these examples of cat predation, *AC* transforms the Samantha-Furball scenes from *FB*. While *FB* tells of the dangers of cat predation from a bird's eye, *AC* rewrites the entanglement from cat, bird, and human perspectives.

Atwood uses humor to keep her younger (and older) readers engaged, but the frequently pun-filled silliness is also tempered with seriousness and fact. Take, as example, the section on cat abandonment and feral colonies. Cate tries to console a young, crying half-cat who has been abandoned by "kitten dumpers" (124). His siblings have died from common causes associated with feral cat populations: wildlife attacks, disease, and parasitical infection. The narration around his needs reveals adult disinterestedness in his plight. In fact, almost every adult character in *AC* sloughs off the duty to help little Fog, and one poet-cat, Catullus, ostentatiously cares more for naming him and reciting a Carl Sandburg poem in his honor: "the fog comes—on little cat feet" (128).

Cate and Atheena-owl's argument over mating with Angel Catbird also details Atwood's tension between humor and sobriety. Anthropomorphized as a quarrel between two human females but complicated by the fact that Cate is part cat and Atheena-owl part bird, this scene draws upon a negative call-and-response to enunciate divisions and differences between cats and birds. To Cate, Atheena-Owl is "beak nose," "kitten stealer," "pellet face," as unattractive as a hairball, and descended "from an omelette" (103). To Atheena-Owl, Cate is an "egg sucker" (103). While, again, marginal text calls attention to how general predation disrupts successful avian breeding—indicated by the note that "breeding season is a vulnerable time for birds. The eggs can get eaten and baby birds are susceptible for predators" (102)—Atheena-Owl's labeling of Cate places the blame squarely in the paws of cats.

Atheena-Owl understands that birds and cats have a common foe in rats, so she, ultimately, convinces the owls to fight with the cats to take the rat-man, Muroid, and his army down. Still, natural suspicions about cats plague the owls, even as they understand their common enemy in Muroid. They question why they might assist "feline pests" who "infest our woodlands," "steal our rightful food," and cause owl starvation because they have eaten "all the mice and voles and shrews" (135). They fight these fears as Muroid appropriates his knowledge about both cats and birds to execute his battle plans against them. First, he entices Angel Catbird's feline side through winged, flame-throwing technology disguised as a huge bird toy. In a show of predation, Angel tries to catch it, strategizing how he will execute, "midair pounce, and then . . . claw! shake! Rend! Predation at its finest!" (151). The educational gloss on this scene is that "pet cats hunt for stimulation, not food" (151). This hyperbolic and comic bird-cat entanglement soon turns devastating as the flying toy lures Angel into a glass window. The bird-with-glass collision also instills fear in Raven (a.k.a. Ray) who, in preparation for liberating Angel from Muroid's lab, worries that "Muroid might use the GLASS WALL—the one Angel smashed into" (171) to harm himself or others. Glass windows interfere with bird habitats and have contributed to bird injuries and deaths, and this scene, again, reveals how human worlds negatively interfere with avian ones.

Atwood returns to birds flying into windows in her poem "Fatal Light Awareness" (2019). Originally published in the image-text *Bringing Back the Birds*, and reprinted in the collection *Dearly* (2020), the poem confronts human awareness of clashing bird-human worlds. Like van Dooren's push to "subvert scale" (2019, 6), Atwood's lyric speaker begins with local knowledge: her own laziness that she attributes to a thrush's death. Instead of turning immediately to the immensity of the bird and window problem, as the marginal facts of *AC* do, the speaker ruminates on a personal crossing into the thrush's world rather than intervening on a grander scale. The speaker's epiphany enacts van Dooren's belief about "multispecies worlds," and how these worlds "are not preexisting, static entities" but are "becomings that must be put together" (van Dooren 2019, 8). Becoming, or worlding, means "acknowledg[ing] the various forms of agency, of very real even if always thoroughly constrained and unequal influence that each of us—and not just the human 'us'—has in the shaping of what is" (van Dooren 2019, 8). Two worlds meet in "Awareness"; two worlds are "put together." In this tension of two worlds coming together, the speaker recognizes how human choice and action has contributed to "unequal influence" over a world not her own. While a human "dark light magic" has confused the birds and they do not know what causes their deaths, Atwood's speaker insists that we do: human "criminal negligence," to use a phrase reminiscent of Phoebe's instruction to Samantha.

Atwood seems sold on Lutwack's belief that literature can make a difference in responsorial approaches to "a diminished natural world" (Lutwack 1994, 225). While she has recently returned to poetry focusing on birds to elicit a more traditional way of using literary art to garner critical and political understanding, she has also enfolded her experience with public activism into a hybrid literature for young readers that merges aesthetic pleasure and educational polemic. Her use of such image-text and paratextual forms provides these younger readers with intriguing paths to best understand their own ethics of care regarding the environment. Like Samantha and Angel Catbird, who learn to see various worlds from multiple perspectives, Atwood invests in all her readers, young and old, by showing them the way toward affective and scientifically informed multispecies appreciation and engagement.

NOTES

1. *For the Birds* and *The Complete Angel Catbird* will be referred hereafter as *FB* and *AC*.
2. *Oryx and Crake* (2003), *The Year of the Flood* (2009), and *MaddAddam* (2013) make up the trilogy.
3. Whether Atwood is also subtly alluding to Isaac Asimov's short story "For the Birds" (1980) is unclear; however, given that Asimov's text admits that humans cannot appropriate exact bird abilities, leaving human flying with wings "for the birds," it is possible that such a subtext is at work.

REFERENCES

Ackerman, Jennifer. 2020. *The Bird Way*. New York: Penguin.
Asimov, Isaac. 1983. "For the Birds." *The Winds of Change and Other Stories*. New York: Del Ray.
Atwood, Margaret. 1990. *For the Birds*. Fire Fly Books.
———. 2003. *Oryx and Crake*. Doubleday.
———. 2009. *The Year of the Flood*. Doubleday.
———. 2010. "Act Now to Save Our Birds." *The Guardian,* 8 January. https://www.theguardian.com/books/2010/jan/09/margaret-atwood-birds-review
———. 2013. *MaddAddam*. Doubleday.
———. 2019. "Fatal Light Awareness." *Bringing Back the Birds*: *Exploring Migration and Preserving Birdscapes Through the Americas*. Seattle: American Bird Conservancy, Braided River.
———. 2020. "Fatal Light Awareness." *Dearly*. Harper Collins.
Atwood, Margaret, Johnnie Christmas, and Tamra Bonvillain. 2018. *The Complete Angel Catbird*. Dark Horse.

Bain, Jennifer. 2010. "Atwood's Coffee is (Literally) for the Birds." *Toronto Star,* 27 January. https://www.thestar.com/life/food_wine/2010/07/27/atwoods_coffee_is_literally_for_the birds.hmtl

"Balzac's Coffee." 2020. https://shop.balzacs.com/blogs/news/balzacs-conservation-of-migratory-birds-with-margaret-atwood

Burrows, Steve. 2016. *A Cast of Falcons.* Toronto: Point Blank.

Carey, Jonathan. 2016. "What's Part Cat, Part Owl, and Out to Save the World? Meet Angel Catbird." *Audubon* 9 September. https://www.audubon.org/news/what-part-cat-part-owl-and-out-save-world-meet-angel-catbird

"Cat Wars: The Devastating Consequences of a Cuddly Killer." 2016. Cornell Lab of Ornithology. 5 December. https://academy.allaboutbirds.org/live-event/cat-wars-the-devastating-consequences-of-a-cuddly-killer/

Dundas, Deborah. 2017. "Birdwatching with Margaret Atwood." *The Star,* 3 June. https://www.thestar.com/entertainment/books/2017/06/03/birdwatching-with-margaret-atwood

Felski, Rita. 2008. *Uses of Literature.* Malden, MA: Wiley-Blackwell.

"Ghosts of Gone Birds: Exhibition Enlists Artists to Save Endangered Species." 2011. *The Guardian* 25 August. https://www.theguardian.com/environment/2011/aug/24/ghosts-of-gone-birds-exhibition-artists

Jackson-Houston, C. M. 2018. "Here's What You Missed at Margaret Atwood's Speech in Vancouver." *Vancouver Courier,* 22 August. https://www.vancouverisawesome.com/2018/08/22/margaret-atwood-vancouver-ornithological

Leber, Jessica. 2019. "Margaret Atwood Insists Birds Matter to Everyone—Whether They Realize It or Not." *Audubon,* 25 November. https://www.audubon.org/news/margaret-atwood-insists-birds-matter-everyone-whether-they-realize-it-or-not

Macdonald, Helen. 2020. "High-Rise." *Vesper Flights.* New York: Grove, 32–40.

Marra, Peter P. and Chris Santella. 2016. *Cat Wars*: The Devastating Consequences of a Cuddly Killer. Princeton: Princeton University Press.

McKibben, Bill. 2006. *The End of Nature.* New York: Random House.

Munroe, Grant. 2017. "How Margaret Atwood and Graeme Gibson Built a Bird Sanctuary." *The Walrus,* 18 August. http://thewalrus.ca/how-margaret-atwood-and-graeme-gibson-built-a-bird-sanctuary/

Nicholson, Paul. 2014. "Atwood, Gibson Birding Role Models." *The London Free Press,* 15 November. https://lfpress.com/2014/11/15/atwood-gibson-birding-role-Models/amp/

Perkins, Martha. 2018. "Cats Killing Birds: Margaret Atwood and Angel Catbird to the Rescue." *Vancouver Courier,* 22 August. https://www.vancouverisawesome.com/courier-archive/news/cats-killing-birds-margaret-atwood-and-angel-catbird-to-the-rescue-3081843

Rosenberg, Kenneth V., Adriaan M. Dokter, Peter J. Blancher, John R. Sauer, Adam C. Smith, Paul A. Smith, Jessica C. Stanton, Arvind Panjabi, Laura Helft, Michael Parr, and Peter P. Marra. 2019. "Decline of the North American Avifauna." *Science* https://www.birds.cornell.edu/home/wp-content/uploads/2019/09/DECLINE-OF-NORTH-AMERICAN-AVIFAUNA-SCIENCE-2019.pdf

Sethi, Anita. 2016. "Birdwatching with Margaret Atwood." *Financial Times*, 26 October. https://www.ft.com/content/9e1e1506-9b04-11e6-568a43813464

"Shade-Grown Coffee Could Help Save Birds, If Only People Knew About It." 2021. Cornell Lab of Ornithology. 2 March. https://mailchi.mp/birds.cornell.edu/release-surveyreveals-the-bird-friendly-coffee-message-is-not-getting-through?e=f0b505020c

Stephens, Steve. 2017. "Love of Birds Leads Margaret Atwood on New Journey." *The Columbus Dispatch*, 21 May. https://www.dispatch.com/entertainmentlife/20170521/books-love-of-birds-leads-margaret-atwood-on-new-journey

van Dooren, Thom. 2014. *Flight Ways: Life and Loss at the Edge of Extinction*. New York: Columbia University Press.

———. 2019. *The Wake of Crows: Living and Dying in Shared Worlds*. New York: Columbia University Press.

Williams, Alicia, Ashley A. Dayer, J. Nicolas Hernandez-Aguilera, Tina B. Phillips, Holly Faulkner-Grant, Miguel I. Gómez, and Amanda D. Rodewald. 2021. "Tapping Birdwatchers to Promote Bird-Friendly Coffee Consumption and Conserve Birds." *People and Nature*, 1 March. doi: 10.1002/pan3.10191

Section 3

ENTANGLED WORLDS

Chapter 9

The Peregrine

At the Intersection of Ecocriticism and New Nature Writing

Debarati Bandyopadhyay

John Alec Baker (1926–1987) devoted a major part of his adult life to the study of nature in his native Essex in the United Kingdom. *The Hill of Summer* (1969) testifies to his patience and perception in this pursuit. However, his primary area of concentration was related to avian life. From 1955 to 1965, the decade of his regular sojourn amid the nature of the Essex coast and countryside, he assimilated the material for *The Peregrine* (1967), an essay entitled "On the Essex Coast," and his *Diaries*. This material was imaginatively compressed into a record of sightings of one year in *The Peregrine*. The compression heightens the aesthetic and epistemological pleasure of learning about avian existence in general, and the peregrine in particular. He never received any training as an ornithologist. Yet the immediacy of his experiences of the birds, both native and migrant, which he viewed through his binoculars and with his naked eyes during these years, have been conveyed with such vividness that it is as if the reader can hear the calls and visualize the wingbeats of every avian species that he presented in his writings.

Salient features of Baker's works include the descriptions of the various birds that he watched. The list that I compiled after reading his published works is by no means either exhaustive or comprehensive, but it at least indicates Baker's dedication as a birdwatcher: we are not counting the pipistrelle and Daubenton's bats; the birds described, more than one hundred and forty when counted, include water-birds, raptors, songbirds, and nightbirds.[1]

But Baker's writing never reads like a dry enumeration of birds. Baker observes each bird with loving care, and always includes a story with his notes on the birds' habits and habitats. For instance, in *The Peregrine* he notices a tawny owl, three yards away, and observes that it had a "helmeted face" that was "ascetic, half-human" (Baker 1967, 78–79). It does not fly away immediately as neither the man nor the bird "could bear to look away," and only when the author moves and breaks this direct eye-contact does it flee (Baker 1967, 78–79). The interspecies encounter surprises and transfixes both. As well, in *The Hill of Summer*, he notices a redstart's orange chest accentuated by the gray at its crown and back, "pipe-clay" white on its forehead and belly, and the "cindery" black of its cheek and throat. Yet the height of Baker's description in terms of individualizing detail is reached when he states that this bird is "finding nest-sites, and showing them to his mate" (Baker 1969, 176). An affinity is immediately established between the reader and the bird. In the *Diaries*, Baker's adoring human gaze characterizes a fat, "preening" mistle thrush in terms of a "roly-poly pudding, speckled with currants" even as he admired the bird for being an "unselfconscious" creature, happy to soak in the sunlight (Baker 2015, 414). Again, in the same *Diaries*, Baker describes gulls flying toward the coast as "almost transparent" at sunset, making them appear to him in that moment of "ethereal light" as "the lightest, freest, most creative of created things" (Baker 2015, 320). The beauty of the bird at twilight is captured with a reverence akin to the poetry of Gerard Manley Hopkins.

It cannot be claimed that Baker is unique in watching birds or recording their habits with such attention. There are glorious precursors. Richard Jefferies, for instance, in *The Life of the Fields*, originally published in 1884, gathers the essence of the life of rooks by mentioning them as the "happiest creatures in the world" when they are "at the acorns," busy not only "eating" but "finding" (Jefferies 1983, 43). He examines in minute detail the kestrel's habit of hovering, as well. Jefferies describes how the kestrel maintains "an altitude a little lower than the tallest elms" for "hours together, and sweep[s] over miles of country" (Jefferies 1983, 175). Furthermore, he notes:

> As he comes gliding through the atmosphere, suddenly he shoots up a little (say, roughly, two or three feet), and then stops short. His tail, which is broader than it looks, is bent slightly downwards; his wings beat the air, at the first glance, just as if he was progressing. Sometimes he seems to oscillate to one side, sometimes to the other; but these side movements do not amount to any appreciable change of position. If there be little or no wind (note this) he remains beating the air, to the eye at least perfectly stationary, perhaps as much as half a minute or more. He then seems to slip forward about half a yard, as if a pent-up force was released, but immediately recovers himself and hovers again. The alternate hovering and slipping forward may be repeated two or three times: it seems to depend on the bird's judgment as to the chance of prey. (Jefferies 1983, 175–76)

We find in Baker's works too this kind of detailed description of the flight of the peregrine in particular and of other species of birds in general. We also find a famous naturalist as his predecessor in writing about avian life through interesting anecdotes. W. H. Hudson, in *Land's End: A Naturalist's Impressions of West Cornwall*, originally published in 1908, describes the gulls at St. Ives, and he conveys their "charm" despite acknowledging the "peculiar fascination" of the jackdaw with its "intelligence and amusing rascalities" (Hudson 2005, 19). He mentions the common, the herring, the black-headed, the lesser black-backed, the great black-back, and a glaucous gull as the varieties he watches there, referring to the last as "large ivory-white," the "famous Burgomaster of the Arctic Sea" (Hudson 2005, 20–21). Hudson declares that the fishermen were fiercely protective of the gull, as they usually thought of gulls as their "friends" and felt that injury to a gull spelt "disaster," possibly because

> gulls gather in vociferous crowds round the boats and in the harbour when the fishing has prospered, and in this way become associated in the fisherman's mind with all those agreeable ideas or images and emotions connected with a good catch [. . .]. On the other hand we may have here a survival of an older superstition, a notion that gulls are in some degree supernatural beings, perhaps drowned mariners and fishermen returned in bird forms to haunt their ancient homes and associate with their human fellow-creatures. (Hudson 2005, 21–22)

Hudson sympathizes with the poor gulls because they were forced to fast during the weekend, as the Cornish fishermen were "strict Sabbatarians" and the birds "are never able to understand the long break in the fishing" so that by "Monday morning they are very hungry indeed" and begin a "tremendous demonstration of the unemployed" (Hudson 2005, 22).

The attempt to present through anthropomorphism the gulls' food crisis in a lighter vein is soon replaced by the description of a tragedy that reveals the nature of the gull society. Hudson describes the gulls happily feasting on a morning when the boats laden with fish come in and then, precisely because of the avian rush and competition, there is an accident. He observes a mature herring gull striking a rope or spar and falling into the water, as "its wing was broken" (Hudson 2005, 23):

> The bird could not understand this; it made frantic efforts to rise, but the whole force exerted being in one wing merely caused it to spin rapidly round and round. These struggles eventually caused the shattered bone to break through the skin; the blood began to flow [. . .]. At length the poor thing became convinced that [. . .] it could only swim, and at once ceasing to struggle it swam [. . .] out towards the open bay.

[. . .]. Then a strange thing happened. Instantly, [. . .] the uproar in the harbour ceased; the hundreds of gulls fighting on the water rose up simultaneously to join the cloud of birds above, and the whole concourse moved silently away in one direction, forming a dense crowd above the wounded bird. (Hudson 2005, 23)

In other words, Hudson presents an intensely pathetic scene which proves dramatic in its emotional effects. We might choose to compare Baker's poetic and spiritual response to gulls with the reality of the moment presented by Hudson.

If Jefferies and Hudson had already presented certain species of birds with great clarity, and *The Goshawk* by T. H. White remains universally admired as a key to understanding the nature of the proximity and the challenges of the bird-human encounter, then why do we return avidly to Baker's writings to learn about the peregrine, other birds, and his view of nature and wilderness? The entire purpose and practice of his birdwatching had already been questioned by others. We learn from the *Diaries* that some men had come in three boats near Joyce's Bay and were on the flats collecting "shell-fish," and a man was by Gore Steps "digging up seaweed": "'What do you do when you've seen 'em?', he asked, when I agreed I was a bird-watcher" (Baker 2015, 368). Presumably, compared to the hard manual labor that involved moneymaking, survival, and sustenance for these rural men, what viable objective, apart from being a hobby, could birdwatching achieve? Yet it remains necessary for us even today to return to Baker's works. The qualities in his works that made his writing about avian life a literary phenomenon might only be understood if we try to understand him as located at the intersection of New Nature Writing and ecocriticism.

New Nature Writing is considered a relatively recent literary development. In fact, Jos Smith, in *The New Nature Writing: Rethinking the Literature of Place* (2017), declares that he made a "case for dating the emergence of the New Nature Writing to the early 1970s" (Smith 2018, 4). While Baker wrote primarily in the 1960s, characteristics of New Nature Writing appear in Baker's works, and these help us to grasp his presentation of a distinctive experience of avian life in the context of his place and time. It is customary in nature writing to visit a place and describe its scenic beauty, the topography, flora, fauna, and even the human characters met amid nature. In New Nature Writing, over and above these characteristics, an attempt at understanding the ecological conditions, the politics governing these, and the malady, if any, besetting the place being visited or inhabited, remain important. The New Nature Writer bears witness to this or becomes an activist who records this experience in her works. In 2008, Jason Cowley, in the Editor's Letter of the "New Nature Writing" issue of *Granta*, points out the differences between the traditional and new approaches to nature writing by declaring that New Nature Writing, "rather than being pastoral or descriptive or simply a natural history essay, has got to be couched in stories—whether fiction or non-fiction—where we as humans are present. Not only as observers, but as intrinsic elements" (Cowley 2008, 12). Cowley's expression suggests that natural historians earlier would have had to be objective in their descriptions of the species they concentrated on. In New Nature Writing, the author often immerses herself in the situation as an active agent and records the experience thereafter, in a narrative. Thus, literary articulation of the experience serves to disseminate knowledge about the place, the human and nonhuman populations, and the adverse conditions besetting them. Joe Moran, in "A Cultural History of the New Nature Writing" (2014), traces the history of New Nature Writing in Britain and points out that such writing is often about a concern for the "human disconnection from natural processes" and takes an active interest in the "small scale and quotidian encounters with nature" (Moran 2014, 50). Human encounters with nature become all the more significant because New Nature Writing stresses how human activities have eroded wildness in the name of exerting order and control. Graham Huggan notes that the wild could signify a range of meanings to different people, including "a quality of self, a relation to the world, an atavistic memory," and that New Nature Writing seeks to reinterpret that range "in the light of a global environmental crisis characterized by [. . .] devastating species loss" (Huggan 2016, 165). In other words, New Nature Writing attempts a conscientious performance of the basic ecological ideal of interrelated and sustained coexistence. And this is what makes it akin to the ethics of sustainability and consciousness celebrated in ecocriticism as well. We learn from Mark Cocker's introduction to Baker's works: "[Baker's] writing has been intimately associated with the resurgence of literature on nature and landscape, the so-called New Nature Writing of authors like Tim Dee and Robert Macfarlane" (Cocker 2015, 4). Hence, we need to search Baker's writings about avian life repeatedly to recognize the value of its content as anticipating the ecological concerns necessary for sustaining birds' lives and habitats.

In "On the Essex Coast," published originally by the Royal Society for the Protection of Birds in *RSPB Birds* magazine (1971), Baker wrote clearly about his view of the wilderness in Essex, not in a poetically wistful tone as in traditional nature writing, but in a language which anticipates New Nature Writing:

> The wilderness is here. To me the wilderness is not a place. It is the indefinable essence or spirit that lives in a place [. . .]. It lives where it can find refuge, fugitive, fearful as a deer. It is rare now. Man is killing the wilderness, hunting it down. On the east coast of England, this is perhaps its last home. Once gone,

it will be gone forever. And of course it is doomed. [. . .] The habitat may look much the same: just a reservoir or two, the hydro-electric temples, the tight clasp of a motorway, the roaring concrete of airports. But the wilderness cannot endure these things. It is the goaded bull at bay, [. . .] awaiting the quietus of the ritual sword. (Baker 1971, 428)

To Baker, the spirit of the wilderness possibly appeared most prominently in the avian life that he tracked in the Essex countryside and on the coast. His focus was on the peregrine that embodied the freedom of the sky and the pinnacle of avian power and glory, but in the 1960s was a doomed species. Cocker, in his introduction to *The Peregrine*, states:

During Baker's life this glorious creature was no more than a rare winter visitor to his portion of Essex. Worse still, the raptor had endured a catastrophic decline in the second half of the twentieth century. [. . .] It is, once more, a breeding bird even in Essex. Today it is extremely difficult for us to recover fully the sense of crisis prevailing in 1960s Europe or North America. [. . .] We must remind ourselves how one of the most successful predators on the planet—exceeded in its transcontinental range only perhaps by ourselves or the red fox—was then so stricken by the toxic effects of organochlorine-based agrochemicals, it was considered at risk of global extinction.

It was that anxiety which charged Baker with his deep sense of mission as he tracked the falcons across the wintry landscapes of Essex. [. . .] This sense of the bird's impending doom supplies the book, not only with its emotional rationale, but also its thematic unity and burning narrative drive. (Cocker 2015, 6)

New Nature Writing was yet to establish its novelty and distinction from traditional nature writing, but Baker had already written about the impending loss of the birds. Like his American contemporary Rachel Carson in *Silent Spring*, who writes about the death and subsequent silencing of birdsong because of the unchecked use of DDT and pesticides, Baker laments bird loss, but in Great Britain. Ecocritical literature is significant for its interdisciplinary presentation of aspects of nature, species, and the causes of destruction and deterioration thereof, especially due to human activity. It can have two aspects, and, consequently, might concentrate on either or both of these: first, the presentation of the positive aspects of the relationship between the human and natural worlds, and, second, environmentally destructive and ecologically disruptive human practices and their effects on nature and nonhuman creatures. It also becomes possible for ecoliterature, at times, to point out the ethical and sustainable way out of the human devastation of nature.

An early ecocritic, Joseph W. Meeker, in *The Comedy of Survival: Literary Ecology and a Play Ethic* (1997, 1974), anticipates Cowley's description of New Nature Writing accounts as embedded in stories:

> Human beings are the Earth's only literary creatures. [. . .] If the creation of literature is an important characteristic of the human species, it should be examined carefully and honestly to discover its influence upon human behavior and the natural environment, and to determine what role, if any, it plays in the welfare and survival of humanity, and what insight it offers into human relationships with other species and with the world around us. Is it an activity that adapts us better to life on Earth, or one that sometimes estranges us from life? From the unforgiving perspective of evolution and natural selection, does literature contribute more to our survival than it does to our extinction? (Meeker 1997, 4)

We comprehend, following Meeker's ideas, that at the very least, viable ecoliterature can issue a timely warning that can help human beings adapt better to their environments by choosing sustainability. Meeker wrote about the comic and tragic ways of leading one's life. While the tragic way could lead one to the destruction of the individual, community, and even species, the comic way, he wrote, is the "path of reconciliation" as it represents a complex vision, "not heroic or idealistic; rather, it is a strategy for survival" (Meeker 1997, 14–15). The aim of some ecologically conscious literary texts is to teach the necessity of continued survival. And New Nature Writing teaches us to spot the fictional and nonfictional narration of experiences as stories that remain rooted in criticism of human activities, sometimes affecting nature adversely, sometimes upholding positive, ecologically sustainable practices. It is, therefore, at the intersection of New Nature Writing and ecocriticism that we seek to understand the distinctive nature of Baker's works.

John Fanshawe, in "Notes on J. A. Baker," contextualizes the writing of *The Peregrine* historically. He invokes Tim Dee who "grew up thinking of Peregrines as sickly" and felt that the "magnificent hunter, the apotheosis of the wild, the falcon on the king's gloved fist, was becoming as helpless as a spastic battery hen, a bird that broke its own eggs" (Fanshawe 2015, 17). Fanshawe records that in the nineteenth century, peregrines were persecuted by gamekeepers, pigeon fanciers, and egg collectors. He notes that during World War II, the Air Ministry's authorization of widespread culling to save carrier pigeons meant extermination of several hundred peregrines. Fanshawe sympathizes with Baker who lamented that in the 1960s the chemical ravages of organochlorine pesticides killed the adult peregrines and thinned their egg shells into fracturing: "Peregrines were totems of a wilderness under siege" (Fanshawe 2015, 18).

From Fanshawe's account, if we come to understand the reason behind Baker's compulsion to track the peregrine painstakingly, then the next question arises as to how he viewed the birds. This perspective is important because we can think of two basic approaches to writing about avian life. Aesthetically speaking, Baker's decision to compress the birdwatching of ten years into a narrative spanning one year meant that an artistic balance could be achieved in juxtaposing these two. One of these two approaches could follow Jennifer Ackerman's *The Genius of Birds* (2016) in which she teaches us to appreciate the power, resilience, and insight of birds. For instance, she notes that among the articles on studies in scientific journals, we may find a title like "Have we met before? Pigeons recognize familiar human faces" (Ackerman 2016, 3). And in Baker's writing, we find moments when birds gradually learn to recognize him as a harmless birdwatcher. Initially, regarding his experience of "October 16th," we read of a tiercel, or the male peregrine, encountering Baker as it flies straight at him, and its "eyes seemed to stare into mine. Then they widened in recognition of my hostile human shape. [. . .] the hawk swerved violently aside" (Baker 1967, 59). But about "October 18th" Baker writes that when the hawk had been feeding and was satisfied: "I went carefully [. . .] towards him. He flew at once, carrying the remains of his prey. [. . .] He begins to know me, but he will not share his kill" (Baker 1967, 61). On "November 2nd," Baker notes: "He is more willing to face me now, less ready to fly when I approach, puzzled perhaps by my steady pursuit" (Baker 1967, 71). By "December 29th," the tiercel recognizes him; Baker writes, "as though I too were a species of hawk" (Baker 1967, 116). Ackerman emphatically declares:

> As a class, birds have been around for more than 100 million years. They are one of nature's great success stories, inventing new strategies for survival. [. . .] To say that humans are more successful or advanced really depends on how you define those terms. After all, evolution isn't about advancement; it's about survival. It's about learning to solve the problems of your environment [. . .]. (Ackerman 2016, 8)

Baker writes: "The peregrine sees and remembers patterns we do not know exist: the neat squares of orchard and woodland, the endlessly varying quadrilateral shapes of fields. He finds his way across the land by a succession of remembered symmetries. [. . .] Everything he is has been evolved to link the targeting eye to the striking talon" (Baker 1967, 46). Baker's assessment of the peregrine finds a later resonance in Ackerman's assertion of birds' abilities. And this adds manifold to the tragedy of the mighty hawk facing extinction during his times. In earlier forms of nature writing, there would be a gentle lament for the vanishing birds. But in New Nature Writing, as in

Baker's work, an analysis of the situations that gave rise to such difficulties in the very existence of these powerful birds prevails.

We will return to this aspect of Baker's writing. But before that, it is necessary to discuss the second approach taken by writers of avian life. It is usual to elide realistic descriptions of the birds killed and eaten by the raptor, possibly due to aesthetic considerations. Baker always presents the reality of the situation. But this is done without reducing the aesthetic experience. He achieves this effect by carefully selecting details. For instance, in the *Diaries* he writes: "There were two peregrine kills by Ramsey, one gull on the wall, and another in the middle of an immaculate green lawn in front of one of the bungalows. A great insult to respectability. A really messy oval of bloody bones, and scattered feathers" (Baker 2015, 322). This gory description is not reflected in the same way in the writings that he had decided to publish in his lifetime. In *The Hill of Summer*, Baker describes the difficulty in coming to terms with scenes of smaller birds killed by bigger and stronger birds, even as he acknowledges this as the truth of avian life. He writes that it felt "sad to see life ending before it has really begun," when he came across "an unfledged starling" that a jay had hunted and dropped, still "twitching" (Baker 1969, 206–207). In his opinion, the truth is: "The woods and fields and gardens are places of endless stabbing, impaling, squashing, and mangling. We see only what floats to the surface: the colour, the song, the nesting, and the feeding. I do not think we could bear a clear vision of the animal world" (Baker 1969, 207). Elsewhere in *The Hill of Summer*, Baker observes that at the "highest point of the moor" there was a small gray stone that seemed to flutter in the wind, but closer inspection revealed that the wings of a snipe were moving on the stone, the leftover of a merlin's meal (Baker 1969, 217). But then, in one of the very rare instances of near-anthropomorphic description, Baker describes that the stone was dark with bloodstains and he believes that it looked like "a place of sacrifice" and possibly that the merlins had been bringing their prey to this stone for many years (Baker 1969, 217). It is possible to imagine an avian parallel to ancient human rituals such as those supposedly conducted at Stonehenge.

In *The Peregrine* Baker highlights the "bloodiness of killing" that has been "slurred over" "too often" "by those who defend hawks," and in this context he reminds us unequivocally that even the thrush is a "worm stabber," the "carnivore of lawns," and we cannot afford to "sentimentalise" its song and "forget the killing that sustains it" (Baker 1967, 31). He describes the sheer predatory prowess of the peregrine in a congratulatory tone regarding the carcass of a great black-backed gull: "That was a remarkable kill, even for a falcon" as this species of the gull weighs "four to five pounds" and the falcon "two to two and a half" (Baker 1967, 156). He notes honestly that the peregrines would not follow the killing-style predicted for them by traditional experts: "I expected to see the two peregrines stoop [. . .] in the spectacular manner so often described in books about falconry. [. . .] The falcon ignored the heron. The tiercel swooped past it and attacked it from below" (Baker 1967, 156). The power of the peregrine itself is revealed when Baker mentions that the hawk breaks the neck of its prey with its bill to kill it and that this reflects that no flesh-eating creature is more "efficient" or more "merciful" than it and that "it simply does what it was designed to do" (Baker 1967, 39). Baker's realistic portrayal of the birds as predators, juxtaposed with the admirable qualities he continued to locate and extol in their behaviors and abilities, incorporates opposite yet twin human impulses. When Baker writes of birds, he combines a spirit somewhat akin to that of Hopkins, and the realistic acumen of Darwin and Ted Hughes. This is natural in the case of Baker, who once aspired to be a poet. Fanshawe notes that Baker's extensive poetry collection included the Romantic poets, the major Victorians like Hopkins, and modern poets like Hughes. Furthermore, Fanshawe records that Baker was "ferocious in his identification with the animal world" (Fanshawe 2015, 22). This identification, moving beyond sympathy for avian existence, prompted Baker to shadow the birds and record their vanishing lives in meticulous detail. For instance, in *The Peregrine*, on "March 28th," he observes the tiercel mentioned earlier arriving in a place inhabited at that moment by two hundred woodpigeons, his possible prey; then the man and the peregrine meet: "To me he was still apparently indifferent, but he kept me in sight, when I moved, by following or flying higher. He has found a meaning for me, but I do not know what it is. I am his slow and moribund companion, Caliban to his Ariel" (Baker 1967, 157). Mere sympathy would have coaxed Baker to commiserate with the fate of the species as going extinct. But for the peregrine, as Ariel, Baker evinces empathy, just as the bird ignores the prey for the moment and recognizes his companionship. This personal connection enhances the value of Baker's presentation of the peregrine individually and as a species in his works.

Baker's analysis of the ecologically adverse situation for birds, as accomplished in New Nature Writing and its critique of human activities, and as presented in ecocritical readings of literary texts, form the groundwork of his evaluation of avian life in that part of Essex. We learn in *The Hill of Summer* of the reality of the hawks when "they hung dead from the gamekeeper's gallows tree" and how the "muted" yet ever-present sense of violence spread from wood to wood with the "minatory crash of the gamekeeper's gun" (Baker 1969, 181). We also learn from Baker the fate of another bird in the same volume, and his choice of words reveals the sense of injustice that he harbors on behalf of the birds against the human perpetrators of such wanton cruelty:

> A little owl has been lynched. He hangs by the neck from a gate-post. [. . .] His head seems shrunken now, lolling judiciously downwards in death, eyeless and light. Nothing can re-awaken the aching purity of his spring call. [. . .] He moves in the wind, a dark plebeian swaying over the doomed patrician pheasants that swagger through the stubble. (Baker 1969, 250–51)

This is a one-on-one feud between raptors and a gamekeeper, but there are other ways in which human beings kill birds. They do not even have the time or intention to mourn these deaths, caused carelessly. Baker says in *The Hill of Summer*: "Blind cars had made their kill. Many birds lay shattered in the road: blackbirds, thrushes, and starlings, were pulped and flattened in the sanded tar" (Baker 1969, 219). Pollution caused by human callousness destroys the habitat of the birds as well: "choking smoke from stubble burning" (Baker 1967, 56). He also alludes to a real-life situation echoing the imaginary condition of Carson's *Silent Spring*, saying that on a spring evening, the air was mild, smelling of damp grass, fresh soil, and "farm chemicals," resulting in "less bird-song now" (Baker 1967, 164). In "On the Essex Coast," Baker writes against other thoughtless human activities that destroy innocent birds:

> I stumble over a dead, mummified object. It is a red-throated diver so matted and bound with oil as to be almost unrecognizable, the mere torso of a bird. It stinks of oil. It is an atrocity, a stumpy victim of our modern barbarity. [. . .] We must not let its death be soothed away by the lullaby language of indifferent politicians. This bird died slowly and horribly in a Belsen of floating oil, as thousands of others have done, as millions more may do in the vile years to come. [. . .] I blunder across the saltings, in too great a rage to see or hear anything clearly. (Baker 1971, 430)

Fanshawe highlights Baker's evocation of the Torrey Canyon supertanker disaster that resulted in an oil spill which flooded oil up to the Cornish coast, after which the government decided to "bomb and napalm" the oil "creating a hellish scene" (Fanshawe 2015, 24). "On the Essex Coast" supports an early conservation campaign, presumably made necessary to counter the building of "the largest airport in the world" in proximity (Baker 1971, 431). He points out the effects of noise pollution on the natural habitat and life in Essex: the "last home of wilderness will be imprisoned in a cage of insensate noise. Cordoned by motorways, overshadowed by the huge airport city, the uniqueness of the place will be destroyed as completely as though it has been blown to pieces by bombs" (Baker 1971, 431). New Nature Writing and ecocriticism might appreciate the specificity and clarity of Baker's warning.

It is possible to find three viewpoints in Baker's works regarding the ways in which human beings and birds approach each other. In the first and the worst, we, the unconcerned human beings, cause the death of innumerable birds: "We are the killers. We stink of death. We carry it with us" (Baker 1967, 113).

The second approach refers to human activities as disturbing to avian life. But birds have learned to find ways and means of survival and sustenance, built around these human practices, albeit cautiously. For example, three tractors plough, and a hawk remains unperturbed. The predators try to derive the benefit of other birds moving along with the tractors continuously in search of the worms that are unearthed as they would find their prey among these birds: "They do not fear machines [. . .] [as] predictable. When the tractor stops, the hawk is immediately alert" (Baker 1967, 98). In the *Diaries*, Baker sees five men, "a hawking party, one carrying a fine female Goshawk on his gloved fist" and remarks on the apparent happiness of both species in working together in this way, although this pertains only to tame birds (Baker 2015, 381). However, more often than not, wild birds would have to endure the disturbance created by human activities. *Diaries* records curlews, dunlins, oystercatchers, redshanks, whimbrels, and godwits coexisting happily and making a "wonderful cacophony," until a "noisy boat came, and disturbed them all" (Baker 2015, 358–59). Elsewhere, swallows, little grebes, and teal fear the planes passing overhead (Baker 2015, 384). The peregrines made compromises to survive. They need to bathe every day to control the lice infestation in their feathers. Otherwise, it is dangerous for the juvenile peregrine's health and life (Baker 1967, 35–36). Baker reports a peregrine taking a bath in a shallow pond containing "the usual human detritus: pram wheels, tricycles, broken glass, rotting cabbages, and detergent containers, overlaid by a thin ketchup of sewage" (Baker 1967, 98). An uneasy attempt on the part of the birds to adapt to human civilization continued.

The third approach, Baker's own practice regarding avian life, remains the best and friendliest approach to these creatures. Baker walks or uses a bicycle to follow the peregrine. He observes them with his naked eyes, with binoculars, or with a telescope. In every case, the approach is completely unobtrusive and does not threaten the well-being of the birds. In this way, Baker watches a male shrike for over an hour while it brings beetles and other insects to feed his two nestlings (Baker 1969, 244–45). He astutely recommends a congenial approach to the peregrine like an ecocritic accentuating ecosustenance:

> To be recognized and accepted by a peregrine you must wear the same clothes, travel by the same way, perform actions in the same order. [. . .] assume the stillness of a tree. [. . .] Be alone. [. . .] Learn to fear. To share fear is the greatest bond of all. The hunter must become the thing he hunts. [. . .] Persist, endure, follow, watch. (Baker 1967, 30)

We feel that the man had taught himself to enter into the spirit and the philosophy of existence of the peregrine itself. He declares himself "possessed" by it as it had been his "grail" for ten years. And so Baker states that he "tried to recapture the extraordinary beauty of this bird and to convey the wonder of the land he lived in" (Baker 1967, 31–32).

In Baker's works, urgent recording of the human threat to peregrine existence, as in New Nature Writing, intersects with the ecocritical emphasis on adoption of humane activities conducive to the survival of the species. In terms of literary aesthetics, Baker's writing inspires humans to "at least imagine" what it is like to be a peregrine, which is vitally necessary for their sustenance (Cocker 2015, 15).

NOTE

1. These are nightjar, sparrowhawk, peregrine, dunlin, finch, fieldfare, kestrel, snipe, thrush, duck, woodpigeon, black-headed gull, shelduck, pheasant, redshank, mallard, lapwing, wigeon, partridge, moorhen, curlew, golden plover, rook, jackdaw, saw bill duck, grebe, swallow, martin, jay, magpie, gray plover, knot, turnstone, ringed plover, sanderling, curlew sandpiper, goldfinch, heron, green sandpiper, starling, skylark, godwit, greenshank, sea-rejoicer, sparrow, bullfinch, blackbird, whimbrel, corn bunting, teal, owl, merlin, wren, swan, red-breasted merganser, green woodpecker, oystercatcher, woodcock, lesser spotted woodpecker, herring gull, marsh harrier, snow bunting, shrew, cormorant, chaffinch, great crested grebe, kingfisher, goldeneye, coot, goldcrest, rock pipit, treecreeper, pied wagtail, meadow pipit, reed bunting, robin, mistle thrush, nuthatch, greenfinch, hawfinch, cuckoo, willow warbler, long-tailed tit, hobby, lesser whitethroat, tree pipit, redstart, swift, garden warbler, turtle dove, blackcap, hedge sparrow, blue tit, yellowhammer, nightingale, great spotted woodpecker, wood lark, fulmar, buzzard, sedge warbler, sand martin, chiffchaff, common tern, black tern, linnet, shrike, stonechat, willow tit, spotted flycatcher, wheatear, little stint, bar-tailed godwit, great tit, coal tit, siskin, lesser redpoll, song thrush, shoveler, pintail, pochard, tufted, twite, black-tailed godwit, redwing, gadwall, goosander, common scoter, stock dove, brent goose, barn owl, tawny owl, garganey, jack snipe, grasshopper warbler, ruff, brambling, yellow wagtail, sandwich tern, stone curlew, black-throated diver, red-throated diver, little owl, and the ubiquitous crow.

REFERENCES

Ackerman, Jennifer. 2016. *The Genius of Birds*. New York: Penguin.

Baker, J. A. 1967. "The Peregrine." In *The Peregrine, The Hill of Summer, and Diaries: The Complete Works of J. A. Baker*, edited by John Fanshawe, 26–169. London: William Collins.

———. 1969. "The Hill of Summer." In *The Peregrine, The Hill of Summer, and Diaries: The Complete Works of J. A. Baker*, edited by John Fanshawe, 170–275. London: William Collins.

———. 1971. "On the Essex Coast." In *The Peregrine, The Hill of Summer, and Diaries: The Complete Works of J. A. Baker*, edited by John Fanshawe, 426–31. London: William Collins.

———. 2015. "Diaries." In *The Peregrine, The Hill of Summer, and Diaries: The Complete Works of J. A. Baker*, edited by John Fanshawe, 276–425. London: William Collins.

Cocker, Mark. 2015. "Introduction to *The Hill of Summer*." In *The Peregrine, The Hill of Summer, and Diaries: The Complete Works of J. A. Baker*, edited by John Fanshawe, 4–15. London: William Collins.

Cowley, Jason. 2008. "Editor's Letter." *Granta: New Nature Writing* 102, July: 7–12.

Fanshawe, John. 2015. "Notes on J.A. Baker." In *The Peregrine, The Hill of Summer, and Diaries: The Complete Works of J. A. Baker*, edited by John Fanshawe, 16–25. London: William Collins.

Hudson, W. H. 2005. *Land's End: A Naturalist's Impressions of West Cornwall*. Stroud, Gloucestershire, UK: Nonsuch Publishing.

Huggan, Graham. 2016. "Back to the Future: The 'New Nature Writing,' Ecological Boredom, and the Recall of the Wild." *Prose Studies* 38(2): 152–71.

Jefferies, Richard. 1983. *The Life of the Fields*. Oxford: Oxford University Press.

Meeker, Joseph W. 1997. *The Comedy of Survival: Literary Ecology and a Play Ethic*. Tucson: University of Arizona Press.

Moran, Joe. 2014. "A Cultural History of the New Nature Writing." *Literature and History* 23(1), Spring: 49–63.

Smith, Jos. 2018. *The New Nature Writing: Rethinking the Literature of Place*. London: Bloomsbury Academic.

Chapter 10

Helen Macdonald, T. H. White, and Hawks

H is [also] for History

Louis J. Boyle

Helen Macdonald's *H Is for Hawk* (2014) defies genre boundaries: more than a memoir, more than a nature study, its scope reaches beyond the limitations imposed by traditional literary categories. By breaking boundaries, it also connects; it melds divisions among often arbitrary literary labels and achieves a harmonious whole. The memoir and the nature study, for example, do not appear as dissimilar classifications or otherwise oppositional categorizations in Macdonald's work. Among its many achievements is a multilayered, unified text that is as informative as any scholarly essay but as accessible as the prose of Annie Dillard.

The book also offers readers a journey encompassing past, present, and future. It is about history, but it is not a traditional history book. As Ann Curthoys and Anne McGrath (2009) have stated in their useful *How to Write History that People Want to Read*, "sadly, historical writing has quite a bad reputation. [. . .] Newspaper reviewers will often praise a history book because it's *not* like a history book [. . .]. It's as if historians have no style, unlike those cool 'creative' novelists" (2). This criticism, unfair as it is to many great historical writers and books, does not apply to Macdonald or *Hawk*. Her handling of personal past, present, and future as well as the sweeping history of time, place, and memory, seamlessly blend in a way that, as stated above, hybridize traditional categories, literary, historical, and otherwise.

One way that *Hawk* accomplishes this feat is to invoke T. H. White's *The Goshawk* (1951). Macdonald's homage to *The Goshawk*, a book that White began writing in 1936 but did not publish until much later (Winn 2007, xi), charts each respective writer's journey as they train a goshawk, a notoriously difficult bird to work with in falconry. Macdonald refers to White's book throughout, filling in gaps and offering commentary on White himself. She also tells her story against the backdrop of *Goshawk*: "The book you are reading is my story [. . .] it is not a biography of Terence Hanbury White [. . .] but White is part of my story all the same [. . .]. [I] have to write about him because he was there" (38). Earlier she writes of White "haunting" her (38).

Both writers effectively draw meaning from their goshawks, a meaning that drastically exceeds the practical mechanics of falconry. The sport of falconry—requiring specialized knowledge that is as much art as it is science—is not the ultimate goal of either text nor is it the only takeaway for the reader. Rather, for both Macdonald and White, the interactions of bird and austringer connect the human to nature and history. Both writers, in their daily accounts of interaction with their goshawks, take the reader on a temporal journey. Hawks and falconry function as a fulcrum of sorts for both writers. Each writer's textual interlacement of history and hawk, rhetorical strategies that represent the type of unification discussed above, is a point of convergence: of histories, personal and otherwise, of texts, and of creatures, human and nonhuman. For each, the act of training and flying a hawk simultaneously connects and disconnects them to and through history; readers become embedded in the same history as they follow both authors' journeys. Ultimately both writers reflect a degree of success navigating the conflicting currents of their histories. Macdonald, referring to her goshawk Mabel, comments in the final pages of her book: "[. . .] there were other scars [. . .] but they were not visible [. . .] they were the ones she'd [Mabel] helped mend, not make" (275). White, while his attempt to train his hawk fails, at one point during the process writes that "part of the joy was that now, for the first time in my life, I was absolutely free [. . .] I was as free as a hawk" (39).

This chapter will attempt to offer an analysis of Macdonald's and White's textual intersectionality through the lens of history. Macdonald's book takes readers back in time to White's book. The fusion of text and history does not stop there, however. Both books take readers even further back: to Babylonian times, to Chaucer, to Shakespeare, and to the Victorian Age. As well, both books refer to early texts on falconry, and both refer to numerous historical events and figures. They recount the personal journeys and histories of each writer. The unique connection falconry has with the past is a linchpin for both. Among the many examples of this is White's comment in *The Goshawk* that "I was trying to reconquer a territory over which the contemporaries of Chaucer had rambled free" (27). Macdonald, in one of her many astute observations of falconry's connection to history, writes that "to public-school men raised on tales of knights and chivalry, the sensation of time-travelling that falconry provoked could be overwhelming" (115).

From the opening of each book, there is an articulation of imagined history, reminiscence, and allusion to recorded history. White begins with a description of the arrival of his bird, which he names Gos. The bird has been transported to him from Germany; it arrives in a sack that has been sewn shut, in a basket, and the first paragraph describes his first sight of the moving sack. By the second paragraph, White recounts what was going through his mind in the form of a history of Gos's life to that point: "imagine what his life had been till then" (11). He offers an imaginary account of the bird's experiences before and during its capture in Germany, before it was shipped to him. At the time, White lived in a former gamekeeper's cottage on the grounds of the Stowe School, an exclusive private school for boys in Buckingham, England. White offers more imagined histories, in this case of earlier life in and around the cottage, noting that it had been built during the time of Queen Victoria (12) and that the gamekeeper would have been raising pheasants "instead of competing at games with tedious abstract tennis and cricket sticks and golfing mallets as they do today" (13). A few pages later he describes how two years earlier, in 1937, he'd found three books on the training of hawks, one of which was Edmund Bert's 1619 edition of *An Approved Treatise of Hawkes and Hawking*, and these gave him "a theoretical idea, and a very out-of-date idea, of the way to man a hawk" (16). On the next page he offers an observation connecting falconry to recorded history, noting that falconry was "perhaps the oldest sport in the world" and that there exists a Babylonian bas-relief 3,000 years old depicting a man with a hawk on his fist, leading White to conclude that "I thought it was right that I should now be happy to continue as one of a long line" (17). Macdonald comments on these lines in her book: White "closed his eyes and imagined reaching back across the centuries" (115). These early examples in *The Goshawk* represent a small sampling; White offers imaginary histories, reminiscences, and connections to recorded history throughout the entire work. The examples presented above demonstrate that White begins his book by looking back.

Macdonald's text opens with her driving to a forest to try and glimpse some goshawks, and, like White, very early on forges connections to history. One of the earliest examples involves the history of place. The forest where she hopes to see some goshawks is where "on wet mornings you can pick up shards knocked from flint cores by Neolithic craftsmen" (6) and in later times was an area used to farm rabbits. She explains that the grazing rabbits, however, along with sheep, eventually led to environmental disaster in the area, and in 1688 strong winds created dunes, turning the area into a type of "*Arabia deserta*" (6–7). Later, in the 1920s, pines were planted for timber (7). She describes her affinity for this area, noting that "it is rich with an alternative countryside history" (7) and begins an overview of how goshawks were raised and therefore plentiful by the seventeenth century but became extinct in England by the nineteenth century, but then were reintroduced in the 1960s and 1970s (7–8). This first chapter concludes with a personal reminiscence of Macdonald watching hawks with her father (9–11), and the last line of the chapter introduces what will become one of the major currents in the book: she receives a phone call from her mother that her father has died (11). Like the opening of White's text, Macdonald's also utilizes this intersectionality of recorded history, personal reminiscence, and imagined past. The love of goshawks is the fulcrum for these narrative lines, and in this sense, hawks serve as both anchor and pivot, enabling the melding of these currents. One of Macdonald's numerous brilliant insights perhaps phrases it best: "Their [goshawks'] history is just as human" (7).

Exploration and analysis of the connection of history to memory is a popular topic in recent historical studies, as Geoffrey Cubbit observes: "In the last quarter century, memory has become, to all appearances, one of the central preoccupations of historical scholarship" (2007, 1). Cubitt has noted that "memory has become, in some quarters at least, a key term in the lexicon of historical study—an almost obligatory concept for the validation of new modes of historical enquiry and for the revamping of old ones" (2). He argues, however, that there are divergent approaches to how historical scholarship employs and even defines memory: "Memory studies are not, and are not obviously in the process of becoming, a coherent and unified field of enquiry, and the kind that possesses agreed definitions" (2). White and Macdonald, though, do not concern themselves with formal definitions of history and memory in their respective books, nor do they burden the reader with the type of prose and terminology found in scholarly journals. This is not to say that these are not scholarly works—White's references to recorded history and literary texts, for example, and Macdonald's well-researched chapters, complete with cited sources, more than qualify their books as impressive scholarship—but the intent of both writers is not to offer formalized, historical analyses. If anything, there is a more holistic and, if the word can be used, natural presentation of the interrelationship between history and memory. Perhaps the most appropriate characterization can be drawn from Georg Wilhelm Friedrich Hegel (1824): "the philosophy of history means nothing but the thoughtful consideration of it" (22). Both White and Macdonald apply "thoughtful consideration" to history—their personal histories and recorded history, and the medium through which this thoughtfulness manifests itself in their interaction with and ruminations upon their hawks.

For each writer, the hawk is a bird with a unique connection to history. This historical uniqueness, though, is through the hawk's interaction with humans, and, in this sense, a bird bridges human and natural history. As noted above, White ruminates that falconry may be the oldest sport in the world (17) and elsewhere comments "every falconer was an historian" (154). He also relates how hawks connected natural history with human legal history:

how the medieval *Boke of St. Albans*, from 1486, details which social classes were permitted to own which hawks—an eagle for an emperor, or a peregrine for an earl. Thus, hawks "are the only creatures for which man had troubled to legislate" (18). He concludes this paragraph with characteristic self-effacing humor: "Well, a goshawk was the proper servant for a yeoman, and I was well content with that" (18). Macdonald sees hawks' unique connection to history through the ideas they produce in the mind: "Trained hawks have a peculiar ability to conjure history because they are in a sense immortal [. . .] there are no breeds or varieties, because hawks were never domesticated [. . .]. The birds we fly today are identical to those of five thousand years ago" (116).

The association of hawks and falconry with history leads both writers to ruminate about the perception of time. That is, both writers discuss a sense of timelessness, a distortion or alteration of their sense of time passage, at different points during their training of and interaction with hawks. It is as if time spent with the hawk alters one's sense of temporality. For example, White, early in the training of Gos, employs what he believed was an old technique, what he refers to as *watching*, essentially depriving the bird of sleep in the belief that this, over time, will bond the bird and handler. White, ever the traditionalist, decides to also deprive himself of sleep since he believed that he must constantly carry the bird to further the bonding process, and recounts how, for days, both man and bird would go with minimal sleep resulting in an unprecedented level of exhaustion. He characterizes these days as a "timeless universe" (61) where "time itself became illusory," and he has "lost all contact with the calendar," ultimately "becoming muddled with chronology altogether" (62). This perception of timelessness is balanced against the numerous historical references White makes throughout the book, and often the overall effect is a merging of past, present, and future: in a passage comparing Gos to a "savage," White recounts the Vikings attacking the last two kings of Northumbria, then refers to the Battles of Hastings and Crecy, then declares "we still lived in the Middle Ages," concluding with references to both Hitler and Mussolini (133). In an earlier and somewhat prescient passage in which he refers to "the march of civilization" (70), he writes that Hitler, Mussolini, and Stalin "would bring us to the preliminary ruin perhaps in our own lifetime" (71). Elsewhere, he alludes to the future, stating that "the ambition of every writer" is to "write something of enduring beauty" (155) and that the artist "yearn[s] to discover permanence" (156).

Macdonald also discusses a sense of altered perceptions of linear time, although, unlike White, grief and her mourning the loss of her father compound the effect. In moving passages early in the book, she describes memories as "heavy blocks of glass" (14), and a few pages later says "time didn't run forward anymore" (16). Regarding hawks specifically, she later writes that "history collapses when you hold a hawk" (116) and, in another moving passage describing her strong bond with Mabel, writes that "she lived in the present only, and that was my refuge" (160). As a testament to Macdonald's research into White's work, she highlights what he wrote in an unpublished journal: "If the hawk dies almost all my present me dies with it" (qtd. in Macdonald, 161). In a later passage, she characterizes White as "certainly interfering with time [. . .] he was turning it backward" (247). She connects this to White's novel *The Once and Future King* in which the character Merlyn lives backward through time; she interprets Merlyn as "White's imagined future self" (247).

Both authors' personal relationships to history are at the forefront of their literary art, but, interestingly, White is a part of Macdonald's history. That is, Macdonald read White's *The Goshawk* when she was nine, and she recounts how, as a young woman fascinated by hawks and falconry, she read numerous books on the subject, among them White's (29). Early in *Hawk* Macdonald remembers her initial reading of White's book and recalls how picking up the book again years later renews her interest in White and his work. Among her many achievements, Macdonald offers a sensitive, perceptive, and thorough discussion of T. H. White through the lens of both biographical and literary analysis. In fact, Macdonald's book represents a milestone in White scholarship. Her research into White—from traveling to America to study his personal journals to visiting the gamekeeper's cottage at Stowe where White lived while writing *The Goshawk*—afford her a level of insight into not only White and his work but also into her own experiences training and interacting with Mabel. An additional, layered consideration is that she engages in these activities while simultaneously attempting to come to terms with the loss of her father. This intersectionality of historical lines—White, White's work, her own memories and experiences, all centered on the love of falconry and hawks and the love and memories of her father—comes forward in Macdonald's book in profound, meditational moments. One such moment is found in chapter 12. In a passage that refers to a section of White's book in which he reminisces about life of the past, Macdonald sees her own connection to history in a different light:

> a hawk let White feel part of the community of a pre-Reformation English village. [. . .] When I was small I'd loved falconry's historical glamour [. . .] but that was a long time ago [. . .] I did not feel like that anymore [. . .] I had no use for history, no use for time at all [. . .] I was training the hawk to make it all disappear. (117)

It should be noted that this describes one point along the journey Macdonald recounts in her book. It is presented here as only one example among many that show the depth of analysis Macdonald offers about White and his work. At this stage in their respective journeys, Macdonald and White seem to approach history from different directions. Macdonald attempts to make history disappear by reasserting the present while White attempts to make the present disappear by going back into history. These conflicting historical currents are the result of each writer attempting to come to terms with personal struggles: as mentioned above, for Macdonald it is the recent death of her father, and for White it is his disillusionment with others and self, including his own family, and his sexuality.

White's life was a difficult one. Macdonald states directly, "T. H. White was one of the loneliest men alive" (33). White suffered numerous personal and psychological struggles during his lifetime, beginning with his childhood. On more than one occasion he writes of his difficult upbringing in India by his hard-drinking father and his tyrannical mother, and he underwent psychotherapy to address his sadistic tendencies and his homosexuality (Brewer 1993, 7). In 1938 White wrote in his diary some verses about his unstable childhood, characterizing his birth as "brutally begun" and concluding "Thus bred without security / Whom dared I love, whom did not flee? (Warner 1967, 21). Other stresses plagued him. Among them was fear; White felt fearful his entire life, a theme Macdonald explores in *Hawk*. As Macdonald points out, White wrote about being afraid in his book *England Have My Bones* (36), and Macdonald, in her exploration of White's fear, notes that "he had been afraid as long as he could remember" (36). Elsewhere she writes that "he had tried so hard not to be a coward" (127). Macdonald is not the first to comment on White's fears. Sylvia Townsend Warner (1978) states that "throughout his life White was subject to fears [. . .] fears from without [. . .] fears from within [. . .] his life was a running battle with these fears" (x). These fears were the result of multiple forces in his life. In addition to his difficult childhood, White saw himself as both a misogynist and a sadist. In a 1940 letter to his friend, L. J. Potts, he compares himself to Sir Bors in Thomas Malory's *Le Morte Darthur*, the source for his book *The Once and Future King*. White writes, "Bors was a misogynist like myself" (Gallix 1982, 115). Another friend of White's, writer and publisher David Garnett (1968), relating a conversation he had with White late in White's life, reports that

> [White] explained to me that he was a sadist. [. . .] Tim [White's nickname] explained that the sadist cannot be happy unless he has proved the love felt for him by acts of cruelty [. . .] it had been Tim's fate to destroy every passionate love he had inspired [. . .] he had found himself always in the dilemma of either being sincere and cruel, or false and unnatural [. . .] whichever line he followed, he revolted the object of this love and disgusted himself. (8)

Garnett goes on to say that White believed he had inherited this from a great-grandfather, but Garnett believed it was attributable to White's "being emotionally maltreated by his mother and ferociously flogged at school" (8). Notably, Garnett adds that White was an "extremely tender-hearted and sensitive man" (8). Macdonald herself quotes these lines (39) and in her view White "could not imagine a human love returned" (39). Finally, another force in White's life affecting his sense of stability was his homosexuality. Macdonald also explores White's discomfort with his sexuality and the challenges faced by a gay man in early twentieth-century England.

He wanted an escape from his troubles, and he wanted isolation: "[my book] would be about the efforts of a second-rate philosopher who lived alone in a wood, being tired of most humans [. . .] to train a person who was not human, but a bird" (27). Macdonald, at times, also voices a similar desire for solitude: "like White, I wanted to cut loose from the world, and I shared, too, his desire to escape to the wild" (38). Elsewhere she describes moments when she does not want to see or be in the company of people (97). The point to be made here, however, is that Macdonald's insight into White and his work, along with both writers' mutual admiration and love of hawks and falconry, provide an avenue for the merging of history, memory, and narrative as well as the conflicting inner struggles for both writers. Daniel Little (2020) writes that "the philosophy of history must pay attention to the nexus of experience, memory and history." He also observes that narrative, when applied to the discipline, provides "an account of how a complex historical event unfolded and even why," and details "the contextual features that were relevant to the outcome." A shared love of hawks provides the kind of nexus that Little describes.

The seamless integration of direct references to White and his work in Macdonald's book provides one type of connection, but there are others. As noted above, both writers allude to the history of falconry, but there are numerous other parallels. Both writers offer the etymology of specific terms, both refer to historical texts for portrayals and depictions of hawks, and both refer to literary works and writers. White mentions Shakespeare on numerous occasions, and offers a particularly interesting, though brief, commentary on falcon imagery in *The Taming of the Shrew* and *Othello* (157–58). In another literary allusion, Macdonald characterizes White's approach to falconry as a "metaphysical battle" and compares it to *Moby Dick* and *The Old Man and the Sea*, as a "literary encounter between animal and man that reached back to Puritan traditions of spiritual contest: salvation as a stake to be won in a contest against God" (33). She considers her perspective of White through her more mature stance, an "older, wiser me," in light of seeing his attempt at falconry in the metaphysical contest she has described, making his "admissions of ignorance" about falconry "brave rather than stupid" (33). Thus,

Macdonald reads White's book against other literary works, which leads to an increased level of admiration for the man and writer.

I conclude this chapter by briefly discussing one more connection involving hawks in both White's and Macdonald's works. Marlene Kadar has noted "life writing as a critical practice [. . .] encourages (a) the reader to develop and foster his/her own self-consciousness in order to (b) humanize and make less abstract (which is not to say less mysterious) the self-in-the-writing" (12). Kadar asserts that the term "life writing" was formerly defined as autobiography but argues that "life writing is not a fixed term, and that it is in flux as it moves from considerations of genre to considerations of critical practice" (3). Both autobiography and life writing can capture the essence of White's and Macdonald's books, as can memoir. Yet none of these terms, strictly speaking, accurately and completely applies to either book. Genre descriptions, such as autobiography, life writing, or memoir, do not adequately encompass the scope of White's and Macdonald's books. Yet Kadar's point about this type of writing fostering self-consciousness in readers in order to humanize the self in the writing bears scrutiny. As we follow Macdonald's reading and research into White, we experience Macdonald's journey of mourning and triumph, of bonding between woman and hawk. Then we also see how Macdonald's experience is informed by White's. That is, readers can appreciate how the *self-in-writing* of *Hawk* is affected and aided by the *self-in-writing* of *The Goshawk*. This layering compounds the final effect for readers and fosters a unique level of complexity and depth. Gos and Mabel help shape the *humanized self*, and thus the reader is doubly affected. As the *self-in-writing* of *Hawk* offers a humanizing of White and the narrative voice of *The Goshawk*, readers of *Hawk* perform the same process and come away with a humanizing of both narrative voices. Readers also see the role Gos and Mabel play in the process, stretching the bonds between human and hawk beyond the text. In the widest sense this elasticity reinforces the importance of nurturing and maintaining the bonds between the avian and the human. Macdonald has shown readers how the separations among history, memory, and narrative can be bridged by an avian-human partnership, and White is the catalyst for that discovery. In this context Gos and Mabel are more than mere literary devices. They guide their human partners and us as well.

White's best-known work, *The Once and Future King*, opens with the section *The Sword in the Stone*, in which hawks figure prominently. In the opening pages of the book a young Arthur, nicknamed Wart, and his brother Kay take their father's goshawk, Cully, into the forest and attempt to fly him. Wart worries that, because Cully is "deep in the moult" (9), it is not the right time to fly him, but Kay insists. The hawk immediately lands in a tree and refuses to return to the boys. After trying to lure him back, a frustrated Kay leaves, and Wart spends the night in the forest attempting to retrieve the bird. Readers are told that, unlike Kay, Wart "had some of the falconer's feelings and knew that a lost hawk was the greatest possible calamity" (11). He is also sensitive to the effect that the lost bird would have on Hob, the man who trained the hawk: "he knew that Hob had worked on Cully for fourteen hours a day to teach him his trade, and that his work had been like Jacob's struggle with the angel [. . .] when Cully was lost a part of Hob would be lost too" (11). It is while Wart is in the forest trying to retrieve Cully that he meets Merlyn, who becomes his tutor and advisor. Later in the book, Merlyn transforms Wart into a hawk, in this case a merlin, so that Wart can spend a night in the mews as a part of his own education (68–78). Macdonald highlights this scene in her own book (228–29).

My point is that hawks in *The Sword in the Stone* serve as guides to Wart. That is, in the opening pages it is a hawk that leads Wart to Merlyn, the teacher who will magically open the world to him and educate him. It is the goshawk Cully that facilitates this; he opens the door to Wart and initiates the necessary preparation for Wart to become the great King Arthur. It is a hawk that shows Wart the way to his own destiny. In doing so, a hawk simultaneously makes possible the greatest king of England and helps humankind throughout the land. Just as Gos and Mabel provide new insights for White and Macdonald and help them along their respective journeys, so Cully occasions new insights for the great King Arthur and guides him on his journey, which will in turn benefit all England. Later, when Wart is transformed into a merlin, hawks again help advance his education toward becoming king. Macdonald argues that here the lesson is bravery and that Merlyn, through the hawks, teaches Wart courage (230). In her recent book *Vesper Flights*, Macdonald (2020) insists that "animals don't exist in order to teach us things, but that is what they have always done, and most of what they teach us is what we think we know about ourselves" (296). Goshawks like Gos, Mabel, and Cully continue to teach young and old readers alike. Hawks are guides and teachers, and in performing that function they solidify the bridge between the human and natural worlds.

REFERENCES

Brewer, Elisabeth. 1993. *T. H. White's The Once and Future King*. Cambridge, UK: D. S. Brewer.

Cubitt, Geoffrey. 2007. *History and Memory*. Manchester: Manchester University Press.

Curthoys, Ann and Ann McGrath. 2009. *How to Write History that People Want to Read*. Sydney: New South Wales Press.

Gallix, Francois, ed. 1982. *Letters to a Friend: The Correspondence Between T. H. White and L. J. Potts*. New York: G. P. Putnam's Sons.

Garnett, David. 1969. "Preface." In *The White/Garnett Letters*, edited by David Garnett. New York: Viking, 7–8.

Hegel, Georg Wilhelm Friedrich. 1824. Rep. 2001. *The Philosophy of History*, translated by J. Sibree. Kitchener, Canada: Batoche. Accessed June 27, 2021. https://socialsciences.mcmaster.ca/~econ/ugcm/3ll3/hegel/history.pdf

Kadar, Marlene. 1992. "Coming to Terms: Life Writing—from Genre to Critical Practice." In *Essays on Life Writing: From Genre to Critical Practice*. Toronto: University of Toronto Press, 3–16.

Little, Daniel. 2020. "Philosophy of History." In *The Stanford Encyclopedia of Philosophy* (Winter 2020 Edition), edited by Edward N. Zalta. Accessed June, 27, 2021. https://plato.stanford.edu/archives/win2020/entries/history/

Macdonald, Helen. 2014. *H Is for Hawk*. New York: Random House.

———. 2020. *Vesper Flights*. New York: Grove.

Warner, Sylvia Townsend. 1967. *T. H. White: A Biography*. New York: Viking.

———. 1978. "Prologue." *The Book of Merlyn* by T. H. White. Berkley: Medallion, ix–xxviii.

White, T. H. 1951. Rep. 2007. *The Goshawk*. New York: New York Review

———. 1958. Rep. 2011. *The Once and Future King*. New York: Ace.

Winn, Marie. 2007. "Introduction." The Goshawk *by T.H. White*. New York: New York Review.

Chapter 11

Across So Wide a Sea

Humans, Seabirds, and the Kinship of Mortality

Keri Stevenson

Writing of nesting Laysan albatrosses on the island of Kaua'i, avian extinction researcher Thom van Dooren conceptualizes these seabirds as a "flight way," an entangled group that consists not just of the physical birds but of their evolution, their fishing habits, and their long labor that, from the laying of eggs to the fledging of chicks, takes months of time and thousands of miles of sea traveled (van Dooren 2014, 34). Yet Laysan albatrosses, and many other kinds of seabirds and shorebirds, are also intimately involved in another entanglement, that of dying and mortality. Due to climate change, human fishing techniques, past human predation, and, perhaps most perniciously, swallowing ocean-borne plastic trash that starves both adults and chicks (van Dooren 2014, 32), seabirds extend mortality across time and space, even as they extend their lives and work of reproduction. Human communities, both those that rest directly on the shore and those that depend indirectly on fish and other food from it, are kin to these birds in their dying. It is not an easy death; it is not one way, as fluctuations of hope, like the retreat and rise of the waves, stave off the extinction of one albatross colony (Safina 2002, "Learning and Luck"), or raise buildings and roads in one city (Miller 2019). This protraction across time and space, I argue, both catches up, as in a fishing net, and attenuates human mourning for seabirds, obscuring the kinship of mortality we share with them. Even the texts directly about possible seabird extinction and shorebird loss of habitat contend uneasily with this mourning, flickering between wonder and loss, striving to direct human attention across the spaces of the sea and to the uncertain numbers of birds left. Both mourning theory and the theory of ocean-oriented criticism known as the blue humanities can help us to structure this kinship and more readily understand it.

As well, nonfiction texts about seabirds and shorebirds cast as popular science can underwrite this endeavor. These texts address the possibility of extinction and the human mourning connected to it more directly than most novels and poetry featuring these birds, which tend, instead, to focus on the life and death of an individual—for example, the death of the single/singular albatross in Samuel Taylor Coleridge's *The Rime of the Ancient Mariner*. Popular science writing is also more accessible to a broader audience than technical scientific articles are, and thus more likely to clarify the work of mourning species and seeing kinship.

In this chapter, I examine a book by the environmental journalist Deborah Cramer, *The Narrow Edge: A Tiny Bird, an Ancient Crab, and an Epic Journey* (2015), which follows the migration of the small shorebird called the red knot from Tierra del Fuego to the Arctic, and two books by the seabird ecologist Carl Safina, *Eye of the Albatross* (2002) and *Song for the Blue Ocean* (1997), which conceptualize the intertwined destinies of human communities and seabirds that nest on remote islands like French Frigate Shoals and Midway. The fact that both Cramer and Safina include other species as part of the entanglement between humans and seabirds shows how desperately needed these conceptualizations are. The idea of the ocean as "impervious to human harm" (Alaimo 2016, chap. 5) due to its vast size and capability to absorb waste has prevented many people from feeling much kinship with creatures of the sea at all, including seabirds. Evolutionary kinship and reminders of our shared bodily past *can* play a part, but "even though such formulations evoke a 'community of descent' across vast temporal and oceanic expanses, their reach may be acquisitive, shoring up human heft" (Alaimo 2016, chap. 5). The idea of bodily kinship, then, is not enough, especially given formulations of the ocean and its beings as "bizarre" and "otherworldly" that often accompany fictional or even documentary explorations; undersea fish, for example, may be "described as nightmares, alien, and monstrous" (Dobrin 2021a, 196). Seabirds, if not alien, may be simply left out. Stacy Alaimo, for example, argues that a "bird's-eye view" (Alaimo 2016, chap. 6) can equal escape, or soaring beyond the problems of earth and sea into a formless atmosphere, positioning a reader or consumer of art as a bodiless and unaffected observer. Sylvia Earle, a well-regarded ecologist and author of *The World Is Blue*, a book that inspired several blue humanities scholars, includes separate sections in her book examining the effects of human hunting and oceanic pollution on marine mammals, fish, and shellfish, but none for birds. Birds, however, *are* part of the ocean's wildlife, *are* affected by human assaults on the supposedly limitless sea, and *are* bound to humans in a kinship of mortality and endangerment. "Animals [who] are cultural beings, enmeshed in social organizations, acting, interacting, and communicating" (Alaimo 2016, chap. 2) include seabirds and shorebirds, and Safina's and Cramer's writings portray and help enact this kinship.

MOURNING THEORY AND THE BLUE HUMANITIES

Many scientists acknowledge that we are in the middle of a sixth great extinction, which has not spared seabirds (van Dooren 2014, 39). Yet it can be hard to grasp so immense a process, as it accelerates a loss of biodiversity on a timescale that continues beyond any single human lifetime. In fact, we may believe that extinction is being staved off if the death is happening out of our immediate vicinity, or if a single member of that species continues to exist. When species cease to exist, relics may take the place of the living. Stacy Otto's study of public mourning in the wake of the Triangle Shirtwaist Factory Fire and the September 11, 2001 attacks includes an account of relics gathered from the dead, "a referent for the one-lost [sic]" (Otto 2014, 581) or a way to hold them in mind with the mourning for them as present-day and ongoing emotional labor, rather than a finite, fixed-time activity. I would argue that the more familiar examples of human mourning for avian extinction are functional relics, such as the body of Martha, the last known passenger pigeon to die, which was shipped to the Smithsonian in a block of ice, fitted with carefully preserved feathers and memorialized in photographs and written descriptions before being skinned (Greenberg 2014, chap. 9). In cases where bodies are not readily available, those who mourn extinct birds may create their own relics, such as models that hang in ornithologists' offices (Lanham 2018). This provides a way to hold the "one-lost" bird in mind, and in hand, before the eyes, a tangible picture of what is gone.

However, this kind of mourning helps less with species that are currently still extant, in the *process* of going extinct, but not yet there. Mortals need a different kind of mourning from the moribund. Thus, our mourning for extinct birds is best used as a spur to save those still alive. "It is tiring sometimes to think of our postmodern grief, but it is a crucial beginning, a necessary grief before the salve of some healing energy" (Cokinos 2009, 2); it is a *beginning,* not an end, not a grief in which we can wallow or rest. To try to prevent the last seabird or shorebird of any species from becoming a specimen or model that can be held in the hand, then, human mourning must be active. In general, "mourning theory's or memory studies' failure to think ecologically, to apprehend the disastrous imbrication of human and nonhuman worlds" (Crownshaw 2017, 133) can be connected in the case of extinct birds to mourning the past, to the exclusion of the future that will in turn have to be mourned *as* relic-laden past if we do not look to it. Adding a grounding, or in this case a watermark, of ecological theory can help reorient one kind of mourning theory to the open horizon.

Blue humanities, also called blue ecocriticism, while not as established as some other branches of ecocriticism, seeks to correct the "ocean deficit" (Dobrin 2021a, 89) its practitioners see in environmental humanities. The most applicable aspect of that deficit to my project here is renewing a sense of scale, specifically of the immense distances that migratory seabirds like albatrosses travel across the seas, and that shorebirds like red knots travel along the coasts. While not a neat one-to-one correspondence, because a bird-focused argument must also take account of the sky, "blue ecocriticism, then, necessarily, rethinks the role of scale in considering the impact of textual representations of ocean upon the cultural imaginary" (Dobrin 2021a, 89), and provides a useful bow wave for this chapter to ride upon. The lack of widespread ecocritical work on oceanic texts matches the lack of widespread ecocritical work on avian texts, despite the work that *has* appeared on the stray bird-focused piece of nature writing or watery literature. While not going as far as to agree "that our planet should actually be called Ocean rather than Earth, because nearly three-quarters of it is covered in water" (Gershwin 2016, 19), I believe that shifting ecocritical attention to the sea is necessary, particularly with the factors of sea-level rise, overfishing, and ocean acidification affecting humans as well as seabirds and shorebirds.

That we are entangled and enmeshed with other oceanic species is shown particularly well by Cramer and Safina. Cramer's work demonstrates the dependence that red knots and humans have on the horseshoe crab, as well as the threats that sea-level rise brings to the beaches where knots rest and feed from their long migrations and to the human communities that live close to these beaches. Safina's *Song for the Blue Ocean* examines the consequences for human communities of overfishing certain species like tuna and salmon and destroying their habitats. These fish also often feed seabirds or help drive their prey to the surface, as with tuna, so crashes in their populations ripple down, or up, the trophic levels to affect avian lives. Meanwhile, Safina's *Eye of the Albatross* looks at both the plastic threat to all of Earth's species that use the oceans and at how local human economies may rise and fall because of seabirds. The necessity to consider what we all have to mourn, and who will be left alive to mourn with us, is also the necessity that drives my application of "thick" ecology, "an ecology that spans all scales of our milieu and is self-reflexively fed back into the material-technological-semiotic process of milieu-building itself [. . .]. Our technological assemblages, cultural narratives, and the ontological assertiveness of the world itself are all compositional elements of our milieus" (Horton 2019, 6).

In these texts, the milieu for humans, seabirds, shorebirds, crabs, and fish must be multispecies—committed to incorporating "technological assemblages" and "ontological assertiveness" into the "cultural narrative" written by the author—and capable of seeing the scale. "Thickness" is likewise the word that van Dooren uses to describe how humans can "gain a 'thicker' sense of who [birds] might be, but also of what is being lost in their disappearance" (van Dooren 2014, 136). As well, thick applies to the tangibility of ocean as medium and milieu, and to the challenges faced by avian species dependent on the ocean. Cramer and Safina, as authors committed to thickness in their texts, elaborate the kinship of mortality for seabirds, shorebirds, and our own species, how much mortality we have ignored, and how much we may still have to confront.

NUMBERING UNCERTAINTY: DEBORAH CRAMER'S *THE NARROW EDGE*

In the beginning of her book that traces the yearly migration of the red knot up the South and North American coasts, Deborah Cramer muses that while she has "a compass, GPS, and radio" to fix her location (Cramer 2015, 4), the birds she tracks have no such visible equipment and yet cross distances and keep to their routes on a scale that defies humans to travel without aid. "By the end of this journey I am more in awe than when I began" (Cramer 2015, 4), and this awe and doubt will haunt Cramer as she travels after, pursues, sees dead, and rarely finds a bird that is currently threatened and likely to reach the edge of extinction (Cramer 2015, 4). The mortality of red knots is consistently at the forefront of Cramer's writing, but so, too, is human mortality. Humans crowd into the same shoreside communities where knots need to eat and rest (Cramer 2015, 4), which means that these communities can also land on an edge of extinction due to sea-level rise and oceanic degradation. Fishermen who make a living gathering horseshoe crabs for biomedical research see the possibility of their livings drying up (Cramer 2015, 85), and sick people in hospitals stand a much higher chance of dying of infections if LAL, a compound taken from the crabs' blood, is not used to detect and cleanse bacteria from medical instruments before use (Cramer 2015, 91). Researchers in the Arctic, where Cramer travels to find nesting knots, are under threat from polar bears who may seek the camp in search of something to eat, which could be human food or human flesh, and who also eat the eggs of shorebirds in enormous numbers, causing colony crashes (Cramer 2015, 197). Mourning for knots is mourning for humans is mourning for crabs is mourning for polar bears. Cramer's text makes kin of the dying processes of all these species across a protracted scale of space and time, using numbers as an example of how humans try to grasp knots and make their continued existence certain. Those numbers, however, flap out of Cramer's grasp like falling feathers, rendering knots' closeness to extinction a matter of guesswork, and thus leaving both the living and the dead literally up in the air. What is certain is their mortality.

Besides accompanying scientists, birdwatchers, and others who try to number the knots and to learn exactly how many visit each beach, how many horseshoe crab eggs they eat, and how many additional food sources they access, Cramer recounts past expeditions to the knots' feeding, nesting, and wintering grounds, and compares past and present numbers to try to get a sense of future ones. Unfortunately, despite the seemingly comfortable solidity of such information and the proof it would offer about whether knots can evade extinction, security proves elusive in this case. Numbers are one way of attempting to understand and live within the world, but they cannot constrain or bind it. The scales involved are simply too great. Instead, Cramer, and ultimately her readers, must attempt to extend their *emotional* comprehension of kinship—mourning, empathy, and awe—further than numbers can reach.

Traces of this appear in the first chapter, when Cramer travels to Tierra del Fuego to see the place where knots spend the (Northern Hemisphere) winter: "As would happen so many times during this trip [. . .] I find myself in a remote place with landmarks I can't read, my companions people I barely know" (Cramer 2015, 8). Both marks specifically made on land—and on human maps, which concentrate more often on land—and human bonds of community have broken for Cramer, prompting her to direct her attention to the birds who *do* know where they are going, and follow paths made of sea and sky. As blue humanities scholars warn, "land-based thinking and ocean-based thinking are not the same" (Dobrin 2021b). Ocean-based thinking means accepting, among other things, that other-than-human animals have ways of navigating the sea and sky that we do not. Humans *can* reorient themselves in these spaces, but only by following the birds, as Cramer does, and acknowledging the kinships between us, rather than by relying on old landmarks of difference.

Cramer, however, has not, at this early point in her narrative, made an out-and-out commitment to oceanic thinking. Instead, she tries to find certainty in the numbers of knots that have existed in the past by recounting Guy Morrison and Brian Harrington's 1979 ornithological expedition (Cramer 2015, 10). Despite having been told they would find thousands of birds easily, Morrison and Harrington only discovered twenty knots within fifteen stops (Cramer 2015, 11). This occurred during a supposedly more productive and prosperous era for the birds, before as much shoreline development and pollution had happened. When Morrison and Harrington did manage to locate a larger flock of four hundred knots, they "saw that 15 had oil-smeared chests and bellies" (Cramer 2015, 12). With numbers such as these, Cramer destroys both the false image of the past as another, safer country where large numbers of knots fed and flew, and the presumption that the species has only become endangered in the past few decades. To encompass a truer sense of the timescale on which shorebirds have been endangered, human mourning must extend backward as well as forward. Thus, Cramer refuses to validate the golden, nostalgic perception of nature as untouched and unpolluted in the childhood or young adulthood of people alive now; it brings humans and shorebirds into a sharper and more expansive sense of kinship to acknowledge that oil pollution and threats to the health of knots, and humans, existed even *then*. In the words of Brooke Jarvis in her investigation of the "insect apocalypse" that is claiming enormous numbers of insects worldwide—a number also difficult to count because of the lack of accurate records for many places and many specialized researchers' tendency to overlook insects in aggregate—"The world never feels fallen, because we grow accustomed to the fall" (Jarvis 2018). Cramer's attempt to find precise numbers on how exactly the fate and survival rate of red knots has changed over time shows that the fall likely began further back than we want to acknowledge and may, or may not, take more time going forward than we can imagine. The stretched-out process of dying forces the acknowledgment of mortality and extension of kinship over time and sea.

The uncertainty continues as Cramer travels into North America to observe red knots on beaches where they feed on horseshoe crab eggs before completing their flight to the Arctic. She explains that many shorebirds were shot in the nineteenth century as scientific specimens, but it is uncertain how many birds were in the flocks before the hunters came (Cramer 2015, 67). Ornithology itself, which now strives to save the knots, "was built on a foundation of dead birds" (Cramer 2015, 67). Our own mortality, and our own mourning, have covered a century or more. Similar doubt clouds the possible numbers of horseshoe crabs, whose eggs red knots feed on at stopping places on the East coast of the United States (Cramer 2015, 55). Simply by not visiting the right beach at the right time, such as Delaware Bay, an important knot stopover, ornithologists may have missed accounting for their true numbers (Cramer 2015, 56), and for the numbers of the crabs that visited the beach to lay eggs and then retreat into the sea. Again, this illustrates an important reason to shed land-based thinking and turn to the oceanic (and the airborne). Knots, and other shorebirds, can take to the wing with speeds that outpace many land animals, and horseshoe crabs can disappear into the sea, which even now is less thoroughly researched than terrestrial habitats (Cramer 2015, 62). Combine this with the dearth of records on knots and horseshoe crabs, with Cramer describing the ones that exist as "frayed and stained, the ink faded" (Cramer 2015, 59), and it becomes clear that the history of shorebirds and crabs is itself mortal. Writing cannot grant immortality here, and neither can stuffed specimens of birds in a museum. Humans again join shorebirds in the kinship of mortality, our history as fleeting as numbers on an ocean.

The crabs that both humans and knots depend on to stave off higher mortality are bound in this kinship as well. Cramer explains the history of how horseshoe crabs' blood began to be harvested for the sake of LAL, a chemical that can signal the presence of toxins from fragments of bacteria remaining in medical instruments after they have been sterilized (Cramer 2015, 91–94). Because the crabs can be bled without being killed, they are regularly gathered from the sea and then returned there after the bleeding to recover (Cramer 2015, 98–99). This process makes horseshoe crabs vital to staving off infections and keeping deaths in hospitals low when patients need intravenous treatment. However, horseshoe crab numbers are declining, particularly numbers of female crabs, which lay the eggs red knots need to survive flight and nesting in the Arctic (Cramer 2015, 105). Part of this may be caused by the fact that horseshoe crabs, once widely used for fertilizer, are still captured in supposedly sustainable numbers for fish bait, but there is also the fact that biomedical companies bleeding the crabs do not have to report the number used, or the number that die in use (Cramer 2015, 109–10). The available independent numbers show "a threshold [of dead crabs] that the industry has exceeded every year since 2007" (Cramer 2015, 110). Here, human secrecy and reluctance to keep track of numbers makes the future survival of both shorebirds and human hospital patients uncertain. This is perhaps the bleakest part of Cramer's narrative of empathy, mourning, and mortality. These numbers and human carelessness with horseshoe crabs show an alarming disregard for the possibility of future mourning. The present, including a resistance to numbering of any kind except the counting of profits, is all that matters. This same carelessness is visible in human reactions to climate change, another slow-moving threat with more impact on the future than the present. Jeff Goodell, in *The Water Will Come,* his book on sea-level rise and its impact on coastal communities, stresses that we as a species are "not wired to make decisions about barely perceptible threats that gradually accelerate over time" (Goodell 2017, 16). But we will need to extend our sense of kinship into the future, and to creatures of the sea, like horseshoe crabs, that might strike us as completely alien to ensure our own survival as a species and the maintenance of mourning for the dying rather than for the dead. This is another example of the move away from land-based thinking, and here Cramer takes fully to the sea, spending nearly a complete chapter of her narrative on threats to horseshoe crabs and the importance of their survival to the survival of shorebirds, creatures of sea's edge and sky. Keeping in mind that horseshoe crabs have survived for millions of years (Cramer 2015, 137), and might last millions more, we will require practice extending our mourning across time for crabs as Cramer does in space for birds, lest it lead to a careless assurance that crabs will always be there when we need them.

As Cramer moves north, her tone becomes more subdued, and metaphors of haunting increase. For example, she investigates a migration route across Texas that red knots once used in much greater numbers, but which now bears only the memory of those flocks; Cramer titles her chapter about this route "Ghost Trail" (Cramer 2015, 140). While knots are still seen along this route, their provenance is uncertain; David Newstead, a dedicated bird researcher, tells Cramer that he doesn't know where the knots who travel through in the fall spend their winters (Cramer 2015, 140). In another return to the past, Cramer evokes Harrington, who saw oil-smeared birds in South America in 1979, and who only managed to locate small flocks in Texas in 1992, "when the population was much higher" (Cramer 2015, 140). *How* much higher is not known for sure, and the knots who once arrived in Texas along this migration route have faded, leaving the whole chapter uneasy with their ghosts, their uncertain numbers. Newstead and other counters who attempt to number the birds are portrayed by Cramer as waiting, hoping, without being sure that the ghosts will ever revive—the scientific equivalent of necromancers. Cramer, telling the history of rebounding sea turtle numbers in south Texas, does insist that the turtles' "history—of abundance, decimation, and restoration—is imaginable for knots" (Cramer 2015, 141). But that restoration has not happened yet, and the lack of firm numbers for knots, especially since they have faded enough to no longer require this migration route, keep the *imagination* in "imaginable." The mortality that keeps the dying *as* dying, not yet dead, not yet extinct, but not yet abundant, and decimated or more than decimated, resonates with the ghostly metaphors in this chapter to render the reader as uneasy as Cramer feels.

Cramer ends the book by summing up the story of the red knot and tying it together with a personal story of human mortality: "The story of red knots begins with loss—loss of large numbers of birds, loss of beach and mudflat, loss of horseshoe crab eggs, and a slide toward extinction. As I began to understand this story, a close friend became seriously ill [. . .] she knew she wouldn't live to read the book" (Cramer 2015, 221). Cramer provides a model of striving forward in the face of mortality—in this case, by continuing her work and discussing the book with her friend even though she would never show her the finished product, and even though the story of red knots did not provide a narrative with definitive triumph waiting at the end. The process continues, flickering toward death, across ocean and land, sky and sea. Although seeing some hope in the attempts to protect seashores and horseshoe crabs for knots' future use, Cramer admits that "whether, in each of their homes between Tierra del Fuego and the Arctic, they will find shelter on quiet and spacious beaches, food in abundance, and marshes where they can roost, hangs in abeyance" (Cramer 2015, 223). Cramer writes a story without an end, one that asks for the extension of kinship, conservation attempts that must not cease, and a mourning that may be tempered, based on the future, for small birds whose dependence on shores and crabs intertwines with our own.

KINDRED ISLES OF MORTALITY: CARL SAFINA'S *SONG FOR THE BLUE OCEAN* AND *EYE OF THE ALBATROSS*

Carl Safina recalls in *Eye of the Albatross*, his narrative of travels to various Pacific islands and other places where albatrosses nest, a central moment that pointed out for him the kinships between humans and seabirds. He watches as an adult albatross attempts to feed her chick but is prevented by a plastic toothbrush that is stuck in her throat (Safina 2002, "Midway"). This moment shakes him: "Seeing a parent albatross gagging up a toothbrush changed my worldview. In my mental map, society no longer stops at the borders of shorelines, or of species. The world is no longer large enough for that" (Safina 2002, "Midway"). Although Safina pictures this moment as a compressing of distance, a rejection of the sizable gap that human exceptionalism imposes between humans and seabirds, this moment also embraces the scale of plastic pollution, sea, and distance in the thick way that Zach Horton discusses. Humans must struggle to comprehend that distance as bridged by plastic, and mourn the connections between seabirds and their chicks, and seabirds and their futures, severed by instruments as various as toothbrushes and fishing lines entangled in their guts and their lives. Safina uses this moment to embody his understanding that albatrosses and humans alike are in the process of dying from the wasting of the seas.

At least since Coleridge's *The Rime of the Ancient Mariner*, the albatross has been an uneasy reminder of death in Western literature, although Coleridge himself might not have meant to establish a kinship of mortality between birds and seabirds; rather, though "the albatross has a central role in the poem as the innocent victim of the Mariner's unmotivated violence, the focus was more on the spiritual and emotional states the Mariner experienced in the course of his ship's journey" (Barwell 2014, chap. 2). And notably, it is the already-dead albatross that is hung around the Mariner's neck as a reminder of his sin—like a crucifix, a relic of a death that has already happened. The albatross in Coleridge's poem has little transition between the dead and the living states, little "dying," which in turn leaves little room for the Mariner or the other sailors to mourn it. It is, in fact, possible to argue that the punishment for the Mariner's killing of the albatross was a "disproportionate consequence" (Barwell 2014, chap. 2), and that the death toll of sailors was useless, given that it could not bring back the dead bird. Safina's writing in *Eye of the Albatross*, in contrast, presents albatrosses and other seabirds as in the process of living, and thus, in the process of dying, as his story of the bird parent presenting a toothbrush to its chick illustrates. Capable of being mortal, they are also capable of being saved, and of being something other than relics of extinction.

I have chosen to consider *Eye of the Albatross* with Safina's earlier book *Song for the Blue Ocean*, which examines the decline of tuna and other fish species and the human communities that depended on them, because these books "tease out the various ways in which loss matters, sometimes drawing distant listeners into a sense of felt connection and so affective involvement in a loss" (van Dooren 2014, 141). Those who might not feel much about seabird losses can be affected by the narrative of human communities that decline and suffer loss because of overfishing and plastic waste in the oceans. Safina's narratives, which are organized by places and maps rather than by numbers as Cramer's is, also work together to give a sense of the immense scales of distance involved and the necessity to continue to think about them.

Song for the Blue Ocean begins with Safina's investigation of the market for bluefin tuna, specifically how it touches on New England fishing communities; turns to a narrative of the losses for salmon and humans in the Pacific Northwest; and looks at how the market for reef fish in various South Pacific islands has depleted local islanders' lives and poisoned coral as well as depriving fish of their lives and freedom. Bluefin tuna were such a valued ingredient for sushi in Japan that a single large fish could sell for hundreds of thousands of dollars, and so they were overfished—which also affected seabirds, some species of which depend on tuna to drive prey fish toward the surface of the water for them (Safina 1997, "The Gulf of Maine"). The collapse of not only the tuna fishery but others, like that for cod along the New England and northeastern Canadian coast, damaged numerous human communities and made them mortal, as they entered the long process of dying of "widespread unemployment" (Safina 1997, "Ogunquit"). Safina blames lack of regulation by bodies charged with protecting the fish, because of focus on temporary and short-term profit instead of a sustainable life for the communities involved, and includes a quotation casting the approach of apparent extinction for the fish in the mode of the passenger pigeon and the dodo, both extinct birds (Safina 1997, "Ogunquit"). Birds here serve as a natural symbol of death and mortality, in this case finished mortality. Safina and the congressman he quotes want to keep the fish and fishing communities from joining the dead.

Safina also traces the journey of bluefin tuna from their spawning grounds in the Gulf of Mexico to the Northeast Atlantic coast and other places where they will feed, become food, and assist other species, like seabirds, to feed

(Safina 1997, "Ogunquit"). While no human can journey with the bluefin, understanding the immense distances involved—and the fact that few young tuna grow up to produce the immense adults that humans and seabirds alike rely on—makes empathy and mourning active. If "we do productive work in undermining human exceptionalism by drawing our own responses to death into an evolutionary continuum" (van Dooren 2014, 136), those like Safina make that work even more productive. They write science-informed narratives that show how *lack* of mourning, and how the conviction that species like bluefin tuna will always be alive to serve human needs, push those species ever close to the brink of motionless death where they will no longer move across the immense distances of migration. Migrating fish, the foraging seabirds that depend on them, and the human fishers who continually increase distance traveled to kill the few survivors of once-immense fish stocks will all suffer consequences in the future of not being seen as kin now.

Distance is also a feature of Safina's *Eye of the Albatross,* which intersperses the travels of a female Laysan albatross, "Amelia," in her efforts to feed her chick, with Safina's own travels to islands like Midway, important seabird nesting grounds, and Alaska, where Safina works with a human fishery under threat of closure if they harm too many albatrosses of the rare short-tailed species (Safina 2002, "Working in Overdrive"). Amelia is fitted with a transmitter to track her positions and distance traveled while in flight (Safina 2002, "Bonding"), an innovation that has only recently become possible; before this, seabirds spent so much time out of sight of land and traveled such immense distances that their lives were essentially unknown outside of the rare times they were on shore, especially since earlier technology was affected adversely by seawater (Brooke 2018, 18). Safina explains that attaching a transmitter to Amelia "let Amelia draw me a map of her world so I could visit her country and its neighboring nations populated by other beings. From what I started seeing, it seemed to me that the basic struggles within the lives of many animals and of people differ mainly in detail" (Safina 2002, "Preface"). While always remembering that "the map *is not* the territory it represents" (Korzybski 1933, 58, emphasis in original), we can also know that "if correct, it has a *similar structure* to the territory, which accounts for its usefulness" (Korzybski 1933, 58, emphasis in original). This similarity of structure is what interests Safina and what allows for kinship with seabirds in place of a facile statement that seabirds and humans are either affected in identical ways by mortality or too separate to permit relation. Safina enters Amelia's world imaginatively in creative nonfiction passages interwoven among those of his own experience, recounting Amelia's travels, why she lingers in a particular area as opposed to another, and how she perceives her food.

This mixture of creative nonfiction, narrative based on personal experience, and narrative based on scientific information, allows the different genres of writing to empower one another, such as when Safina discusses what Amelia might smell as she travels, based on scientific discoveries about the powerful sense of smell albatrosses and other "tubenosed" seabirds have (Safina 2002, "Letting Go"). This makes the albatross's attempt to feed her chick, disrupted by the toothbrush, all the more upsetting and brings humans and seabirds closer in the kinship of mortality. It might be tempting to think that seabirds as big and long-lived as albatrosses, capable of traveling such immense distances as 917 miles in two days (Safina 2002, "Letting Go"), would be separated comfortably from humans, not only in the sense of human exceptionalism but also in that they could be immune to our killing of the oceans. Safina's narrative aims to crush this possibility and show how closely tied we are despite the distance. We cannot fly hundreds of wind-borne miles as the albatross does, but we can and must try to understand those distances, that great sense of scale, to understand their dying and, if we can, stem it. Admiration is not enough; neither is gathering the relics of the dead. At one point, Safina describes a memorial ritual for short-tailed albatrosses held by ornithologist Dr. Hiroshi Hasegawa, who labored for decades to restore the species, slaughtered by the millions for their feathers and oil (Safina 2002, "Working in Overdrive"). After gathering "some of the numerous albatross bones from the surrounding ground, he placed them gently on a large stone beside two memorial cairns, lit candles and incense, and knelt. As an offering to the spirits of the millions of dead albatrosses, on the stone he poured seawater for their drink, and set out dried squid and flyingfish" (Safina 2002, "Working in Overdrive"). But the memorial would not have been important if it was the only effort Hasegawa made for albatrosses. Instead, he labored on the island of Torishima to replant native grass species, smooth the land to encourage nesting success, and lure the remaining albatrosses back with decoys and recordings of mating calls (Safina 2002, "Working in Overdrive"). Hasegawa could not construct the memorial and consider his mourning done; he had to work for the mortal, not only the dead. It is for his work in keeping short-tailed albatrosses among the living that Safina writes, "We salute you, Hiroshi" (Safina 2002, "Working in Overdrive"), with perhaps an echo of the Roman salute supposedly used by gladiators to the emperor, "We who are about to die salute you" (Yale University Art Gallery 2021). We who are about to die, who are dying, who are living, everyone, birds and humans, must salute those who take the kinship of mortality seriously and continue to try to stave off the day when the mourning finishes.

Safina ends his book with ruminations on four flights. Three of them, Amelia's, her chick's, and Safina's as he leaves French Frigate Shoals, are successful; the fourth, that of several young albatrosses who take off from the island only to land in the atoll's lagoon and be eaten by tiger sharks, is not (Safina 2002, "Learning and Luck"). Mortality is always close to both humans and seabirds in the dying world we have created; even the plane that takes Safina away must land carefully so as not to strike any albatrosses on the island's only runway (Safina 2002, "Learning and Luck"). Safina reflects, "Are we not little kindred isles adrift a sea of time, on a conveyor of space?" (Safina 2002, "Learning and Luck"), and glances ahead to the inevitable end of being kindred, of being alive: "We are sucked back in, to be reintegrated, recast in the continuing saga of our singular island home afloat the oceanic universe" (Safina 2002, "Learning and Luck"). We cannot conquer immense scales of time and space, but must bridge them with empathy and kinship, accepting that seabird lives are worth mourning, that we are all kindred isles of mortality.

REFERENCES

Alaimo, Stacy. 2016. *Exposed: Environmental Politics and Pleasures in Posthuman Times.* Minneapolis: University of Minnesota Press. Kindle.

Barwell, Graham. 2014. *Albatross.* London: Reaktion. Kindle.

Brooke, Michael. 2018. *Far From Land: The Mysterious Lives of Seabirds.* Princeton: Princeton University Press. Kindle.

Cokinos, Christopher. 2009. *Hope is the Thing with Feathers: A Personal Chronicle of Vanished Birds.* New York: TarcherPerigee. Kindle.

Cramer, Deborah. 2015. *The Narrow Edge: A Tiny Bird, an Ancient Crab, and an Epic Journey.* New Haven: Yale University Press. Kindle.

Crownshaw, Rick. 2017. "Climate Change Fiction and the Future of Memory: Speculating on Nathaniel Rich's *Odds Against Tomorrow.*" *Resilience: A Journal of the Environmental Humanities* 4, no. 2–3 (Spring-Fall): 127–46. doi:10.5250/resilience.4.2-3.0127

Dobrin, Sidney I. 2021a. *Blue Ecocriticism and the Oceanic Imperative.* New York: Routledge. Kindle.

———. 2021b. "Where is the Ocean?" Features. Last modified April 12, 2021. https://www.asle.org/features/where-is-the-ocean/

Gershwin, Lisa-Ann. 2016. *Jellyfish: A Natural History.* Chicago: University of Chicago Press. Kindle.

Goodell, Jeff. 2017. *The Water Will Come: Rising Seas, Sinking Cities, and the Future of Civilization.* New York: Little, Brown and Co. Kindle.

Greenberg, Joel. 2014. *A Feathered River Across the Sky: The Passenger Pigeon's Flight to Extinction.* New York: Bloomsbury. Kindle.

Horton, Zach. 2019. "The Trans-Scalar Challenge of Ecology." *ISLE: Interdisciplinary Studies in Literature and Environment* 26, no. 1 (Winter): 5–26. doi:10.1093/isle/isy079

Jarvis, Brooke. 2018. "The Insect Apocalypse is Here: What Does It Mean for the Rest of Life on Earth?" *The New York Times Magazine*, November 27, 2018. https://www.nytimes.com/2018/11/27/magazine/insect-apocalypse.html

Korzybksi, Alfred. 1933. *Science and Sanity: An Introduction to Non-Aristotelian Systems and General Semantics*. New York: International Non-Aristotelian Publishing.

Lanham, J. Drew. 2018. "Forever Gone: How Bird Lives and Black Lives Intertwine Under the Long Shadow of History." *Orion Magazine*, Spring 2018. https://orionmagazine.org/ article/forever-gone/

Miller, Sarah. 2019. "Heaven or High Water: Selling Miami's Last 50 Years." *Popula*, April 2, 2019. https://popula.com/2019/04/02/heaven-or-high-water/

Otto, Stacy. 2014. "A Garden from Ashes: The Post-9/11 Manhattan City-Shrine, the Triangle Fire Memorial March, and the Educative Value of Mourning." *Journal of Social History* 47, no. 3 (Spring): 573-92. http://www.jstor.org/stable/43305950

Safina, Carl. 2002. *Eye of the Albatross: Visions of Hope and Survival*. New York: Holt Paperbacks. Kindle.

———. 1997. *Song for the Blue Ocean: Encounters Along the World's Coasts*. New York: Holt Paperbacks. Kindle.

Van Dooren, Thom. 2014. *Flight Ways: Life and Loss at the Edge of Extinction*. New York: Columbia University Press. Kindle.

Yale University Art Gallery. 2021. "Ave Caesar! *Morituri te salutant* (Hail Caesar! We Who Are about to Die Salute You)." European Art Collection. https://artgallery.yale.edu/ collections/objects/9187

Chapter 12

Window Collisions in Contemporary American Poetry

Calista McRae

The most famous literary window collision appears in a poem within a novel: Vladimir Nabokov's *Pale Fire* (1962). Its opening couplet remembers a "waxwing slain / By the false azure in the windowpane," with a rhyme that tidily binds glass to one of its consequences (Nabokov 1989, 33). As the poem's fictional editor matter-of-factly spells out, these lines depict "a bird knocking itself out, in full flight, against the outer surface of a glass pane in which a mirrored sky [. . .] presents the illusion of continued space" (Nabokov 1989, 73). Wild birds see the illusions of glass as sky or as shelter, and, when they fly to it, most die on impact. Those who survive are left concussed. Some have wing fractures, broken beaks, or bruised eyes. Because of untreated glass, between 365 and 988 million birds die each year in the United States by colliding with glass (Loss 2014, 18). It is thus unsurprising that window collisions appear again and again in late twentieth- and early twenty-first-century American literature: collisions have become part of our lives, even if we have not consciously noticed.

This chapter explores the handling of window collisions in recent poetry. Songbirds—tiny, beautiful, normally able to sing and fly at heights humans can only dream of—appear frequently in metaphors. When people literally make contact with a bird, by picking it up off the ground, the poems they produce speak to the emotive power of the window collision: it can work as a subdued objective correlative, or, in other words, a pointed deflection of feeling. The collision presents aesthetic challenges: the emotions it provokes can border on cliché or on rhetoric that is still deprecated in mainstream literary criticism. And the collision also points to a challenge that extends beyond poems: how to contextualize the affecting, personal encounter alongside other, more insidious problems birds now face. My chapter, beginning with incidental depictions and moving to poems in which collisions are the main subject, explores this mixture of aesthetic, ethical, and rhetorical problems. It also indirectly considers questions relevant to writing in the environmental humanities more broadly: How does one evaluate a poem to which one's primary response is far from neutral? How does one critique poems when the text under consideration seems to involve a real-world misunderstanding about window collisions? Though poetry is still considered a genre far removed from more-social worlds, the poems gathered here entwine with problems and reactions that bear on our relation to those worlds.

A few years before Nabokov published *Pale Fire,* Robert Frost took up birds and glass in a six-line poem entitled "Questioning Faces": a "winter owl" checks her flight and turns at the last minute to avoid colliding with a window. The poem emblematizes window collisions in that it lets us get closer to a bird than we usually can. In its first couplet, when the owl suddenly tilts sideways "to [. . .] save herself" (Frost 1995, 456), we are so close as to see from the owl's perspective. Catching at her sudden realization that she is about to confront an object she should not hit, these lines understand an owl as having a mind and a "self."

When the owl swerves, plumage normally unseen becomes visible, fleetingly. The view and perspective shift slightly to the other side of the window so that the bird's wings, illuminated and tinted red by the sunset, are glimpsed by the "glassed-in children." Frost compresses an intense number of sensory polarities: cold outdoors and warmth inside; extremely swift action and a stationary audience; draining color and gathering dusk; hard glass and soft feathers. The owl is both in motion—gone by the poem's end—and a static "display," like a specimen in a natural history museum. For a second, the startled, transfixed observers (those actually "glassed-in") see the undersides of a wing, nearly able to feel the softness of "underdown and quill" on a startled, formidable raptor. The poem, like the encounter, ends almost as quickly as it begins; appropriately, this six-line poem about a sudden turn includes a turn. It is as if it cuts everything out of a sonnet except the volta that—in many sonnets—appears at the start of the last six lines.

Frost describes an increasingly uncommon exchange of glances. In "Why Look at Animals?", John Berger reconstructs what was, prior to modernity, the "look between animal and man," a "similar, but not identical, abyss of non-comprehension" felt when human and nonhuman animals met each other's eyes (Berger 1980, 5). That gaze has largely vanished today; as animals become rarer, they become something to observe, so that "what we know about them is an index of our power, and thus an index of what separates us from them" (Berger 1980, 16). The looking in most windowstrike poems is, necessarily, even more lopsided. But the owl retains some power, seeing the glassed-in children from both outside and inside. Frost doesn't give the owl a species label: she escapes being classified as one of the "objects of our ever-extending knowledge" (Berger 1980).

Frost and Nabokov write as window collisions begin to occur more widely. As Nadia Berenstein (2015) relays in "Deathtraps in the Flyways: Electricity, Glass and Bird Collisions in Urban North America, 1887–2014," the late nineteenth century's progress in electrical engineering was followed by developments in glass: large transparent or reflective glass facades became possible on a new scale by the mid-twentieth century. Each season, this glass takes a varyingly hidden toll. Throughout the United States, window collisions occur mainly during fall and spring migrations, and are most intense in the hours just after daybreak (though birds continue to collide throughout the day, while seeking food or after being startled by human activity). The number of birds who hit the ground and vanish before being documented is high: some are carried off by cats, gulls, crows, and raptors, all of whom can come to recognize a particular building as a good site for prey. And most other carcasses are removed as soon as they are noticed by a person connected with the building, whether a homeowner or manager. At office buildings, for example, the people who most often see the consequences of glass are guards and especially custodians, who sweep sidewalks early before residents emerge or employees arrive.

In cities, almost always those who do see window collisions or their aftermath are pedestrians. Morgan Parker's first book, *Other People's Comfort Keeps Me Up at Night*, repeatedly notices birds in situations that suggest windowstrikes, though the connection isn't spelled out. In one early poem, birds make a surreal appearance: "seven birds have fallen dead at my feet / right out of the sky" (Parker 2015, 3). While the poem takes self-performance as one of its subjects, and intimates that the speaker herself could have been supernaturally responsible for these birds, the sense of fatefulness also makes sense in the actual world. When even one bird lands at your feet "right out of the sky," it sticks with you as a bizarre portent. If the incident is rooted in a real event, the seven birds who fall near the speaker could be a gregarious species, like cedar waxwings—who tend to hurtle through the air in groups, calling to each other as they go, and who are more likely to hit glass near each other. Perhaps Parker once walked past a glass-heavy building during a fallout, when the intensity of collisions can be so great that birds essentially collide simultaneously. Or these incidents might not have been simultaneous but cumulative, from one structure passed multiple times during the long autumn migration in New York. A similarly inexplicable dead bird appears later in *Other People's Comfort*, when the speaker sees "another bird dead head / in a snow pile dull claws / in the air" (Parker 2015, 48). The disjointed, percussive style gets at something glimpsed only for a few off-putting seconds. Instead of lingering over detail or culminating in an epiphany, the poem moves on, as a pedestrian might continue down the street after a moment of consternation. But before the subject changes, the speaker imagines what the bird might say: a mordant "what the fuck." This sentiment seems implicitly shared by the observer, who has seen too many dead birds.

These passages from Parker exemplify the *likely* window collision in contemporary poetry. The link between glass and its byproducts is not spelled out (in the hundreds of poems that come across dead birds, as in the actual world, the observer may attribute the death to West Nile Virus or poison). These subsidiary window collisions are not discussed explicitly but are glancing, and often embedded within metaphor. In "Boys' Bodies in Flight (are also a kind of text)," for example, Patrick Rosal indirectly compares growing children to "small bodies / crashing into glass" (Rosal 2018, 22). Until the figurative collision, the children he sees are lively, gregarious, and unaware of how they are threatened.

In "how many of us have them?", Danez Smith draws a correspondence between birds and the precarious lives of black children and adults in the United States. The poem is sparked by seeing "two boys—yes, black" as they cycle by laughing and playing (Smith 2018, 520). From there, Smith's speaker meditates on close friends and the loss of one. Mourning takes place through a game of the dozens: "I got a crush on each one of your dumb faces / smashing into my heart like idiot cardinals into glass" (Smith 2018, 521). The simile fits with the poem's compression of love, friendship, jocular insults, and understated pain. Though birds hit glass at high speeds with great force, the simile exposes where the correspondence *ends*: the speaker's heart feels these collisions. And the death mourned around the poem's edges delicately links to the collisions: the mournful metaphor "my friends / is some birds" is mitigated by the comic heckling of "some chicken-head muhfuckas" (Smith 2018, 522).

The windowstrikes suggest how the phenomenon of birds hitting glass has worked itself into American culture. In Dexter Booth's elegy for his grandmother, birds are a part of ordinary life; their "shit polka dots / my car" (Booth 2017, 4). While omnipresent, their numbers seem to diminish: Booth writes of "an emptying sky, / everything with wings restless and sinking" (Booth 2017, 4), in a line that could suggest a gathering storm or a broader loss. On a windy night, imagining grackles that "fall from the clouds," Booth's speaker faintly invokes windowstrikes in a metaphor that sees grackles as "bloated bodies that rise to the surface after a shipwreck" and as "reverse firecrackers that explode when they hit the glass dome of night" (Booth 2017, 4). Although buried in layers of figurative language, these images are likely informed by memories of birds hitting glass.

In the poems considered so far, the situation remains somewhat vague: either the cause or consequence of the windowstrikes goes unarticulated.

In the next set of poems, collisions are treated more directly, though they are not main subjects. Victoria Chang introduces collisions explicitly at the conclusion of a poem from her fourth book, *Barbie Chang*. "Barbie Chang Can't Stop Watching" opens with the protagonist following the *Pao v. Kleiner Perkins* trial (in 2015, Ellen Pao sued her former employer, a venture capital firm, for gender discrimination). The core of the poem considers how frequent injustice may be taken for granted. At the poem's end, Chang's speaker describes an empty office building, one that—despite being vacant—kills several birds each day. The unnamed structure could be one of countless office buildings around the United States: "dead / birds lie in the grass new // ones each day hit the glass" (Chang 2017, 17). The avian dead are an inadvertent product of either imperceptiveness or callousness, and of capitalism, as emphasized by the deliberately stilted syntax of "new // ones each day hit the glass." Like Parker, Chang stresses repetitiveness: here birds collide morning after morning. Like Parker, she avoids vivifying detail: they are simply "birds." And like Parker, she captures a realistic scenario: in both suburbs and cities, commercial buildings designed to signal wealth and power often have floor-to-ceiling glass walls on their lowest floors. In "Barbie Chang Can't Stop Watching," which identifies window collisions as a form of anthropogenic death, the collision holds ethical weight. The gratuitousness of the deaths is underlined by the lack of people: nobody uses the office, and nobody sees the birds. Though unoccupied, the building will do damage as long as it stands unaltered. When Chang's speaker remarks "the same expression // forever frozen" on each bird (Chang 2017, 17), that repeated expression underscores the number of casualties; here death is not a one-off but something permanent and replicable.

The implicit but pointed reproach in Chang's conclusion brings abiding questions about poetry and its relation to rhetoric. Songbirds have long been poignant symbols in poetry, and indeed persistent figures *for* poetry in English, evoking some combination of words like *inspired, transcendent, ephemeral, melancholy, private,* and *beautiful*. The bond between birds and poems solidifies over the Romantic era, as poets hear the songbird's music over the mundane. Consider the speaker of John Keats's "Ode to a Nightingale," listening to the bird sing in "full-throated ease" (Keats 1820, 107), who declares he will "fly to thee" "on the viewless wings of Poesy" (Keats 1820, 109). For many poets, the union of art and birdsong persists: the longstanding idea that birds embody unachievable beauty and transcendence clashes with the sudden sighting of one dead or in distress. The birds of window collisions are earthbound and songless—and all too literal. The pathos of a collision is somewhat overdetermined. It risks a clichéd sentimentality, and even quick metaphorical references can become a shorthand for emotion.

It is also worth reviewing the expectations and critical desiderata surrounding the genre in which these birds appear. As lyric poetry becomes defined as a deeply personal, intensely expressive utterance, avian song represents what poets long for and cannot achieve. When writers project a "pure expressive capacity" (Jackson 2005, 27) onto birdsong, it is of a piece with theorizations of poetry as intensely subjective. Percy Bysshe Shelley describes a poet as "a nightingale, who sits in darkness and sings to cheer its own solitude with sweet sounds" (Shelley 1923, 135). The idea of poetry that springs from and speaks to one's "own solitude" becomes central to twentieth-century definitions of poetry. Poetry is free of any vulgar awareness of an audience, and, indeed, of any social or historical context. As codified by mainstream criticism and pedagogy, it is supposed to be the private utterance of a universal human self. Poems tainted by trying to reach someone are not poems at all. W. B. Yeats distinguishes poetry from rhetoric, declaring that we "make out of the quarrel with others, rhetoric, but out of the quarrel with ourselves, poetry. Unlike the rhetoricians, who get a confident voice from remembering the crowd they have won or may win, we sing amid our uncertainty" (Yeats 1918).

Yet a window collision frequently draws a poem toward rhetoric: it entails the emotive force of seeing a vulnerable and culturally significant animal hurt concretely by human activity. Rather than the ambiguity Yeats seeks, a collision can risk outrage or didacticism: described even neutrally, it can resemble an argument with a building manager rather than with oneself. Thus, for poets, a collision is a demanding subject.

The import of the deeply subdued window collision in W. S. Merwin's "Shore Birds" is one of reproach—tacit but forceful—that occurs in the context of large-scale population decline. Merwin depicts a flock of unnamed shorebirds taking off to migrate, "pulled" by moon and earth. Soon they reach developed areas, where "the glass curtains kept falling around them / as they flew in search of their place before / they were anywhere" (Merwin 1999, 124). Instead of "their place," the habitat where they have been nesting for millennia, they are confronted by the "glass curtains" that suddenly cut off their routes. Because regular glass is essentially invisible to birds, Merwin portrays these structures as just suddenly there, as obstacles that randomly materialize with no warning. He only briefly sketches the toll, noting that the migrants "passed the tower lights where some vanished": the deaths are confined to a relative clause, and glass is one of many threats, such as poaching and hunting. The poem ends by bringing together two perspectives in an intricately hypothetical clause, in which the speaker compares his memories of their former numbers to the few birds who now experience the shore at the end of the summer. Merwin frames the poem with the cumulative loss he feels, but also imagines what the shorebirds may experience on their journey. Implicitly, their numbers decline because of human actions.

Another complex network of guilt and loss appears in Srikanth Reddy's serial prose poem *Underworld Lit*. Reddy introduces window collisions when passing traffic ruffles the pages the narrator is grading. The pages "flutter and settle like a stunned wren rearranging itself on my lap" (Reddy 2020, 4). This simile resonates later, as the narrator and his spouse fix the silhouette of a raptor onto their glass door. In the real world, however, the raptor silhouette does not stop birds from colliding with glass, because the birds get used to it and because it does not break up the illusion of open space. There are likely to be more "stunned wren[s]" there in the future. And besides, just as the couple puts it up, they hear "a feathery thud against the window next door" (Reddy 2020, 179)—a sound that calls to mind the relative uselessness of individual acts, as well as the frequency of window collisions at single-family homes (a point returned to at the end of this chapter).

Birds marked by the Anthropocene recur in *Underworld Lit*: the one buried in the yard to teach a daughter about death; the initially bizarre metaphor that compares a pyramid to "the broken black beak of a badly buried bird" (Reddy 2020, 93); and the "burning papers" that "fluttered out like hurt birds from the window" (41). Reddy depicts the ways humans are indirectly responsible for harm even when they are passive (e.g., funding wars through their taxes or doing nothing about climate catastrophe), how ineffective their attempts are, and how difficult it is to recognize the consequences. Through multiplicity, however, the poem avoids moralizing. This heavily allusive book spans not only the poignancy of the small, stunned wren, but the alliterative grotesqueness of the broken beak. The leitmotif of windowstrikes contributes to a meditation on what one person can or can't or won't do, and on the knowledge that poetry holds little power in contemporary culture.

Window collisions often entangle with guilt. For instance, Warren Woessner's "What's An Angel Like?" features melancholic culpability. The speaker's young grandson asks the title's question. When the speaker tries to answer, he first turns to swallows, who "cut the sky to pieces with sharp wings" (Woessner 2021). He remembers a swallow that hits glass outside his building. The poem turns to the kind of detail that stems from an act of witnessing: the swallow's body landed on the roof just beyond his window, where it remained in sight for months, "one wing / fluttering—like it could take off / any minute, or at least blow away" (Woessner 2021). This grisly, haunting memory causes the speaker to seek a different analogy; he thinks next of a snowy egret, a bird perhaps less likely to hit windows. This poem partly exemplifies how our longstanding cultural associations with birds are under new pressures because of what we have done to them. Here the figurative idea of birds' proximity to angels gives way to the all-too literal and present. And the poem as a whole considers, indirectly, how to convey the damage done by humans: the speaker ends by thinking of what else his grandson might ask, and though the speaker's open-ended final line—"won't be so easy to explain"—is technically about subjects other than extinction or climate change, it nevertheless evokes these topics.

The windowstrike is called up by a question about angels in Woessner's poem; in many others, the strike gives rise to metaphor, as demonstrated by Michael Collier's "Bird Crashing into Window." Collier's speaker recalls how cartoons show birds getting knocked out. For a minute, their heads are temporarily flattened and accompanied by "a carousel of stars, asterisks, and question marks" in "a caption bubble"; then they are back to normal (Collier 2006, 11). But the bird in front of him, on a porch floor, does not bounce back; its neck appears broken since "its head hangs like a closed hinge." Collier's speaker documents what may be the last few minutes of the bird's life, noticing how it still blinks but cannot stop "scrabbl[ing]." After this close, graphic look at a stunned bird, the speaker glances over at a friend sitting on the porch. Though Collier does not make an explicit connection between the bird and the friend—they are connected merely by their proximity—the friend is very ill. As if averting his eyes from both timeframes of likely death, the speaker then looks out the window, to the turbulent natural world renewing outside. In one final sudden cut, "Bird Crashing into Window" ends with three futile imperatives to someone who can neither understand nor act on them: "'Get up! Fly away!' / my caption urges. 'Get up, if you can!'" (Collier 2006, 11). Although the poem's title focuses on the collision, the understated way that Collier places the friend in the middle of the poem shifts the emphasis to the friend's situation, as though the collision forces the speaker to recognize the severity of his friend's illness. This poem demonstrates a stylistic peril of collisions—that a comparison made between kinds of damage could open the poem to cliché—and an attempt to offset that peril by reaching for less-expected tonalities, here by splicing sorrow with comics.

The symbolic and emotional potency of window collisions is also suggested by their role in a novel, a novel that has affinities with lyric in its lack of traditional plot and in its centripetal force: Teju Cole's *Open City*. In the final paragraphs, the narrator looks at the Statue of Liberty and reflects on its previous history as a functional lighthouse, one that attracted birds in large numbers. After fourteen hundred birds died at the lighthouse in one night in 1888—some circled the torch until exhausted and drenched, others hit its panels—the island's superintendent tracked subsequent deaths systematically. Cole closes by echoing the neutral statistics of his source:

> The average, Colonel Tassin estimated, was about twenty birds per night, although the weather and the direction of the wind had a great deal to do with

the resulting harvest. Nevertheless, the sense persisted that something more troubling was at work. On the morning of October 13, for example, 175 wrens had been gathered in, all dead of the impact, although the night just past hadn't been particularly windy or dark. (Cole 2011, 259)

Unlike the poems just discussed, there is not much explicitly subjective here. Instead, Cole stays close to Tassin's own account as published in contemporary newspapers: "On clear nights there are none or very few, but on dark nights the harvest is very large. On the 12th [of October] 175 wrens were gathered in, although it was not a particularly dark or windy night" ("Killed By Liberty's Torch" 1887, 2). *Open City* ends quantitatively, enigmatically, and a bit flatly, with a sentence grounded in the nuances of what might have caused the volume. And yet the affecting fate of these tiny birds, with "their dark wings and throats, their pale bodies and tireless little hearts" (Cole 2011, 4), comes through; the passage attests to the emotive intensity of collisions. This lyrical novel, like so many short poems, thus registers the affective force of window collisions.

A third set of poems makes collisions explicitly central. Anne Pierson Wiese's "Birds Hitting Glass," for example, is grounded in naturalistic detail: after a pigeon flies into the glass of a bus shelter, Wiese's speaker remembers other windowstrikes, among them the "half thud, half flap" of a hawk, the "sleek, freckle-feathered, hollow-boned / body" of a partridge, and, in a long penultimate sentence, chickadees foraging dangerously near the plate glass face of a library (Wiese 2008). For most of the poem, the speaker's attention is on the birds themselves, and on the problem itself; near the end, with the chickadees, she describes the library, which opens out into a stark delineation of the threat: a low-rise building with foliage nearby. The sense of hazard is accurate, since a structure's surroundings do affect the windowstrike rate (buildings with native plants may attract birds; areas that seem to promise but in fact lack real shelter or nourishment also attract them, then force them back to flight out of necessity). But "Birds Hitting Glass" exemplifies how a poem centered on an actual incident still draws to metaphor. Only the poem's final lines turn to a moral, admitting that "The shock of slamming up against / reality happens more slowly when you don't have wings" (Wiese 2008). While this insight works on a literal level (that humans don't usually kill themselves when they walk into glass doors), it demonstrates how a window collision, especially in a poem, gravitates toward a significance beyond the solitary incident. Because of the symbolic resonances of birds, it is almost impossible to write about a window collision without being pulled toward broader reflection.

Near the end of Jorie Graham's bird-filled *Swarm*, a poem's speaker hears an actual windowstrike: the clipped opening line, "Painful to look up," is followed by a correction: "No. Painful to look out" (Graham 2000, 59). The speaker hears the collision, and she hopes her ears are wrong as she did not hear it hit the ground. Eventually, though, she finds the body, still surrounded by life: "there is sun all over it" (Graham 2000, 61). Dismay is followed by avoidance, followed by an unstated, conflicted emotion. Graham's poem is one of many that documents the feelings of the person who saw or heard it happen. Because you are likely to witness a collision where you spend the most time—that is, your own home—those feelings often involve consternation, regret, and denial. And they are difficult to express successfully in a poem, partly because those feelings are fairly predictable. Graham's elliptical sentences, which record the impulse not to acknowledge what has occurred, avoid predictability through the sheer amount of material they bring in: not only the collision but a welter of other images, which do not necessarily relate to the dead bird but to the other thoughts and impressions in the speaker's head. This multiplicity is also present in Reddy's *Underworld Lit*: one way to handle collisions is to disperse them.

In "for the bird who flew against our window one morning and broke his natural neck," Lucille Clifton uses the opposite approach: extreme brevity. Though the poem is about her reaction, it avoids any explicit reference to emotion. Her speaker sees the bird's death as "a crash of / birdpride," a phrase rhymes to "his suicide" (Clifton 1972). Initially, this language suggests that the bird hit glass deliberately; but, if he breaks his neck, it is unlikely to be territorial aggression, and thus unlikely to be intentional. Accordingly, Clifton's speaker notes how the bird not only "breaks" his neck (as in the long title), but also discerns "the arrogance / of my definitions." The repeated verb compels her to change the way she sees her relations to the nonhuman world: what she thought of as "our window" was, for the dead bird, a "wall." As if the speaker is forced to take responsibility for it herself, the "our window" of the title becomes "my window" in the first line.

Other poems stemming from windowstrikes entail varying ratios of knowledge or confusion. In Nathaniel Bellows's "The Bargain," a step-by-step account of a hummingbird hitting a window on a house, the encounter is permeated by misunderstanding. After the speaker relays how the hummingbird "let me" stroke their plumage, he immediately corrects himself: "No. It / was helpless to keep me from / helping" (Bellows 2013, 313). As with many window collisions, the bird is so stunned as to not react to human touch (which often causes people to think that the bird senses their kindness and trusts them). Correction occurs on a more dramatic scale in the poem's final lines: the speaker, who has been preparing to dispatch the injured bird, realizes they have "somehow lived, / vanished" (Bellows 2013, 314). That the bird has flown off changes the tone of the encounter and poem; but the low recovery rates of window-collision patients—who may succumb to brain swelling days after their crash, even if they are able to fly well soon after the incident—suggest that the hummingbird probably still died.

Bellows's ending thus raises, for me, a problem in reading: that one layer of misunderstanding may not be intentional and yet is hard to ignore. Eamon Grennan's "On a Cape May Warbler Who Flew Against My Window" raises other critical difficulties. In the first stanza, the speaker knows enough about the natural world to note that the warbler, a "she" rather than an "it," flies from a "tall spruce" before breaking her neck (Grennan 1989, 17). After he watches his children bury the warbler, however, he reflects on vulnerability, wondering how to protect "my own young, their migrations" (Grennan 1989, 17). The line of thought here implies that it is impossible to protect warblers—which may be true broadly, in that one person has little control over population-level threats—but the poem's title insists that the speaker owns the window and would therefore be able to protect at least those who migrate through his property.

This poem leaves me hesitant to write about its apparent realization, and so do several other poems here: How to evaluate what might, in part, be misinformed? Is the ineffective raptor silhouette applied in Reddy's *Underworld Lit* a knowing insertion? When the hummingbird in Bellows's poem flies off, are we supposed to read it as wholly affirmative, as a testament to a tiny bird's resilience? Unlike the mistakes discussed in Erica McAlpine's *The Poet's Mistake* (2021), the moments I become stuck on in these poems keep pulling me to real-life consequences. Some of the questions that intrude are not stylistic but logistical, or even moral: Why didn't Collier's speaker do anything to help the bird flailing on the porch floor? (To ask that question here seems more justified than to ask it of Bellows's poem: that collision victims may need medical support even when they can fly is not common knowledge; a few years ago, I didn't know). It could be possible to read almost all of these assertions as deliberate—for instance, Grennan's speaker may self-consciously stage a failure to protect both children and songbirds. And pointing out ignorance or inaccuracy may "com[e] across as too literal or even pedantic" (McAlpine 2021, 11).

This quasi-critical uncertainty is elicited, for instance, by Chard Deniord's "Confession of a Bird Watcher." Deniord begins with a self-consciously poetic image of windows covered in feathers, and of bones in "the flowers" below. His speaker explains: "I have sat at my window now for years and watched a hundred birds / mistake the glass for air and break their necks, wondering what to do, / how else to live among them and keep my view" (Deniord 2015, 12). The sudden move into rhyme—"what to do," "keep my view"—fixes a lack of action to a refusal to mitigate the glass. The speaker, and perhaps the poet as well, may be under the impression that the only solution is to cover the window completely, although this level of misprision seems improbable. Or he may not want to break up the transparency. In the latter case, the poem underscores how even those who are aware of the problem (having watched "a hundred birds" die because they cannot see clear glass) and who own their own houses (and could therefore fix the problem) are reluctant to make changes.

In either case, the poem dramatizes much broader forms of selfishness: the general recognition that humans are selfish, and the more specific recognition that birders often harm birds, whether through immediate intrusions (e.g., disturbing an owl through photography) or more gradual ones (e.g., driving to see rarities, taking flights to other countries). The role of the individual person runs through many of these poems but is complicated by our still-evolving understandings of windowstrikes. Many people who witness collisions may not understand their severity or solutions. In "Confession of a Bird Watcher," though, the speaker does not consider relinquishing even the feeder that attracts the birds.

The poem that comes nearest to an explicit call for action is Margaret Atwood's "Fatal Light Awareness." Atwood takes her title from FLAP, the Toronto-based Fatal Light Awareness Program, but omits "Program," thereby implying both knowledge and a lack of action. The poem begins with self-recrimination, mourning a thrush as "one lovely voice the less" killed "by my laziness: / Why didn't I hang the lattice?" (Atwood 2019). From the one-off death of the thrush, Atwood moves out to make a larger critique of light pollution and contemporary design, laying blame primarily on "the high rises": "music dies / as you fire up your fake sunrises." It is aggressively poetic in terms of assonance and alliteration, but assonance and alliteration are powerful rhetorical devices, too, and the poem's turn to a "you" and "your" brings lyric into contact with persuasion. It ends with collective self-accusation: seeing birds as "melting away," Atwood's speaker asserts that "No bird knows this"— the short lifespans of most birds mean they would not realize their populations are diminishing—but that "we know" and do nothing.

The inaction that Atwood's speaker bewails, and that Grennan's and Deniord's speakers seem to consider the only options, similarly prevails in real life. Often the people with the power to modify buildings—to add seasonal tape or netting, to retrofit them permanently, or to invest in fritted glass in the first place—are far removed from the effects of unaltered glass, do not recognize the collective damage, or do not care about the issue. Developers and building owners tend to prefer more familiar, heavily reflective or transparent materials, on both aesthetic and financial grounds (Hill, 2017; "Wisconsin Developers Sue to Keep Designing Buildings Deadly to Birds," 2021).

More significantly, the popular understanding of window collisions places blame almost entirely on tall, urban structures, despite evidence that birds mainly collide with glass below tree line. While homeowners might see their windows as innocuous, the few strikes a year add up: it is estimated that residences three or fewer stories tall are responsible for about 44 percent of fatalities, and low-rise buildings—between four and eleven stories tall—for about 56 percent (Loss 2014, 8). Fewer than 1 percent of collisions occur at high-rises (Loss 2014, 8).

Atwood's move from the glass of the house to the glass of the supertall thus encapsulates one of the thorniest problems around windowstrikes: "the high rises" take most of the blame, especially in mass media reports. For example, Kaitlyn Parkins, Associate Director of Conservation and Science for NYC Audubon, remarks that "Mass mortality at famous tall buildings gets news coverage, but low and mid-rise buildings are responsible for the vast majority of bird strikes" (@kait_lorraine, 17 September 2021). As of September 2021, there is no Wikipedia page for bird-glass collisions, although there is one for "Bird-skyscraper collisions." Even conservation groups devoted to protecting birds sometimes blame the dense city itself (Jamaica Bay-Rockaway Parks Conservancy, 2021). The narrative of *height* as destructive to birds is quite powerful. Berenstein's wonderful essay on window collisions, for example, begins with a vivid one-sentence paragraph on "what happens when cities get in the way of birds, when artificial bulbs out-burn the stars and windows duplicate the skies" (Nagai et al. 2015, 79). Berenstein emphasizes cities in part because she is interested in public responses to bird collisions, and most concerted responses have been in cities. And she also clearly distinguishes between the problems of light pollution (which attracts migrating birds to cities) and of glass itself. But a slightly later image, of "stilled bodies briefly [coming] to rest beneath the massive structures that arrested their passage" (Nagai et al. 2015, 79), also draws near to conflating glass with height. Though Charlotte Sleigh's preface to Berenstein's essay notes that "indeed high-density urban living is arguably more environmentally responsible than sprawl" (Nagai et al. 2015, 76), one easily could come away with the impression that cities themselves are the menace. My own previous writing on window collisions inadvertently contributed to Twitter-narratives about "how skyscrapers have decimated bird populations" (@poetswritersinc, 6 January 2020).

Thus, the very visibility of window collisions—and the resultant reaction against tall buildings, a reaction that positions density and urbanism as culprits—may exacerbate one of the most insidious problems facing birds, that of habitat loss. A surprising number of environmental advocates fail to realize or articulate that the alternative to urban density is suburban sprawl, a more dire threat. Even if a new single-family home does not literally cut into birds' remaining swamps and fields, it generates a carbon footprint likely to be significantly larger than that of a home in a population-dense area (Jones

2014, 895), and it contributes more to climate change—which has ongoing and increasingly negative effects on almost every species. When writing of window collisions, whether in a poem, in literary studies, or in advocacy, we need to resist potentially misleading references to urban density and to avoid eliding the effects of suburban sprawl.

Collisions ask us to look at individual birds and global statistics. They demand we consider automatic responses, impercipience, and overpowering feelings—and how to circumvent or harness them. They bring questions of style and rhetoric into dialogue with outreach. And they remind us that consideration of human emotion and error can be useful at many intersections among the environmental humanities, wildlife conservation, and design policy—whether at the scale of a single building, a neighborhood, or a municipality as a whole.[1]

NOTE

1. I thank Adam McGee, arts editor at *Boston Review*; Adam made distinct improvements to a shorter essay on window collisions, which appeared there in January 2020. This longer chapter stems from that essay. I am also very grateful to Danette DiMarco and Tim Ruppert for their edits and probing questions.

REFERENCES

Atwood, Margaret. 2019. "Fatal Light Awareness." *LitHub,* July 17. https://lithub.com/fatallightawareness-a-poem-by-margaret-atwood/

Bellows, Nathaniel. 2013. "The Bargain." *The Massachusetts Review* 54 (2): 313–14.

Berenstein, Nadia. "Deathtraps in the Flyways: Electricity, Glass and Bird Collisions in Urban North America, 1887–2014." 2015. In *Cosmopolitan Animals.*, ed. Kaori Nagia, Karen Jones, Donna Landry, Monica Mattfield, Caroline. Rooney, and Charlotte Sleigh et al., 2015. New York: Palgrave Macmillan, 79–92.

Berger, John. 1980. *About Looking.* New York: Vintage.

Booth, Dexter. 2017. "Remedios, Flying a Kite." *Obsidian: Literature in the African Diaspora* 43 (2): 3–5.

Chang, Victoria. 2017. *Barbie Chang.* Port Townsend, WA: Copper Canyon Press.

Clifton, Lucille. 1972. *Good News About the Earth.* New York: Random House.

Cole, Teju. 2011. *Open City.* New York: Random House.

Collier, Michael. 2012. *An Individual History: Poems.* New York: Norton.

Deniord, Chard. 2015. *Interstate.* Pittsburgh: University of Pittsburgh Press.

Frost, Robert. 1995. *Collected Poems, Prose, and Plays.* New York: The Library of America.

Graham, Jorie. 2000. *Swarm.* New York: The Ecco Press.

Grennan, Eamon. 1989. *What Light There Is & Other Poems*. San Francisco: North Point Press, 1989.

Hill, Tim. 2017. "Minnesota Vikings' New Glass-plated Stadium Becomes 'Death Trap' for Birds." *The Guardian*. 28 February. https://www.theguardian.com/sport/2017/feb/28/minnesota-vikings-stadium-deadly-birds-glass

Jackson, Virginia. 2005. *Dickinson's Misery: A Theory of Lyric Reading*. Princeton: Princeton University Press.

Jamaica Bay-Rockaway Parks Conservancy. 2021. "Help Stop Bird Collisions in Jamaica Bay." March 15. https://charity.gofundme.com/o/en/campaign/help-stop-bird-collisions-in-jamaica-bay

Jones, Christopher, and Daniel M. Kammen. 2014. "Spatial Distribution of US Household Carbon Footprints Reveals Suburbanization Undermines Greenhouse Gas Benefits of Urban Population Density." *Environmental Science and Technology* 48 (2): 895–902.

Keats, John. 1820. *Lamia, Isabella, The Eve of St. Agnes, and Other Poems*. London: Taylor and Hessey.

"Killed By Liberty's Torch." 1887. *The Sun*. October 15: 2.

Loss, Scott, Tom Will, Sara S. Loss, and Peter P. Marra. 2014. "Bird-building Collisions in the United States: Estimates of Annual Mortality and Species Vulnerability." *The Condor* 116 (1): 8–23.

Merwin, W. S. 1999. *The River Sound*. New York: Knopf. Kaori Nagai, Donna Landry,

Karen Jones, Monica Mattfield, Caroline Rooney, and Charlotte Sleigh, eds. 2015. *Cosmopolitan Animals*. New York: Palgrave Macmillan.

Nabokov, Vladimir. 1989. *Pale Fire*. New York: Vintage.

Parker, Morgan. 2015. *Other People's Comfort Keeps Me Up at Night*. Denver: Switchback Books.

Rosal, Patrick. 2017. "Boys' Bodies in Flight (are also a kind of text)." *The American Poetry Review* 46 (6): 21–22.

Shelley, Percy Bysshe. 1923. *Poetry and Prose*. Edited by A. M. D. Hughes. Oxford: Oxford University Press.

Smith, Danez. 2018. "how many of us have them?" *Poetry* (March): 520–22.

Wiese, Anne Pierson. 2008. "Birds Hitting Glass." *Pif Magazine* 128 (January). https://www.pifmagazine.com/2008/01/birds-hitting-glass/

"Wisconsin Developers Sue to Keep Designing Buildings Deadly to Birds." 2021. American Bird Conservancy. July 22. https://abcbirds.org/article/wisconsin-developers-sue-to-keep designing-buildings-deadly-to-birds/

Woessner, Warren. 2021. "What's An Angel Like?" *On the Seawall*, May 25. https://www.ronslate.com/whats-an-angel-like/

Yeats, W. B. 1918. *Per Amica Silentia Lunae*. New York: Macmillan.

Section 4

CONSUMERS CONSUMING BIRDS

Chapter 13

"Their Little Brethren of the Air"

Rhetoric of Youth Birding in the United States, 1890s–Present

Laura McGrath

It is little wonder that birds are ubiquitous in American culture, from our songs and children's stories to our state birds and the bald eagle on the Great Seal of the United States. Whether at the shore or in the city, country, or suburbs, birds are our constant companions. Wild yet familiar, we seek closer connection with them through behaviors like bird watching and bird feeding. Given the long history of birding[1] in the United States, discourses related to bird watching and wild bird care and protection provide ample evidence of how esteem for bird life becomes rhetorically significant, shaping public opinion, laws, and approaches to educating and engaging young students.

In this chapter, I focus on the rhetoric of youth birding in the United States between the 1890s and the present, a discourse colored by the values, preoccupations, and prejudices of various time periods but remarkably consistent in its aims and arguments. My analysis examines children's fiction and nonfiction, field guides, periodicals, material for families and educators, and digital resources. Within this literature, bird study is presented as a wholesome, accessible, fun, and life-enhancing pastime for young people, an activity with aesthetic, moral, and practical benefits. Bird study is promoted as an activity that strengthens bonds between children and nature, engages their minds and bodies, and enlists them in protecting America's wildlife and natural resources.

My analysis begins during a heyday of bird study and bird-protection activism, when conservation-minded women and men used state Audubon groups, printed materials, curriculum guides, and youth groups to educate and recruit children to their cause. In the mid-1890s, picking up where George Bird Grinnell left off, "a new Audubon movement [. . .] spearheaded by women" was established for the purpose of wild bird protection (Merchant 2016, 38). This "movement to protect the birds of America and prevent them from being transformed into millinery in such prodigious numbers" required its members to combat "public ignorance regarding the value of birds in the economy of nature and especially to human life" (Marble 1898, 20). One strategy employed by women and men involved in the movement was to educate children about bird life—its beauty, interesting features, and practical importance—while encouraging them to view birds as friends and fellow citizens. By winning the hearts and minds of young people, bird protectionists could strengthen children's connection with nature—a connection weakened by industrialization, city living, and "ignorance"—and increase their desire to protect the creatures they would come to love like neighbors and members of their own human families. With this goal in mind, nature writers, Audubon group members, and other bird protectionists of the 1890s and the early twentieth century authored a prodigious amount of bird-related material for young readers.

Fictional bird stories—often narrated by the birds themselves—were one means of engaging the imagination and eliciting the sympathy of young readers. Three children's books illustrate this common approach and its rhetorical intent: *Citizen Bird* (1897), *Dickey Downy* (1899), and *The Burgess Bird Book for Children* (1919). While these authors endeavored to present accurate information about birds in story form, they also humanized the birds, a technique that proved controversial. On one hand, as Caroline G. Soule (1899) argued in "Humanizing the Birds": "To 'humanize' the birds by ascribing to them human qualities which they do not and cannot possess, is only to misrepresent them, and stories which so humanize them are of no more value, as nature-study or bird-study, than so many fairy-tales" (193). This viewpoint was also articulated by John Burroughs in *Ways of Nature* (1905): "so far as [. . .] writers awaken an interest in the wild denizens of the field and wood, and foster a genuine love of them in the hearts of the young people, so far is their influence good; but so far as they pervert natural history and give false impressions of the intelligence of our animals, catering to a taste that prefers the fanciful to the true and the real, is their influence bad" (14). On the other hand, as *Citizen Bird* author Mabel Osgood Wright (1899) explains: "In teaching children, I believe in striving to humanize the bird as far as is consistent with absolute truth, that the child may, through its own love of home, parents, and its various desires, be able to appreciate the corresponding traits in the bird" (100). Whether humanizing birds is truly "consistent with absolute truth," the sheer number of anthropomorphic birds in stories of this period suggests that the persuasive effect on children was worth the disdain of certain naturalists.

Mabel Osgood Wright and Elliott Coues's (1897) *Citizen Bird: Scenes from Bird-Life in Plain English for Beginners* instructs children on how to conduct bird study and encourages them to develop love and sympathy for their feathered friends. *Citizen Bird*, dedicated to "all boys and girls who love birds and wish to protect them," is told through dialogue among humans ("House People") as well as among bird characters ("Bird People"). The book begins with a conversation between "Bird People" at Orchard Farm who worry over threats like cats and boys who might have "a pocket full of pebbles and a *shooter*" (5). When the story shifts from "Bird People" to "House People," readers learn that naturalist Dr. Roy Hunter has invited his niece and nephew to join him on the farm because they "have seen so little of Nature and the things that creep and crawl and fly" (12). "House People," Uncle Roy explains, "are apt to grow selfish and cruel, thinking they are the only people upon the earth, unless they can sometimes visit the homes of the Beast and Bird Brotherhood, and see that these can also love and suffer and work like themselves" (12). Thus, the young main characters reconnect with nature as they are educated by their uncle and other characters about bird life, methods of bird study, and the importance of bird protection. *Citizen Bird* also includes a justification of its authors' humanization of birds: Young Nat tells his uncle, "It's the way you tell us about birds that makes us remember. You talk as if they were real people," to which Uncle Roy replies, "Birds *are* people, though of another race from ours" (78). Considered together, these excerpts reveal the authors' persuasive strategy: if children observe how birds love, suffer, and work *like* people and are encouraged by adults to see them *as* people, then children can more readily sympathize with birds and are less likely to harm them or to allow others to do so.

Virginia Sharpe Patterson's (1899) *Dickey Downy: The Autobiography of a Bird* uses a bird narrator's harrowing experiences, along with overheard human conversations, to elicit readers' sympathy and provide children with a moral education about the sin of animal cruelty. *Dickey Downy* offers a strong indictment of naughty cats, wicked ladies who wear "hats trimmed with dead birds" (33), cruel boys with their "'savage, brutal impulse to kill'" (188), misguided young people who keep wild birds as pets, and merciless hunters who slaughter birds for the plume trade.[2] Patterson's storytelling is not subtle:

> The quick sharp boom, boom of the guns had been echoing through the swamp for some time, and the men were now coming nearer. The efforts of the poor mother to shield her babies were piteous, but the hunters did not want them. Their scant plumage is worthless for millinery purposes. Possibly the mother might have escaped had she been willing to leave her dear ones; but she would not desert them, and was shot in the breast as the reward of her devotion. The nestlings were left to starve. (101)

Within the story, such memorable scenes of cruelty contrast with moments of human kindness and examples of reformed thinking leading to benevolent action. *Dickey Downy* relies heavily on pathos and uses emotional appeals to encourage young readers to reform their own behaviors and become bird protectionists.

Twenty years after the publication of *Citizen Bird* and *Dickey Downy*, authors continued to forge bonds of sympathy and understanding between children and birds. In fact, Thornton W. Burgess (1919) dedicated his enduringly popular *The Burgess Bird Book for Children* "to the children and the birds of America that the bonds of love and friendship between them may be strengthened." Recognizing that "there is no method of approach to the child mind equal to the story," Burgess created a resource that is "at once a story book and an authoritative handbook" (Preface). In Burgess's book, birds and other creatures do the teaching, with the curious Peter Rabbit playing the role of an inquisitive child. In response to one of Peter's questions about Little Friend the Song Sparrow, Jenny Wren explains,

> It wouldn't do for everybody to like the same kind of a place. He isn't a tree bird, anyway. He likes to be on or near the ground. You will never find his nest much above the ground, not more than a foot or two. Quite often it is on the ground. Of course I prefer Mr. Wren's song, but I must admit that Little Friend has one of the happiest songs of any one I know. Then, too, he is so modest, just like us Wrens. (Chapter 3)

Through the dialogue between birds and other creatures, Burgess accomplishes his goal of providing facts about bird life in an appealing and sometimes humorous way (although little brown wrens may be "modest" in appearance, children will know the character Jenny is anything but humble and unpretentious). In addition to teaching bird facts, Burgess also uses his storytelling to depict human acts of kindness toward birds, such as when Farmer Brown's boy removes a "cruel twig" from Redcoat the Tanager's shoulder (Chapter 28). Redcoat's predicament and the boy's gentle heroism appeal to the emotions of young readers, and this scene illustrates how Burgess uses pathos to elicit compassion for bird life.

A prolific children's writer, Burgess won many young fans with his books and syndicated columns, and, through the Green Meadow Club children's feature in *People's Home Journal*, he recruited young nature protectionists for a remarkably successful "grass-roots conservation effort" to establish bird sanctuaries (Lowrance 2013, 139). As the Burgess example illustrates, periodicals' broad reach makes them important tools for educating young audiences about bird life. A periodical titled *The Youth's Companion* (1827–1929) frequently featured bird-related content for children. As seen in various publications of the time, arguments from economic ornithology—which studies birds in relation to agriculture—are repackaged for young readers in fiction and nonfiction. For example, in Ruth Mowry Brown's (1923) "Frank's Banded Robin," the character Uncle George tells his nephew, "I am employed by the United States government to care for birds and to learn all that I can about them. [. . .] Birds are valuable help to farmers and to people who have gardens. We ought to have more song birds to destroy the insect pests that eat the crops" (626). In addition to showing children why birds are helpful and should therefore be protected, some contributors focused on making bird study attractive to young readers. For example, ornithologist Bradford Torrey, who regularly contributed nonfiction articles to the magazine, emphasized the pleasures of birding, connecting bird migration patterns to the "charm" of bird study: "It is precisely this endless shifting of the scene, with its numberless opportunities for novelty and surprise, that makes field ornithology—the systematic observation of birds out-of-doors—one of the most delightful of human pursuits; new every season, and the more keenly enjoyed the longer it is followed" (Torrey 1901, 155). As these examples show, the rhetoric of bird protection and bird study appeals to logic, shared values, and young people's desire for "novelty and surprise."

Unlike *The Youth's Companion*, which covered a variety of topics, Frank Chapman's *Bird-Lore* (1899–1940) was exclusively "devoted to the study and protection of birds," featuring sections "For Young Observers" and "For Teachers and Students." In these sections, readers could find observation reports from children, stories about various feathered friends, bird house designs, book reviews, suggestions for bird study, opinion pieces, and strategies for conducting field study and keeping students interested in bird life. The importance of getting children out into nature for fieldwork is reinforced in many selections. In her advice on conducting field classes, Florence Merriam Bailey (1900) advises on the necessity of going "to nature with open heart as well as mind" (83), and Olive Thorne Miller (1900) argues that nature study should "lead the student to Nature herself; to acquaint him with the delights to be found in woods and fields, and the benefit to mind and heart, as well as to body, of close friendship with the great Mother" (151). Thus, bird study engages heart, body, mind, and spirit, drawing the student into a friendship with "the tribes of the air" and a deeper connection with nature (Miller 1900, 151).

Bird-Lore also published news about Audubon groups' endeavors to educate children, efforts that emphasized appealing to children's hearts. For example, an October 1901 report from the Connecticut Society reveals why members felt compelled to "interest [school children] in bird protection": "often people live all their lives among birds and hardly see them or hear them, because no one has 'called their attention' to them, and the children continue thoughtlessly to stone birds and rob their nests, because no one has spoken a few simple words that will touch their hearts" (Glover 1901, 181). Uncle Roy made a similar point in Wright and Coues's *Citizen Bird*, and the same idea clearly informed Patterson's approach in *Dickey Downy*. Calling attention to birds in ways that touch children's hearts and reform young people's behavior emerges as an important technique during this time period.

In the early twentieth century, school was yet another place where many children encountered bird study, a practice that complemented the aims of progressive education, with its emphasis on active learning and pursuing pupils' interests. As explained in "Bird Study: Its Educational Value and Methods," "Perhaps no subject is better adapted to develop the moral or humane features of a child's character than the properly conducted study of birds; and there is no other subject in which children naturally take a greater interest" (*Journal* 1908, 608). During this period, educators were encouraged to lead Junior Audubon clubs, arrange Bird Day programs, and engage pupils in "[erecting] bird houses and [taking] other practical steps for the careful protection and study of these interesting creatures" (*Journal* 1908, 608).

Bird Day, attributed to Charles A. Babcock, a Pennsylvania school superintendent, provided an opportunity for bird study and celebration in schools. A letter in *Ladies' Home Journal* praises the "new holiday": "It is suggested that Bird Day take the form of bird exhibitions, of bird exercise, of bird studies—any form of entertainment, in fact, which will bring children closer to their little brethren of the air, and in more intelligent sympathy with their life and ways" (Mott 1896, 4). Whereas Hamilton Mott (1896) emphasizes "the cultivation of an intimate acquaintanceship with our feathered friends" as "a source of genuine pleasure" for children (4), other sources emphasize a more utilitarian rationale. In a 1922 Bird Day pamphlet from the Commonwealth of Pennsylvania's Department of Public Instruction, Governor William Cameron Sproul underscores educators' duties to "the great army of two million school children upon whom the responsibility will soon fall for the management of the State's resources and conservation," proclaiming that every teacher should devote "at least two hours" on Bird Day "to the study of wild birds, and the best methods through which the conservation and increase of useful birds may be secured" (42). Thus, bird study and related activities were represented as practical, engaging, character-building undertakings essential to the education of future stewards of America's wildlife and natural resources.

Before moving on to youth birding rhetoric in the 1930s and 1940s, I want to mention one additional context for bird study: extracurricular activities. From the early twentieth century to the present day, youth clubs and scouting organizations have played a significant role in promoting bird study and involving children in bird protection. Camp Fire Girls, established in 1910, required bird study for Nature Lore honors, and Girl Scouts, established in 1912, continues to feature badges and patches for completing bird-related tasks. The Boy Scouts of America, established in 1910, offers a Bird Study merit badge and has long been a proponent of bird study and bird conservation. *Boys' Life* (1911–2020), the monthly magazine of the Boy Scouts, consistently covered topics related to bird watching, bird photography, and care of wild and pet birds (e.g., pigeons, parakeets). While *Boys' Life* encouraged early twentieth-century Scouts to admire birds as "the most eloquent expression of Nature's beauty, joy and freedom" and loyal friends (Chapman 1916, 4), the magazine also foregrounded a Scout's duty to conserve and protect wildlife and appealed to cultural ideals of manliness. William T. Hornaday (1914) argued that the "ruthless destruction of the past must not be permitted to continue. It is both wasteful, wicked and suicidal" and called on Scouts not simply to "study the birds and delightfully observe their habits" but to "manfully take up and carry their share of [the conservation] burden" (11). Employing a similar logic, "Scouts and the Birds" reminded readers, "You can't call it a man's game, sneaking up on a pretty little thing and dropping him in the middle of his song—but it used to be done. We're more sensible now. We take care of our friends even if they are little and weak" (*Boys'* 1916, 26). This emphasis on manliness, duty, and heroism certainly informed much of the content in *Boys' Life*, and it foreshadowed a coming shift in the way bird-protection rhetoric attempted to persuade young readers to take up the cause.

Approaches and arguments established during the early twentieth century influenced bird study and bird-protection rhetoric in the 1930s and 1940s. During the Great Depression and wartime, for example, economic ornithology continued to inform arguments for protecting birds, emphasizing that protecting American birds meant protecting America's food supply in fields and gardens. While fathers and other family members were away at war, such calls to action gave young people a role to play in helping their country and their fellow citizens, both feathered and human. The connection between bird protection and patriotism had been established in the nineteenth century and was evident in *Citizen Bird* when Uncle Roy tells his niece and nephew, "I know it is not easy to keep your hands off such pretty things as birds' eggs; but if by doing so you can be patriotic and useful, it is an act of self-denial that you will be glad to do for the good of the country" (Wright and Coues 1897, 50). In *Boys' Life*, National Scout Commissioner Dan Beard frequently invoked patriotism for persuasive purposes. In a 1916 article, Beard called John James Audubon "one of the most loyal, enthusiastic and patriotic of Americans" and challenged Scouts to "prove" their patriotism by doing "something for the birds," "our friends in feather coats," such as creating houses, feeders, and bathing pools (18). Beard's (1938) "Let the Eagle

Scream!" provides a particularly interesting example of how masculinity, duty, and patriotism continued to infuse bird-protection rhetoric in *Boys' Life*. After making some dubious claims about how "the Indians" "with their bare hands, plucked the quills from the living bird's tail," a practice he frames as honorable, Beard laments, "today any chump, any boob, any sissy, any mollycoddle who has the price can buy them. Shame on us! We have commercialized them, thus putting a price on the head of our national bird—more shame on us!" Beard then tells the Scouts that "on your shoulders rests the responsibility of preserving for America our national bird" while offering this assurance: "I know you have got the vigor, I know you have the pluck, and I know you have the intestinal fortitude and the brains to save the bird whose golden image perches on top of every flagpole" (15). Following this call to action, Beard tells Scouts to "appeal to the conscience of thoughtless gunners" and get lawmakers to "champion the cause" (15). "You boys," Beard claims, "by personal pressure, may have more influence with them than any political body of men or women, because your appeal will reach their hearts" (15). Like other bird protectionists before him, Beard recognized the strategic advantages of pathetic appeals. Pathos helped recruit children to the cause and could be used by them to advocate for wildlife. Although not entirely attributable to the valor, manliness, and patriotism of the Scouts, by June 1940 the Bald and Golden Eagle Protection Act had become law.

In contrast with Beard's fiery rhetoric, some children's authors of the time made more subtle arguments for bird protection. For example, Robert McCloskey's (1941) *Make Way for Ducklings* shows the dangers birds face in urban areas, with "horrid things rushing about" like boys on bicycles (who almost run over Mr. Mallard) and speeding cars on the highway (where Mrs. Mallard and her ducklings want to cross). The benevolent police officer Michael saves the day by directing traffic and enlisting other officers' help, thereby providing young readers with a bird-protection role model. Overall, however, storybooks did less to guide bird study during this period than nonfiction books like Hazel Lockwood's (1943) *The Golden Book of Birds* or field guides like Roger Tory Peterson's (1934) *A Field Guide to the Birds* and Herbert Zim and Ira Gabrielson's (1949) *Birds*, a pocket-sized Golden Nature Guide.

Although the aesthetic pleasures of bird study remained present in some youth birding rhetoric, the benefits of bird study for mind and body had, to some extent, won out over heart and spirit by the late 1940s. Ongoing anxieties about masculinity and cultural expectations surrounding how boys should spend their time certainly influenced how *Boys' Life* talked about birding. Between instructions for muscle builder set construction and an ad indicating that Harley-Davidson is "Built for Red-Blooded American Boys," Louis Fink's (1949) "Bird Study's Not So Bad" addresses the waning popularity of bird study among Scouts: "Maybe it has been unpopular because people thought it was a sissy sport, too easy to bother with" (12). To counter this misperception, Fink writes, "Honestly, no one would call birding a sport for weaklings if they'd ever watched a man like Joe Cadbury climbing a 100-foot pine tree in Maine to put aluminum identification tags on young herons" (12). Fink continues, "Bird study really can be fun. It's done in the open; it's an exciting game; it costs very little. And you get a big thrill every time you add a new bird to your list" (12). This argument was repeated in a 1956 review of *My Hobby Is Bird Watching*: "bird watching is fun—and can be [an] adventure. Bird watching can lead men up mountains and into wilderness. The sport of birding is not for the birds—it's for he-men" (Smith 1956, 64). Thus, birding is aligned with sport, adventure, fun, and excitement. For boys, at least, building a bird list became a competitive game and a chance to impress friends.

After World War II, America experienced a "postwar nature boom" (Dunlap 2011, 120), with suburban families spending leisure time out in nature and spending money attracting nature to their backyards. Books like John Terres's (1953) *Songbirds in Your Garden* provided guidance on attracting and feeding birds, creating a bird-friendly garden, and knowing when birds need human help and how to take care of them. Whether in the garden or further afield, a bird guide, notebook, and pencil were the essentials for young students who were encouraged to engage in careful observation and thorough and accurate notetaking. Hands-on projects, like building bird houses, remained popular activities at home and in extracurriculars. To attract young people to the hobby, birding continued to be promoted as a fun game, often using the metaphor of investigative work: "Finding birdnests is like playing detective. The untrained sleuth stumbles over his clues, but the trained investigator knows where to look for them" (Taylor 1954, 50). By "playing detective," young birders could use field guides and their growing knowledge of bird life to speed up identification work and build their lists.

A nature boom was also evident in mid-century books, with bird life appearing in nonfiction, like Robert Lemmon's (1952) *Our Amazing Birds*, and the children's series Little Golden Books and Rand McNally's Junior Elf Books. Popular anthologies also introduced young readers to bird study and conservation, which was to take on renewed significance in the decades ahead. The anthology *Through Golden Windows: Man and His World* (Beust et al. 1958) includes bird poetry and nonfiction, biographies of Audubon and John Muir, and "The Story of Wildlife Conservation" by Edward Graham and William Van Dersal. Bird life and conservation also appeared in story books like Meindert DeJong's (1954) Newbery Award-winning *The Wheel on the School*. DeJong's book tells the story of the residents of a Dutch fishing village who, marshalled by school children, bring storks back to the roofs of Shora. The story uses children's curiosity about bird life as a catalyst for conservation action. As the children's teacher states, "sometimes when we wonder, we can make things begin to happen" (DeJong 1954, 6). Since the late nineteenth century, bird protectionists have encouraged young people to wonder about bird life and to help the birds, including persuading other children and adults to take up the cause.

During the 1960s, 1970s, and 1980s, books and television increased public awareness of environmental issues, and once again the Boy Scouts were called on to protect eagles and other endangered birds. The July 1961 issue of *Boys' Life* features a bald eagle on its cover: the "proud old eagle," the issue reports, "is now in a back-against-the-wall fight for its very life" (3); "he's in real trouble and needs friends—in a hurry" (Allen 1961, 14). Bird protectionists had long realized that children can indeed be friends to birds when their hearts and minds are engaged, and here we see the focus shift from birding as a sport and game back to promoting sympathy and a sense of personal responsibility. Other magazines reached girls as well as boys with cause-oriented, pro-environmental messages. When the National Wildlife Federation began publishing *Ranger Rick's Nature Magazine* in January 1967, the first issue featured a colorful cover illustration of birds at a snow-blanketed backyard feeder. The popular magazine served as a source of bird study information for children, with "Ranger Rick, the National Wildlife Federation's friendly raccoon character, [helping] children [. . .] discover and connect with nature so that they, too, become good stewards of the environment" (National n.d.). Thus, young people were once more represented as "stewards" of America's wildlife and natural resources.

In December 1969, President Richard Nixon signed the Endangered Species Act into law, and in November 1970, *Boys' Life* published an "Endangered Species" issue that again featured a bald eagle on the cover. This issue illustrates a return to the kind of storytelling that engages young readers' sympathy and sets an example for them to follow. A short-fiction piece titled "The Friend" employs a familiar technique: readers see bird life from the perspective of humans as well as birds. Although bird humanization is less evident here than in Wright's, Patterson's, and Burgess's storytelling, the narration does invite perspective-taking: "Now that he was airborne and soon flying well, the young loon was free to enjoy the pleasures of flight as well as the pleasure he took in the underwater world" (Murphy 1970, 16). Primarily, however, the story fosters care for birds through its human main character. The boy has "a warm place in his heart for loons" after an earlier encounter, so when a loon "becomes covered in an oil slick on the beach," the boy enlists the help of his parents: "Dad, we've got to do it. After I heard them in Canada I feel like they're friends" (42). From Beard's patriotic Scouts to DeJong's committed village children to Murphy's loon-loving boy, a theme emerges: when children feel passionately about bird life, they have the power to persuade adults to save the birds.

Saving the birds has been a key theme of bird-related children's literature from the 1970s to the present, with appeals to the mind, heart, and senses evident in fiction, poetry, and picture books that introduce even the youngest readers to the wonders of bird life. While children's writers in the 1990s and 2000s have used storytelling to spark wonder and elicit sympathy, nonfiction bird books and periodicals tend to include plenty of fun facts as well as quizzes, games, and challenges to keep young people interested. Many nonfiction resources for kids and educators also present bird study as science. For example, *Watching Our Feathered Friends* teaches that "bird-watching is more than just fun. Bird-watching also helps us keep track of bird populations" (Spaulding 1997, 38). Material for educators emphasizes the benefits of birding as a tool for teaching scientific inquiry, observation skills, and standards-aligned science content.

From Sputnik-era prioritization of science education to the present-day emphasis on STEM and citizen science, bird study has frequently been promoted as an activity that sharpens valuable skills, prepares young people for in-demand careers, and allows them to contribute to current research. Proving that citizen science is not, however, a new concept, the August 1899 issue of *Bird-Lore* reminded young people that there "are hundreds of facts regarding the distribution of birds [. . .] which are still unknown, and you should make it your aim to become an authority on the birds of your region, and keep records of your observations as to migration, habits, abundance" (Stone 1899, 126). Witmer Stone (1899) continues that "there is a vast amount of bird work that you can do to help the science of ornithology and gain a reputation for yourself" (126). The annual Christmas Bird Count, which Chapman started in 1900, continues today, and now a variety of websites and apps make it easier than ever for young people to put their "interest in science and nature to work" to "help scientists with real research" (Brackney 2010, 44). Currently, the Cornell Lab of Ornithology runs several citizen science initiatives: BirdSleuth, eBird, Great Backyard Bird Count, BirdCams, NestWatch, Project Feederwatch, Habitat Network, and Celebrate Urban Birds, a project that "strives to co-create inclusive, equity-based citizen science projects that serve communities that have been historically excluded from birding and citizen science" (Cornell 2016).

The Cornell Lab's efforts to include missing voices in bird-related citizen science reflect current conversations about representation. While "birding is becoming more diverse and inclusive, particularly among young outdoor enthusiasts" (Kuta 2020), there is still a "lack of children's books about African American kids enjoying nature" (Fetters 2019). The voices and characters present in the literature I examined represent a fairly homogenous group of Americans, and I encountered offensive stereotypes and epithets, especially in late-nineteenth and early to mid-twentieth-century publications. Many diverse voices contribute to youth birding rhetoric now, especially via online publications and social media, and ornithologist J. Drew Lanham has reflected on the importance of reconnecting "young people of color" to nature. In *The Home Place: Memoirs of a Colored Man's Love Affair with Nature* (2016), Lanham writes,

> The wild things and places belong to all of us. So while I can't fix the bigger problems of race in the United States [. . .] I can prescribe a solution in my own small corner. Get more people of color "out there." Turn oddities into commonplace. The presence of more black birders [. . .] will say to others that we, too, appreciate the warble of a summer tanager [. . .]. Our responsibility is to pass something on to those coming after. As young people of color reconnect with what so many of their ancestors knew—that our connections to the land run deep, like the taproots of mighty oaks; that the land renews and sustains us—maybe things will begin to change.

Here, the argument for reconnecting young people with nature emphasizes inclusion and visibility and reinforces important connections with the land and the past.

In the 1990s and 2000s, many writers have sounded a familiar alarm: American children are perilously disconnected from nature, and this disconnection threatens their well-being as well as the future of our natural environment. Modern discourses about reconnecting children with nature have often emphasized challenges related to place (e.g., life in urban areas) or to technological distractions (e.g., television, gaming systems, cell phones). In the introduction to *Sharing the Wonder of Birds with Kids*, Laura Erickson (1997) recounts a friend's experience working with "inner city children who are bewildered and frightened on their first walks into even small woodlots" and then goes on to say, "even suburban and rural children who have easy access to field and forest may spend more time watching television indoors than they do playing outside" (Erickson 1997, vii). Richard Louv's (2005) *Last Child in the Woods: Saving Our Children from Nature-Deficit Disorder* argues similarly, warning that "the bond is breaking between the young and the natural world," with consequences for "mental, physical, and spiritual health," as well as the "health of the earth" (3). Still, even Louv recognizes that technology, especially nature apps and citizen-science tools, can be beneficial. In *Vitamin N: The Essential Guide to a Nature-Rich Life*, Louv (2016) encourages parents and children to become birders, "birdscape" their property (78), and "study bird behavior to demonstrate predicting, observing, and analyzing" (191). He also supports "high tech, high nature" birding, such as using cell phones to record nature sounds or for accessing birding apps (44). Additionally, in his foreword to *Citizen Science*, Louv writes, "An expansion of the citizen scientist movement, particularly if it reaches out directly to recruit the young, will be a powerful antidote to what I've called the nature-deficit disorder of our species" (2012, x). Therefore, while technology can contribute to disconnection, it can also be part of the solution.

In the introduction to *Vitamin N*, Louv (2016) mentions a "new nature movement" (xiv). While it is true that the idea of nature-deficit disorder has sparked public conversations and inspired Leave No Child Inside programs, neither the disorder nor the remedy sound new; rather, these are catchy ways of summarizing a main theme of nearly a century and a half of discourse on nature study for children. What my analysis of youth bird study and bird-protection rhetoric reveals is that Americans who care about children and the natural world have always worried over young people becoming disconnected from nature; becoming, therefore, less well—physically, emotionally, spiritually—and, as Uncle Roy warns in *Citizen Bird*, "selfish and cruel" if they do not develop compassion for wildlife (Wright and Coues 1897, 12). Adults who have loved and delighted in nature want the same pleasures for children, and adults who fear for the future of the environment recognize children as persuasive allies in the fight to save the birds. Children are tomorrow's activists, scientists, journalists, or children's writers who we hope will carry forward the long legacy of conservation and biophilia in this country.

Although some claims in favor of nature study seem exaggerated, I do not believe that Americans have oversold the benefits of youth birding. To some extent, birding is good for kids for all the reasons presented in the large body of literature I studied. It encourages them to pay attention to and appreciate nature, to develop knowledge of and compassion for living things, and to get involved in an enjoyable hobby. Nonetheless, I come away from this project with concerns about how we tend to enlist children in bird protection, and sometimes, by extension, in saving the planet. In many cases, bird-protection rhetoric, after eliciting sympathy, presents young people with manageable ways to help (e.g., create bird-friendly habitats, contribute to citizen-science initiatives, write a letter). Still, the kinds of threats facing today's birds are complex and cannot be easily remedied or eliminated—a fact that may become apparent, especially to older children, as they learn about climate change and biodiversity loss. What happens when sympathy, love, and small actions can't fix things? As Erickson (1997) suggests, "What children love, they love with intensity, and when something they love is in trouble, they want desperately to help it. If they don't know how to help, they may feel overwhelmed by powerlessness" (159). As a rhetoric scholar and a parent of a youth birder, I wonder if pairing bird study with an education in how local government works, how citizens can hold corporations and governments accountable, and how individual and collective action has resulted in lasting change might complement efforts to empower the next generation of nature protectionists.

NOTES

1. From bird students, to bird watchers, to birders, the terminology used to describe people who engage in observing and learning about bird life has varied over time (Dunlap 2011). I use these terms interchangeably.

2. Bird-protection discourses blamed women, "poor whites," "cats, immigrants, pot hunters, [and] minorities" for the destruction of birds (Taylor 2016, 190, 210), and this was certainly evident in the material I examined.

REFERENCES

Allen, Durward L. 1961. "Emblem Eagle." *Boys' Life*. 51 (7): 14, 23, 25.
Bailey, Florence Merriam. 1900. "How to Conduct Field Classes." *Bird-Lore* 2 (3): 83.
Beard, Dan. 1916. "Dan Beard Tells You How to Make Bird Houses and Lunch Baskets and Bathing Pools." *Boys' Life* 6 (3): 18.
———. 1938. "Let the Eagle Scream!" *Boys' Life* 28 (9): 15, 41.
Beust, Nora, et al., ed. 1958. *Through Golden Windows: Man and His World*. New York, Grolier.
Boys' Life. 1916. "Scouts and the Birds." 6 (4): 26.
Brackney, Susan. 2010. "Be a Citizen Scientist!" *Boys' Life* 100 (11): 44–47.
Brown, Ruth Mowry. 1923. "Frank's Banded Robin." *The Youth's Companion*, October 18, 1923.
Burgess, Thornton W. 1919. *The Burgess Bird Book for Children*. Boston: Little, Brown, and Company.
Burroughs, John. 1905. *Ways of Nature*. Boston: Houghton Mifflin.
Chapman, Frank M. 1916. "Older Scouts to Younger Scouts on Camping." *Boys' Life* 6 (4): 3–4.
Cornell Lab of Ornithology. 2016. "What is CUBs?" Accessed May 14, 2021. https://celebrateurbanbirds.org/about/what-is-celebrate-urban-birds/
DeJong, Meindert. 1954. *The Wheel on the School*. New York: HarperCollins.
Dunlap, Thomas R. 2011. *In the Field, Among the Feathered: A History of Birders and Their Guides*. New York: Oxford University Press.
Erickson, Laura. 1997. *Sharing the Wonder of Birds with Kids*. Minneapolis: University of Minnesota Press.
Fetters, Ashley. 2019. "Where is the Black Blueberries for Sal?" *The Atlantic*, May 27, 2019.
Fink, Louis. 1949. "Bird Study's Not So Bad." *Boys' Life* 39 (8): 12, 37–38.

Glover, Helen W. 1901. "Report of Connecticut Society." *Bird-Lore* 3 (5): 181.
Graham, Edward H., and William R. Van Dersal. 1958. "The Story of Wildlife Conservation." In *Through Golden Windows: Man and His World*, edited by Nora Beust et al., 162–65. New York: Grolier.
Hornaday, William T. 1914. "Conservation! The Great Task for Boys." *Boys' Life* 4 (4): 11.
Journal of Education. 1908. "Bird Study: Its Educational Value and Methods." 67 (22): 608.
Kuta, Sarah. 2020. "Why Birding Is Taking Flight with a New Generation." *Lonely Planet*, April 22, 2020.
Lanham, J. Drew. 2016. *The Home Place: Memoirs of a Colored Man's Love Affair with Nature*. Minneapolis: Milkweed Editions.
Lemmon, Robert. 1952. *Our Amazing Birds*. New York: Doubleday.
Lockwood, Hazel. 1943. *The Golden Book of Birds*. New York: Simon and Schuster.
Louv, Richard. 2005. *Last Child in the Woods: Saving our Children from Nature-Deficit Disorder*. Chapel Hill: Algonquin.
———. 2012. "Foreword." In *Citizen Science: Public Participation in Environmental Research*, edited by Janis Dickinson and Rick Bonney, ix–x. Ithaca: Comstock.
———. 2016. *Vitamin N: The Essential Guide to a Nature-Rich Life*. Chapel Hill: Algonquin.
Lowrance, Christie Palmer. 2013. *Nature's Ambassador: The Legacy of Thornton W. Burgess*. Atglen: Schiffer.
Marble, Charles C. 1898. "Birds in the Schools." *Birds* 3 (1): 20.
McCloskey, Robert. 1941. *Make Way for Ducklings*. New York: Viking Press.
Merchant, Carolyn. 2016. *Spare the Birds! George Bird Grinnell and the First Audubon Society*. New Haven: Yale University Press.
Miller, Olive Thorne. 1900. "The Study of Birds—Another Way." *Bird-Lore* 2 (5): 151–53.
Mott, Hamilton. 1896. "A New Holiday for the Children." *Ladies' Home Journal* 14 (1): 4.
Murphy, Robert. 1970. "The Friend." *Boys' Life* 60 (11): 13–16, 40, 42.
National Wildlife Federation. n.d. "About Ranger Rick." Accessed May 14, 2021. https://www.nwf.org/about-us/history/about-ranger-rick
Patterson, Virginia Sharpe. 1899. *Dickey Downy: The Autobiography of a Bird*. Philadelphia: A. J. Rowland.
Peterson, Roger Tory. 1934. *A Field Guide to the Birds*. Boston: Houghton Mifflin.
Smith, Fran. 1956. Review of *My Hobby Is Bird Watching*, by Mary P. Pettit. *Boys' Life* 46 (4): 64.
Soule, Caroline G. 1899. "Humanizing the Birds." *Bird-Lore* 1 (6): 193.
Spaulding, Dean. 1997. *Watching Our Feathered Friends*. Minneapolis: Lerner.
Sproul, William Cameron. 1922. "Proclamation." *Arbor Day and Bird Day*. Pennsylvania: Commonwealth of Pennsylvania Department of Public Instruction. 27 Oct. 1922.
Stone, Witmer. 1899. "Hints to Young Bird Students." *Bird-Lore* 1 (4): 125–27.
Taylor, Dorceta E. 2016. *The Rise of the American Conservation Movement: Power, Privilege, and Environmental Protection*. Durham: Duke University Press.

Taylor, John. 1954. "Know Your Nests." *Boys' Life* 44 (7): 50.
Terres, John K. 1953. *Songbirds in Your Garden*. New York: Thomas Y. Crowell.
Torrey, Bradford. 1901. "Migration of Birds." *The Youth's Companion*. March 28, 1901. 155.
Wright, Mabel Osgood. 1899. "A Bird Class for Children." *Bird-Lore* 1 (3): 100.
Wright, Mabel Osgood, and Elliott Coues. 1897. *Citizen Bird: Scenes from Bird-Life in Plain English for Beginners*. New York: Macmillan.
Zim, Herbert S., and Ira N. Gabrielson. 1949. *Birds: A Guide to the Most Familiar American Birds*. New York: Golden Press.

Chapter 14

Birds Aren't Real

Narrative and Aesthetic Irony in For-Profit Conspiracy

Lauren Shoemaker

The robin digging for worms in the front yard, the cardinal swooping into shrubs for cover, and the acrobatic nuthatch dangling upside down from a tree branch are all very detailed imitators, but they are not real. They are drones with accurate programming to replicate the bird species they supplant, or so the theory goes.

Birds Aren't Real (hereafter BAR) is a community of self-proclaimed American patriots that use slick, minimalist stickers and apparel to recruit "truthers" to their cause: their belief is that the US government has killed billions of birds since 1959 and continues to replace them with identical surveillance drones for collecting data on citizens. According to the official narrative, the originating motive for the annihilation was localized annoyance caused by bird droppings on vehicles in Washington, DC, but as the drones proved to be effective surveillance mechanisms, the project scaled nationally (*Birds Aren't Real* 2021). Is this just an entertaining theory related through humor writing? And what does it have to do with aesthetics?

Contemporary academic study does not allow such an easy dismissal of conspiracy theory as a cultural product. Michael Butter and Peter Knight (2020) write in an introductory chapter to the *Routledge Handbook of Conspiracy Theories* that "cultural studies scholars around the turn of the millennium challenged the psychopathologizing interpretation," or debunking of conspiracy theories, instead viewing them "as increasingly justified, creative and potentially radical challenges to the status quo" (28). Butter and Knight recognize a shift in conspiracy theory scholarship that does not seek to condemn popular manifestations of conspiracy theory, "but to understand their appeal and assess their cultural significance" (31). The growing assumption among such cultural studies scholars is that conspiracy theories constitute logical responses to technological and social changes, especially in a globalized, corporate world. Both Timothy Melley and Kathryn S. Olmsted read conspiracy theory as a legitimate response to global capitalism and centralized government power. The presence of real government conspiracies (MK-ULTRA, the Iran-Contra affair, CIA involvement in Latin American and Caribbean coups, state-sanctioned medical experimentation on minority groups like Tuskegee, and sterilization policies for black, brown, and disabled women) have diminished trust in institutions of authority. Uneasy with this cultural studies lens, I aim to describe and critique the current methodology applied to conspiracy theory study, connect contemporary issues and events that establish the BAR theory's appeal, and discuss the consequences of ironic narrative and aesthetics in driving consumerism, rather than bird activism and habitat conservation, in the context of environmental threats caused by humans. Ironic or nihilist online discourse and its commodification, of which BAR is an example, runs the risk of reinforcing helplessness rather than stoking agency when time is of the essence for action on climate change and agricultural practices, two large threats to birds.

STUDYING CONSPIRACY THEORY

BAR fits into a long narrative tradition blurring satire and seriousness that has been a hallmark of conspiracy theory for the last half century. BAR debuted in 2017 as a video stunt on Instagram with a sign-carrying BAR activist at the Women's March in Washington, DC, but it gained traction on Reddit, a collaborative social media website more prone to attracting conspiracy theorists. Many engaged with the narrative as satire, but the author of the subreddit (r/birdsarentreal) quickly defended it as earnest. This staunch position to refuse the theory's classification as a running joke has a history in conspiracy theory writing, as Robert Anton Wilson, coauthor of *Illuminatus!* with Robert Shea in 1975, established. Wilson created what he called "guerilla ontology," a literary style requiring the reader to consistently evaluate the truth of the information offered in an ironic tone (Walker 2013, 234). The BAR official narrative from the movement's website is a literary descendent of *Illuminatus!* in style and content: the federal plot to kill all birds integrates JFK's assassination, Cold War and Vietnam conspiracy, the Denver International Airport's underground tunnels, Area 51, and other conspiracy theory touchstones, much like Wilson and Shea's trilogy that blended multiple, already circulating conspiracy theories to attribute them to the Illuminati, an internationally omnipotent small group of people influencing all of history. BAR is not very original as a text, nor is it original in its antiestablishment worldview marketed through products that communicate an ironic stance. Jaron Harambam (2020) studies Alex Jones and David Icke as conspiracy theory entrepreneurs, those who have "made a living out of spreading their conspiracy theories in both the off- and online worlds, [while] their websites also have shops that sell, besides their own videos and books, many different products, mostly in the realm of alternative healing and food supplements" (282). Over the last few years, Jones's InfoWars shop items have included virility pills and body armor for the coming race war he totes, and T-shirts designed to imitate campaign aesthetics but that ironically read "Hilary for Prison 2016" (*Frontline* 2021). Though the BAR store is nearly all apparel, Peter McIndoe, the author and entrepreneur behind it, communicates a worldview suspicious of government and the technology industry, reveling in the post-truth environment of online discourse with T-shirts that read "The Birds Work for the Bourgeoisie" and "Bird Watching Goes Both Ways." Interviews with both *Newsweek* and *Audubon* detail McIndoe's deadpan delivery and ironic style (Alfonso 2018; Crowley 2021). As the *Audubon* article points out, irony is a highly effective marketing scheme because it sells products to believers and those laughing at them alike (Alfonso 2018).

Jesse Walker (2013) chronicles the ironic style in *The United States of Paranoia: A Conspiracy Theory*, attributing it to Wilson and his band of pranksters, known as the Discordians. Walker describes the rhetoric: "In the ironic style, the most interesting thing about a conspiracy theory isn't that it might or might not be true; it's that it constructs a story out of the everyday truths we only hazily perceive" (221). The distillation of perceptions into an improviseable myth is a creative process akin to poetry for ironists like McIndoe. The inconsistency of the movement's beginnings (in some places it is listed as 1976 and in others 1959), as well as local chapters' own web presence in five major cities, further iterate the BAR theory. Participation of others fuels this improvisation and helps spread contemporary conspiracy theory online.

When we think of the spread of ideas online, we typically think in the metaphor of virality, as in the phrase *going viral*. But Henry Jenkins, Sam Ford, and Joshua Green argue in *Spreadable Media* that while "viral metaphors do capture the speed with which new ideas circulate the Internet," they "do little to describe situations in which people actively assess a media text, deciding who to share it with and how to pass it along" (2013, 17–20). In short, messages are not static items infecting crowds, but are remixed and recontextualized in participatory cultures of online social circles. Online texts are consistently adapted and appropriated by these cultures. BAR as a retailer is frequently recontextualized on social media platforms where it advertises, appearing between friends' and family members' photos and other shared content, but the site of most improvisation is on Reddit, where users contribute photos of drones in the wild and further extrapolate on the theory. The participatory nature of conspiracy theory narratives and texts is one reason literary study takes interest in conspiracy theories. However, perhaps a more central reason is that literature and its methodologies of ideological critique share some uncomfortable parallels with conspiratorial thinking (Butter and Knight 2020, 37–38).

Conspiracy in literary studies has been pervasive since the 1960s. Fiction of the post-Kennedy era featured conspiracy as an explicit organizing principle, "embrac[ing] the apparent irrationalism of paranoia as a creative, workable stance against the mystifying power of large institutions, public relations schemes, state propaganda, disinformation, advertising and other forms of mass mediated deception and social influence" (Melley 2020, 427). Some of the most widely read examples include Thomas Pynchon's *The Crying of Lot 49*, Don DeLillo's *Libra*, Ishmael Reed's *Mumbo Jumbo*, and, more recently, Dan Brown's *The Da Vinci Code* and Philip Roth's *The Plot Against America*. Similarly, paranoid reading processes' intent to reveal secret or hidden significance in the events, symbols, or allusions within texts has, according to Brian McHale, even become the norm since the standardization of the New Critical approach in literary studies (1992, 87–114). Paul Ricoeur's well-known characterization of critical theory starting in the nineteenth century as a "hermeneutics of suspicion," as Butter and Knight recognize, is "the driving force behind the tradition of critique that begins with Marx, Nietzsche and Freud [. . .] who (respectively) sought to reveal the hidden economic, moral and psychological forces that govern human behavior and the unfolding of history" (2020, 37). This argument culminates in the idea that, at their core, institutionalized disciplinary methods of literary critique drive readings of texts toward acceptable grand narratives—for example, the details are explained by capitalism or unconscious desire—whereas conspiracy theory drives readings similarly toward less academically legitimate grand narratives. Literary critique in its ideological approach is merely the institutionally recognized form of conspiratorial thinking.

Richard Hofstadter's 1965 essay "The Paranoid Style in American Politics" drew the line in the sand for historians; it "pathologized belief in conspiracy theory as a form of paranoia" and claimed that "while conspiracy theories had a long history in the U.S.A., they had always 'been the preferred style only of *minority movements*'" (Butter and Knight 2020, 29). Hofstadter dismissed engagement in conspiracy as something only a minority of Americans would pursue, minimizing its reach and failing to recognize how it could serve those in positions of power. The absence of such pressure to denounce conspiracy theory in literary studies has allowed the same tools to develop legitimate unified readings of texts and anti-Semitic global conspiracy alongside each other, despite how uncomfortable that is for literary scholars. The nascence of English Studies already had a messy, racist inception in institutionalizing the study of imperialist culture in England's colonies, creating British citizens by systematically devaluing native language and literature and replacing native literary values and traditions with hegemonic ones. Perhaps it should not come as a surprise that academic literary study remains ambivalent to the unified readings it produces. Hofstadter's essay is now considered an obstacle for postwar historians because it pathologized not just conspiracy theory believers as paranoid, but also halted any serious study of the theories' historical impacts, likely because of the wrong assertion that they have always represented the beliefs of minority movements and have not had significant historical consequences. The riot and forced entry of hundreds into the US Capitol on January 6, 2021 to overturn election results may have been based on a conspiracy believed by a minority of Americans, but the deadly effects of the QAnon conspiracy will likely prompt more historical analysis of conspiracy theory and its serious impacts on democracy. Former President Donald Trump's unofficial involvement demonstrates that *minority* does not inherently mean *harmless*.

Recent publications like Talia Lavin's *Culture Warlords: My Journey into the Dark Web of White Supremacy* (2020) and the HBO documentary *Q: Into the Storm* (2021), about QAnon, trace several conspiracy theories' relationships with white supremacy, also making the argument for their increasing incitement to violence. The long history of entanglement between conspiracy theory and white supremacy in the United States is as old as the nation itself, from circulating fears of uprisings of enslaved people like the New York Slave Conspiracy of 1741 to Timothy McVeigh's call to action from *The Turner Diaries*, which generated the white genocide myth. When compared to the bombing in Oklahoma City, an inane conspiracy theory like BAR seems harmless; however, I argue that the cultural studies trend to isolate conspiracy theory as a cultural product while withholding value judgment, either to its truths or consequences, no longer serves us, if it ever did. BAR, in commodifying its narrative in its apparel store, replaces activism with helplessness and critique with irony. At best, BAR is a missed opportunity to turn an Internet joke into a site of conservation and activism. At worst, it reinforces ambivalence toward ecological devastation caused by climate change and ignores its own role in consumerism driving that devastation.

SURVEILLANCE FEARS

The appeal of conspiracy theories is their ability to explain problems or rationalize fears. A major appeal of the BAR conspiracy theory is that it stokes people's fears of constant surveillance; current pervasive surveillance procedures justify US citizens' apprehensions. Tracing the anxiety of surveillance by the state is a lengthy project, but its presence in literature and popular culture texts can be used to identify historical moments of intensified interest. Melley names postwar writers like Thomas Pynchon, Don DeLillo, Margaret Atwood, William S. Burroughs, Philip K. Dick, Ishmael Reed, and Joseph Heller as purveyors of a "culture of paranoia," reflecting a "crisis of public knowledge fomented by a mushrooming security state, corporate capitalism and mass-mediated society" (2020, 427). Writers and producers of the new millennia found the postwar paranoia resonant in expanding cellular and Internet technology. Surveillance fears perhaps surpass the central conflict of free will and determinism in the adapted feature-length Steven Spielberg–directed film *Minority Report* (2002), originally a novella by Dick from 1956. Films of the late 1990s and 2000s represent a significant portion of the films featuring surveillance as a central plot arc or theme, many of which adapt Dick. Fears of government surveillance through increasingly regular video recording, cell phone, and Internet technology drove the popularity of the Jason Bourne saga (2002, 2004, 2007, 2016), techno-thrillers like *Enemy of the State* (1998), *Equilibrium* (2001), *V for Vendetta* (2006), *Eagle Eye* (2008), and *Eyeborgs* (2009) to varying degrees of critical success. This trend in film serves as evidence of a peak in interest in government surveillance in the 2000s, and it corresponds with the establishment of the Patriot Act, passed in response to the September 11, 2001 attacks and which has since been used to justify increasingly intrusive government data collection on law-abiding citizens in the name of counterterrorism.

Tracking citizens' location, relationships, employment status, and purchases to surveil and discipline for purposes under discretion of the state was merely paranoia and science-fiction conspiracy until it was not. If COINTELPRO's exposure validated the fears of the postwar era in 1971, Edward Snowden's whistle-blowing disclosure of the National Security Agency confirmed the cultural paranoia of the 2000s. Cell phones, browser history, and smart devices in our homes and workplaces are indeed collecting and storing data about citizens, and the government is "intent on making every conversation and every form of behaviour known to them" according to Snowden (qtd. in *The Guardian*, 2013). Snowden felt compelled to disclose government secrets about data collection because he saw them as eroding privacy and democracy. His concerns encompassed both Cold-War fears of totalitarian government with suspicion of big government in general favored by the right, and the fears of corporatocracy where government is one powerful arm of an oligarchy favored by the left. Recent scholarship and reporting on technology and data suggest that government surveillance should likely be secondary to outrage aimed at private companies' surveillance processes and uses that have grown by misleading or misinforming citizens, sometimes burying what they are forthcoming about in immense terms of service policies and tech euphemisms (Zuboff 2019, 61–97). In fact, *Forbes* reported in 2019 that government surveillance is done mostly by private corporations. The Snowden disclosures revealed that (Leetaru 2019). BAR's narrative names the government as *they* who spy through birds, but online audiences, acclimated to the slipperiness of *government* as synecdoche for the alliance of government and private industry, do not need to distinguish between them.

Some examples found in recent publications on data collection and algorithms as products to sort and influence populations best explain how this line between government and private enterprise is not just difficult to draw, but also meaningless in application. Media scholars, like Siva Vaidhyanathan and Shoshana Zuboff, have catalogued ways that Google collects search terms not merely to improve their technology, as they initially claimed, but to sell access to large banks of user data and the algorithmic tools that turn that data into profitable delivery systems of individualized advertisements or consumer profiles. However, advertising is possibly the least nefarious of the mechanisms used to collect and sell surveillance data. Cathy O'Neil (2017) in *Weapons of Math Destruction* describes at length myriad applications of those algorithmic products on various activities in our lives, ranging from job applications and insurance coverage and cost to the likelihood of a police presence in our neighborhoods to prison sentencing. Receipt scanning apps that pay for a peek into your shopping cart could transform opinion into enforceable policy, mandating that those on welfare assistance should only buy cheap food or risk suspension of Access cards. Health insurance companies could lock a smart refrigerator to keep people from cheating on a diet. What difference does it make if the person bought the insurance on the marketplace established by the Affordable Care Act or Medicare (federally provided) or the insurance is through their employer (privately provided)? Distinguishing between government and private corporation surveillance is difficult, maybe even impossible. The clearest example of the seamlessness of corporation and state surveillance is thus: Amazon Ring's surveillance footage from the doorbells of millions of private homes is accessible to police departments without a warrant (Bridges 2021). Conservative fears of large overreaching government and liberal fears of a corporatocracy are both realized. Generalized fears of surveillance are nonpartisan and explain why a conspiracy theory that posits birds are government drones spying on us appeals to both the right and the left.

BAR capitalizes on anxiety about how many eyes the corporate-government surveillance complex has in our homes and yards already. One of the clever slogans, "Bird Watching Goes Both Ways," is accompanied by artwork on a T-shirt illustrating an anthropomorphized blue pigeon, with surprisingly muscular arms, who holds a pair of binoculars. From the binoculars, dotted lines project a pair of yellow and red human eyes. In "Conspiracy Theories and Visual Culture," Ute Caumanns and Andreas Önnerfors (2020) apply transmedial narratology methods to analyze visual tropes belonging "to the basic repertoire of conspiratorial thinking," and act as introductions to a "larger narrative, which the viewer in a concrete historical context is familiar with" (2020, 444). One of the visual tropes Caumanns and Önnerfors identify is "symbolical anthropomorphism." Although its major purpose is typically dehumanization of an Other, there is also an "inbuilt reference to imaginations of their essential qualities" that seems more relevant to the snooping pigeon image (2020, 444). Pigeons are perceived as nuisance birds by many, and are strongly associated with one of the most basic functions: defecating. The image on the T-shirt aligns government security agents with pesky pigeons as such nuisances. The muscular arms of the pigeon encode masculinity, even the military strength of the state, while the yellow-red eyes, maybe a coincidental design choice to stick to primary colors, are more likely an on-the-nose association with communist iconography, solidifying BAR in a larger narrative of Cold-War spy anxiety. The narrated history of the BAR *movement* starts with President Dwight D. Eisenhower working with Allen Dulles, the director of the CIA, to "put cameras in the sky," specifically to catch un-American activities (*Birds Aren't Real* 2021). (This analysis is bordering on conspiratorial, no?) Hatred of pigeons and pigeon feces supposedly rationalized Eisenhower and Dulles's murder and replacement of all birds. The birds on BAR apparel are not graceful beings but enemies of the people. The snooping pigeon image distills the corporate-government surveillance complex into an immediate and familiar adversary.

THREATS TO BIRDS, NOT BIRDS AS THREATS

The suggestion that birds are enemies of the people reverses what ornithologists and conservationists claim. People in industrializing and radically altering ecosystems have become a serious threat to birds. Industrial agriculture and artificial light interrupt the migration of songbirds, and the changing climate disrupts their food and water sources. The examples that follow are only a small sampling of studies on specific threats to birds. Neonicotinoids, a popular insecticide sprayed on seeds at industrial farms, are toxins that, when ingested in nonlethal doses, cause birds to lose body mass rapidly. Too fatigued to continue flying, for an average of 3.5 days, white-crowned sparrows delayed their departure from a stopover when they were intoxicated by neonicotinoids in a controlled experiment (Eng et al. 2019). Challenges experienced in migration have species-wide consequences and compound other problems like changing or scarce food supplies. According to a study published in 2017, migratory birds have adjusted their migration schedules to account for earlier spring "green-up"—when new plant leaves emerge, and insects abound—but only 9 of 48 species on the Eastern coast of the United States reached their breeding grounds in time for this moving window, thanks to a rapidly warming climate (Mayor et al. 2017). These human-caused problems associated with climate change and industrial agriculture likely contribute to the songbird population decline. A 2019 network analysis of songbird population reports a loss of nearly 3 billion birds or 29 percent of 1970 abundance (Rosenburg et al. 2019). The same article reports even the most common species are now less common. In this context, BAR is an irresponsible satire that takes too lightly the gravity of such profound species loss and what that portends across ecosystems globally.

Unfortunately, members of the BAR movement are likely to explain this profound avifauna decline as proof of the government's knowing annihilation of birds, suggesting that the production of drones cannot keep up with birds' demise. Such are the improvisations to this conspiracy theory and another significant appeal of it. Even the methods of studying avian behavior and population decline could serve as fodder for the theory. Since 2007, ornithologists have been using tiny solar geolocators that look like small backpacks strapped to purple martins and other larger songbirds in order to research migration flight patterns (Dean 2009). Such futuristic devices, weighing less than 1.5 g, could be startling to see on birds in the wild, but appropriating their presence for BAR requires reversing their purpose. These new instruments of supposed spying give scientists insights by which to develop plans to increase bird survival rather than record people's locations to a centralized database as BAR truthers claim. However, the ironic narrative and aesthetics of BAR anticipate naysayers' attempts to educate anyone on the purpose of geolocators. Another image available on the BAR retail website stacks the words "Birds Aren't Real" in the color and style of *Schoolhouse Rock!* cartoons. *Schoolhouse Rock!* was interstitial programming that aired on the US television network ABC during their Saturday morning children's block of cartoons from 1973 to 1984. It initially consisted of three-minute-long animated educational musical short films but was revived in the mid-1990s and again in 2009, releasing new episodes direct to video. The BAR shirt features smiling children holding signs reading "If it flies, it spies" and "Research bird surveillance," while small blue and yellow birds with tiny antennae on their heads perch on electrical lines, supposedly charging, signified by lightning bolts between their antennae. The appropriation of *Schoolhouse Rock!* aligns the mission of BAR with that of the primary school public access children's program, one with a wholesome mission of reinforcing multiplication tables,

English grammar, and civics lessons. The T-shirt design evokes nostalgia and attempts to put BAR beyond reproach because the familiar cartoon style has the cultural trust of multiple generations of teachers and parents. In other words, appropriating *Schoolhouse Rock!*'s aesthetic and cultural meanings are examples of ironic style; the tenets of BAR are made to appear as elementary and above scrutiny as the process of passing a bill or finding a sentence's subject. More importantly, to argue or try to debunk the premise of the movement is as silly as taking issue with how generators produce electricity.

A more subtle T-shirt design applies the ironic style to images familiar to birders and conservationists. Detailed field-guide images of a dozen birds' heads are labeled with their common names under the heading "Bird Drones of North America." Instead of a Latin name in italics below, anglicized descriptors like "Night Surveillance" or "Shore Surveillance" appear under the owl and seagull respectively. The design clearly imitates posters and apparel sold by retailers associated with conservation efforts, yet it mocks the idea of bird conservation in commodifying a message that demonizes birds. Fear and even anger at the corporate-government surveillance complex is understandable but scapegoating animals struggling to cope with their rapidly changing environments is a cruel joke from which to profit. Blaming the victim is hardly a new rhetorical device. The ironic stance and aesthetic, however, protect BAR truthers from having to admit it is a joke at all. This exemption, besides being obnoxious, allows truthers to feel superior to bird activists or anyone who cares about bird diminishment. In his twenty-year retrospective on the popular American television series *South Park*, which popularized the ironic stance on all cultural issues, Sean O'Neal (2017) writes that series creators Trey Parker and Matt Stone have "taught their most devoted followers that taking anything too seriously is hella lame." *South Park* primed a generation to mock homophobes alongside environmentalists, according to O'Neal, and the show's own plotlines regularly dive into conspiracy theory to explain contemporary issues. BAR appeals to the audience of *South Park*, utilizing a similar brand of satire that shrugs at its consequences. The ironic style may have been created by a small minority with Wilson's Discordians, but Parker and Stone brought it to the masses and legitimized it as cultural commentary.

Cultural studies scholars objectively approaching conspiracy theory and withholding judgment in their analyses have good intentions. Perhaps suspension of the drive to debunk theories was important to allow discussion of the sociopolitical meaning of individual conspiracy theories without pathologizing their believers. I also concede that, especially in literary studies, the line between legitimate unified readings and conspiratorial ones can be relative. Yet the consequences of giving particular conspiracy theories credence can do significant harm. Without debunking something like Pizzagate—the theory that Democratic political figures were meeting in the basement of Comet Ping Pong, a DC-area pizzeria, to engage in child sexual abuse and trafficking—we can expect gunmen like Edgar Maddison Welch to continue to endanger the public's safety (Kennedy 2017). BAR is unlikely to cause violence, at least toward people, but what of the violence we inflict on nonhuman species and the role our purported objectivity plays in perpetuating that violence? Rob Nixon (2011) coined the term "slow violence" to identify and theorize environmental devastation like anthropogenic climate change that does not inspire urgency because it does not register in our fast-paced, visual characterizations of violence (2011, 2–3). Narratives have the power to make these unseen processes that unfold over decades or centuries visible, and they have the power to obscure them. BAR's ironic style obscures humans' threats to avian life by scapegoating birds as surveillance mechanisms, all the while profiting from people's apathetic stances.

REFERENCES

Alfonso III, Fernando. 2018. "Are Birds Actually Government-Issued Drones? So Says a New Conspiracy Theory Making Waves (and Money)." *Audubon.org*, November 16, 2018. https://www.audubon.org/news/are-birds-actually-government-issued-drones-so-says-new-conspiracy-theory-making

Birds Aren't Real. 2021. "The History." About the Movement. https://birdsarentreal.com/pages/the-history

Bridges, Lauren. 2021. "Amazon Ring is the Largest Civilian Surveillance Network the U.S. Has Ever Seen." *The Guardian*, May 18, 2021. https://www.theguardian.com/commentisfree/2021/may/18/amazon-ring-largest-civilian-surveillance-network-us

Butter, Michael and Peter Knight. 2020. "Conspiracy Theory in Historical, Cultural, and Literary Studies." In *Routledge Handbook of Conspiracy Theories*, edited by Michael Butter and Peter Knight, 28–42. London: Routledge.

Caumanns, Ute and Andreas Önnerfors. 2020. "Conspiracy Theories and Visual Culture." In *Routledge Handbook of Conspiracy Theories*, edited by Michael Butter and Peter Knight, 441–56. London: Routledge.

Crowley, James. 2021. "Leader of Viral 'Birds Aren't Real' Movement Swears He's Not Joking." *Newsweek*, March 17, 2021. https://www.newsweek.com/birds-arent-real-conspiracy-theory-parody-movement-internet-1573915

Dean, Cornelia. 2009. "Tracking the Flight of Birds, with Tiny Backpacks." *NY Times*, February 12, 2009. https://www.nytimes.com/2009/02/13/science/earth/13webbirds.html

Eng, Margaret L., Bridget J. M. Stutchbury, and Christy A. Morrissey. 2019. "A Neonicotinoid Insecticide Reduces Fueling and Delays Migration in Songbirds."

Science Magazine 365, no. 6458 (September): 1177–80. doi: 10.1126/science.aaw9419

Frontline. 2021. "United States of Conspiracy—Full Documentary." Public Broadcasting Service, *YouTube*, January 21, 2021. https://www.youtube.com/watch?v=hDXJ9OUco04.

Harambam, Jaron. 2020. "Conspiracy Theory Entrepreneurs, Movements and Individuals." In *Routledge Handbook of Conspiracy Theories*, edited by Michael Butter and Peter Knight, 278–91. London: Routledge.

Hoback, Cullen. 2021. *Q: Into the Storm*. HBO Documentary Films, March 21, 2021.

Hofstadter, Richard. 1965. "The Paranoid Style in American Politics." In *The Paranoid Style in American Politics and Other Essays*, 3–40. New York: Knopf.

Jenkins, Henry, Sam Ford, and Joshua Green. 2013. *Spreadable Media: Creating Value and Meaning in a Networked Culture*. New York: New York University Press.

Kennedy, Merrit. 2017. "'Pizzagate' Gunman Sentenced to 4 Years in Prison." *NPR.org*, June 22, 2017. https://www.npr.org/sections/thetwo-way/2017/06/22/533941689/pizzagate-gunman-sentenced-to-4-years-in-prison

Lavin, Talia. 2020. *Culture Warlords: My Journey into the Dark Web of White Supremacy*. New York: Hachette.

Leetaru, Kalev. 2019. "Much of Our Government Digital Surveillance is Outsourced to Private Companies." *Forbes.com*, June 18, 2019. https://www.forbes.com/sites/kalevleetaru/2019/06/18/much-of-our-government-digital-surveillance-is-outsourced-to-private-companies/?sh=26fcd5ff1799

Mayor, Stephen J., Robert P. Guralnick, Morgan W. Tingley, Javier Otegui, John C. Withey, Sarah C. Elmendorf, Margaret E. Andrew, Stefan Leyk, Ian S. Pearse, and David C. Schneider. 2017. "Increasing Phenological Asynchrony between Spring Green-up and Arrival of Migratory Birds." *Scientific Reports* 7, no. 1902: 1–10. Doi: 10.1038/s41598-017-02045-z

McHale, Brian. 1992. *Constructing Postmodernism*. London: Routledge.

Melley, Timothy. 2020. "Conspiracy in American Narrative." In *Routledge Handbook of Conspiracy Theories*, edited by Michael Butter and Peter Knight, 427–40. London: Routledge.

Nixon, Rob. 2011. *Slow Violence and the Environmentalism of the Poor*. Cambridge, MA: Harvard University Press.

Olmsted, Kathryn S. 2009. *Real Enemies: Conspiracy Theories and American Democracy, World War I to 9/11*. Oxford: Oxford University Press.

O'Neil, Cathy. 2017. *Weapons of Math Destruction: How Big Data Increases Inequality and Threatens Democracy*. New York: Crown.

O'Neal, Sean. 2017. "*South Park* Raised a Generation of Trolls." *The AV Club*, July 25, 2017. https://www.avclub.com/south-park-raised-a-generation-of-trolls-1798264498

Ricouer, Paul. 1970. *Freud and Philosophy: An Essay on Interpretation*. New Haven: Yale University Press.

Rosenburg, Kenneth V., Adriaan M. Dokter, Peter J. Blancher, John R. Sauer, Adam C. Smith, Paul A. Smith, Jessica C. Stanton, Arvind Panjabi, Laura Helft, Michael

Parr, and Peter P. Marra. 2019. "Decline of the North American Avifauna." *Science Magazine* 366, no. 6461 (October): 120–24. doi:10.1126/science.aaw1313

Vaidhyanathan, Siva. 2011. *The Googlization of Everything (And Why We Should Worry)*. Oakland: University of California Press.

Walker, Jesse. 2013. *The United States of Paranoia: A Conspiracy Theory*. New York: Harper Perennial.

Zuboff, Shoshana. 2019. *The Age of Surveillance Capitalism: The Fight for a Human Future at the New Frontier of Power*. New York: PublicAffairs.

Chapter 15

Laying Eggs

Ludothematic Resonance and the Birds of Wingspan

Christopher Moore

Wingspan is a board game that involves collecting food resources to play bird cards into appropriately themed habitats. Players guide their animals to lay eggs and provide synergistic bird powers to achieve randomized goals. Designed by Elizabeth Hargrave, the first edition was published in 2019 by Stonemaier Games, and it features 170 pencil color illustrations of North American birds by Ana María Martínez Jaramillo[1] and Natalia Rojas. *Wingspan* is a multiple-award winner, achieving the best "Connoisseur" game of the year at the 2019 Spiel des Jahres, the prestigious annual industry awards in Germany. The game's success has grown to include the European and Oceania expansion sets that increased the number of birds to play with and altered elements of its mechanical dynamics to match the different settings.

The global games industry is second only to the combined film and television industries, generating approximately USD $159.3 billion in 2020 (Field Level Media 2020). In comparison, the tabletop or board game industry is a niche creative industry, which has increased sales by 8–12 percent year-on-year over the past decade as streaming media and online resources have made the pastime more accessible (Grand View Research 2019). The tabletop industry (including puzzles and games) benefited from the global pandemic reaching an estimated USD $11 billion revenue in 2020 (Jarvis 2021). The tabletop industry can be roughly divided into four sections: mass-market games dominated by retail favorites like *Monopoly* and *Pictionary*; collectible card games (CCGs) including *Magic: The Gathering* and *Pokémon*; pen-and-paper-style games such as *Dungeons and Dragons*; and niche hobby games that range from miniature wargame systems to specialist board games and other tabletop experiences.

Wingspan is considered a specialist board game bestseller, with more than 740,000 sales since 2019 (Stonemaier Games 2021), and it has become a transmedia enterprise. The game's popularity supports an aftermarket of products for players to personalize their physical copies, including miniature wooden *meeples* of the birds and food resources. The digital version of the board game was released for Windows and macOS via the digital distribution platform Steam in 2019, and on mobile devices in July 2021. *Celebrating Birds: An Interactive Field Guide Featuring Art from Wingspan* by Rojas and Martínez is due for publication in 2021. A few important factors contribute to the game's success, including its high-quality physical materials and its *Eurogame* design that features a low degree of player competition. It is undeniable that the theme, art, and attention to the birds and their environments captured the imagination of board game fans and bird enthusiasts worldwide, introducing thousands of new players to the medium.

Wingspan has revitalized interest in commonplace birds and has introduced players to many species not previously encountered. Hargrave says she was "sick of playing board games about castles and trains" (qtd. in Evans 2020) and wanted to make a game that featured something she cared for. This care manifested itself in the game's theme and design, revealing an intriguing correlation between human knowledge about birds and game mechanics. The Oceania expansion, for example, introduces players to the Australian ibis (*Threskiornis molucca*) and its infamous reputation as a bin chicken, which gives players the ability to select cards from the discard pile. The New Zealand pūkeko (*Porphyrio melanotus*) is a communally minded addition whose special ability encourages neighboring birds to lay eggs. Activating the fearsome gray butcherbird (*Cracticus torquatus*) requires the player to compare the butcherbird's 40 cm wingspan against others, and smaller birds are converted into extra points and food resources. The ground-dwelling kākāpō (*Strigops habroptilus*) is so critically endangered that its presence provides end-of-game bonus cards to the player lucky enough to encounter it. Australia's superb lyrebird (*Menura novaehollandiae*), when activated, shows off its remarkable mimicry ability and can copy the bird powers of other players' birds. Some birds are exceptional hunters, like the tawny frogmouth (*Podargus strigoides*) who collects additional food resources every activation, and the southern cassowary's (*Casuarius casuarius*) presence is so dominating that it forces other birds to leave but gains a clutch of eggs and bonus food as a result.

This chapter introduces readers to approaches from the field of game studies relevant to analyzing the representation of birds in analogue game texts. This means less attention to the insights available from animal studies and more attention to the way analogue games operate practically and philosophically. However, one important lesson from animal studies is to recognize that *Wingspan*'s theme is not about the experience of birds on their terms. The game represents birds through human frames of knowledge, and the humans' experience of birds is expressed in terms of what can be described as the relationship between representational theme and game mechanics. To examine this relationship in detail, the chapter will propose the concept of "ludothematic resonance" and will consider how effective the relationship is by building on Nathan Altice's (2016) model for analyzing the playing card game as a hardware platform or what can be described as cardware. The central argument proposed by this chapter is that the relationship between what players do in the game, and what that represents, enacts what Michel Foucault (1984) described as a heterotopia.

FROM LUDONARRATIVE DISSONANCE TO LUDOTHEMATIC RESONANCE

Ludology is the act of studying games and their play. The concept of *ludus* refers to the calculated and structured rules-based experience. The *ludic* form of play is compared to the spontaneity of *paidia*, free-form play typically associated with young children or improvisational theater, where the structure is less important than enactment (Caillois 1958, 27). The term "ludonarrative dissonance" was first used by Clint Hocking (2007) to explain the jarring inconsistency between what the game *mechanics* are about and what a digital game's *story* is about. Hocking's concept has been used in game studies to identify the distance between the ludic and narrative features of digital games. He describes two competing contracts of a game, the ludic and the narrative. The ludic contract expresses the games' underlying values through specific game mechanics, while the narrative contract operates experientially for the player and ideologically through its representational signification. Hocking (2007) notes that game designers do not necessarily seek to align these contracts, and, in his analysis of the video game *Bioshock*, he describes how their dissonance and direct opposition effectively mock the player.

Leslie Howe (2017) describes the conflict between the ludic and narrative contracts as "emersion," as opposed to "immersion" because the dissonance effectively throws the player out of the game. This might be true for digital games, where computer-generated and interactive graphics and sounds draw the player in, but it is rarely the case for board games and other tabletop game experiences, due to their analogue material and social contexts. Pen-and-paper role-playing games (RPGs), for example *Dungeons and Dragons*, do not require digital technologies to facilitate complex ludic and narrative play within an immersive shared world. Board game techniques of immersion are not reliant on digital code enacted by silicon-based processes, but rather the game's algorithm (rules and mechanics) being enacted by the embodied cardboard-human machine hybrid. This means that board games provide both immersive and emergent narrative experiences (Tidball 2011).

The emergent narrative of the board game experience occurs simultaneously within the game world and around the table. The players' experience of the text is less a narrative contract, to use Hocking's term, but rather a relationship between the ludic contract and the thematic contract. The question of what counts as a theme is hotly contested among board game players, complicated by generic conventions used to differentiate products in the marketplace. *Wingspan*'s thematic contract, for example, is shaped by the genre of Eurogames, which descend from the work of German game designers who helped to popularize niche hobby games in the 1990s and 2000s. Eurogames are usually characterized by an abstracted design, low degrees of player interaction, high-quality wooden materials, and minimal random elements such as dice. Eurogames are typically distinguished in opposition to *Ameritrash*-style hobby games (or *Amerigames*), an affectionate term for games that feature high randomization, player interaction, and plastic components. By providing an alternative to the interpersonal conflict of tabletop wargames and minimizing the complexity and time commitment of RPGs, Eurogames appealed to families and social gatherings (Woods 2012, 58).

Game studies have long argued that the ludic elements of games are equally capable of expressing representationally as their aesthetics, setting, and narrative elements (Bogost 2006, 2007; Frasca 2003; Begy 2010, 2013). Therefore, it is equally important to examine the philosophical and ideological complexity of board game mechanics in association with their themes. A ludothematic relationship can be arranged in a spectrum of dissonant, resonant, and harmonious designs (Pynenburg 2012), which in Eurostyle board games has distinct material and social dimensions. The sociality of contemporary board games is performed around the tabletop and online through social-media sites and Internet forums. One of the largest online communities of *Wingspan* players outside the Facebook group is the Board Game Geek (BGG); their page for the game includes 46,890 votes for the game, rating it 8.1 out of 10. The page includes the official game description of *Wingspan* as "a competitive, medium-weight, card-driven, engine-building board game," in which players are "bird enthusiasts—researchers, bird watchers, ornithologists, and collectors—seeking to discover and attract the best birds to your network of wildlife preserves" (BoardgameGeek, n.d.). This description outlines the representational schemata in which the ludic contract is balanced against the thematic and sets the Eurogame mechanics in association with players occupying professional roles organizing birds into an artificial habitat.

Wingspan is not a simulation but a simulacrum. One comment in the Board Game Atlas forum aptly describes the ludothematic resonance of *Wingspan*: "I don't feel I'm playing an Eagle, instead, I have learned about Eagles" (rlupino 2020). Hargrave (2020) explains that this was deliberate as she sought to mirror economic systems in the natural world, specifically the supply and demand of resources. The simulacra of economic systems as virtual spaces are common to Eurogames, making them highly effective heterotopias. Heterotopias are liminal spaces based in objective reality that mirror concrete spaces while providing an abstract locale to act out experiences, especially during times of crisis (Hazan 2001). Devin Wilson (2016) explains:

> In Foucauldian terms, the heterotopic space of a [E]urogame—like the mirror has us "reconstitute [ourselves] there where [we are]" [. . .]. The [E]urogame's specular abstraction can allow the player to look at themselves if they are willing to do so. With [E]urogames, if we can pass this Foucauldian mirror test, we can open up a realm of personal meaning previously ascribed primarily to more traditional art forms and more explicitly expressive digital games. (Wilson 2016, 49)

Wingspan's heterotopia is construed in a period of intense ecological collapse, global warming, and extreme threats to bird populations and habitats. The game provides a space of enclosure without perceivable cages or predators, in which humans can expand and reflect the accumulation of knowledge about birds while appreciating their aesthetic qualities through a highly abstract economic management system that rewards effective decision making.

Wilson (2016) engages in heterotopology, the systematic description that takes a space as the object of study, analyzing, describing, and reading these sites as being in relation to others "in such a way as to suspect, neutralize, or invert the set of relations that they happen to designate, mirror, or reflect" (Foucault 1984). Wilson applies the concept to the analysis of *The Castles of Burgundy*, arguing the Eurogame has the capacity to reflect the identities, ambitions, and dreams of players because of the synthesis among material, algorithmic, and thematic components. The key to the heterotopia embodied during play is how the abstracted representational aspects of the game rules, parts, and setting offer a "quasi-historical grounding" (Wilson 2016, 47) that lacks specific historicity and enables a high degree of agency in its interpretation. In collecting various types of animals represented in the game by cardboard tiles with stylized images of cattle, pigs, sheep, and chickens, the rules are explicit in the procedures for amassing the animals on the player's individual tableau (game board) represented by a stable. Wilson argues that although the player might assume the animals are livestock and destined for use as typical farmyard commodities, the game omits any deliberate agricultural mechanics aside from their pasturing, leaving a heterotopic space for the player's projection of the self: "When I play *Castles of Burgundy* , I stipulate that these animals are being rescued and protected from the very agricultural practices that dominate the relationships human have with these nonhuman animals in reality" (Wilson 2016, 48). Comparatively, the heterotopic space of *Wingspan*'s tableau (see figure 15.1) is divided on the play face into three sections of different bird habitats (forest, grassland, and wetland), organizing the ludic placement of cards and resources. On the reverse, the tableau represents a visual artist's leather portfolio case.

Wingspan's heterotopia represents birds through the player tableau, the beautiful pencil color artwork on the cards, the bird powers of each species, food resources, and other game mechanics. The human is representationally implied in the knowledge of birds inscribed in the game, including the Latin taxonomic names on the tops of the cards (see figure 15.2), the trivia and fun facts at the base of the card, and the wooden blocks that represent the number of decisions the human players, during their turns, make for the birds. The heterotopia creates a virtual space wherein players may take pleasure in bird watching and ornithological knowledge, without the accompanying endangerment and erosion of avian habitats and experiences. It produces a perfect

Figure 15.1 Wingspan Player Tableau, Featuring Bird Cards and Egg Counters Played in Three Distinct Habitat Zones. *Source:* Photo by author, used by permission from Stonemaier Games.

Figure 15.2 **An Example of a Single Wingspan Bird Card.** *Source:* Photo by author, used by permission from Stonemaier Games.

enclosure for the human enjoyment of birds without the guilt of the human impact. When asked if Hargrave set out to create a game that specifically drew attention to conservation issues, she answered "No" (The Cardboard Herald, 2020). As a self-described birder, she intended to make a game that gamers would enjoy but birders would find interesting. Hargrave's view was that if the game gets players interested in birds (and, from the feedback and participation online, it does) that may lead to an interest in conservation. It is clear from the number of posts that the player community, particularly on Facebook, has increased the conversation about the overlap between human and bird lives.

Although the *Wingspan* heterotopia is a virtual space enacted as a text during play, Jason Begy (2017) argues that games can also be cultural memory "objectivations," contributing to the ways cultures materially construct their pasts. Begy argues that board games' unique contribution to the historically situated, structural metaphor of remembering is their effectiveness as simulations (734). Begy's account reveals the effectiveness of two railroad-themed tabletop games, *1830* and *Age of Steam*, for representing "the annihilation of time and space, the creation of new spaces, and the loss of geographic aura" for generations who were not present for the "advent of the railroad" (734). In the case of *Wingspan* and the high degree of abstraction in the representational elements of its ludothematic resonance, the game is less simulation than it is simulacra. *Wingspan*'s heterotopia is a carefully constructed space to explore the imagined ecology of birds' cultural and scientific orderings and hierarchies of importance in a world created for them by humans. Interestingly, this heterotopia arises from the shift in game design from narrative to thematic, as the designer initially sought to tell a story in which the human player managed a park that was attended overtly by humans (Hargrave 2020). Hargrave responded to early playtests and feedback on the design by shifting the material layout of the game from a centrally managed board to the individual tableau because players reported, "the thing that I care about is the birds, don't make me look at the middle of the table [. . .]. I want to be all in my tableau [e.g., aviary] because that is where the fun is" (Hargrave 2020). By doing away with the narrative contract, the heterotopia of *Wingspan* focuses attention on human knowledge of birds and, perhaps, care for the real world.

REPRESENTATION IN CARDWARE CHARACTERISTICS: PLANARITY, UNIFORMITY, ORDINALITY, SPATIALITY, TEXTURALITY

To examine the *Wingspan* heterotopia and the ludothematic resonance in the game's representation of birds, the following will expand on Altice's (2016) model for examining the platform specificity of card games. Altice's approach takes inspiration from Ian Bogost and Nick Montfort's (2009) innovations in platform studies, exploring the design process of games as a correlation between the constraints of form, materiality, and underlying systems, and the shaping of creative expression and player experience. Altice provides a detailed analysis of the *Magic: The Gathering* and how a simple "rotational gesture" adds new representational and algorithmic potential, a tactic that "exploded the playing card design space" (2016, 36). Altice's model focuses on five interleaved platform characteristics of the playing card: planarity, uniformity, ordinality, spatiality, and texturality. These cardware characteristics are not discrete categories but overlapping features useful in building the analytical framework for a close study of the representation of birds in *Wingspan*'s materiality and ludothematic resonance.

Planarity

The planarity of the flat rectilinear form of the player's tableau and the bird cards creates a representational duality of strategic information and avian aesthetics. Players can select from three face-up cards and from the deck of face-down cards, creating hidden information, random encounters, unpredictability, and replayability (Altice 2016). This planarity enacts Foucault's (1984) second principle of heterotopias, which describes how spaces change "according to the synchrony of the culture." Zoos and aviaries have changed over time from exhibition spaces to centers of conservation and research, but *Wingspan*'s tableau offers an idealized simulacrum of the bird sanctuary, wildlife preserve, zoo aviary, private aviary, rather than a simulation of those spaces. There is clearly a place for conservation, but that is not constituted during play. Instead, care for birds is a carefully curated, almost fashionable aesthetic that exists somewhere between the ethic of Victorian-era zoos as displays of the exotic and the more contemporary perspective that zoos play a role in breeding and extinction prevention.

The planar surface of *Wingspan* cards is high-quality cardboard stock with the look and feel of embossed canvas. When placed into the tableau environment, they double representationally as both playing cards and canvases added to a scientific artist's folio. The cards feature traditional hand-drawn scientific illustrations that represent both what is known about the bird ornithologically but also what the artist feels about the bird:

> I do my research and try to learn as much as possible about the image I want to create. However, I don't really think about how to approach it. I just jump on it and figure it out as it progresses. I like to experiment and try different ways to achieve certain effects, but I never know if it'll work until it does. With the birds I always start with the beak and the eyes; they need to look alive for me to move forward. I love details and I am a perfectionist, so I won't stop drawing until that piece feels right to my eyes and in my heart. (Rojas qtd. in Hook 2019)

The positions of the birds' heads are also mapped into the game mechanics, as some bonus cards reward players for animals facing in similar or different directions.

The planarity of the *Wingspan* cards includes design innovations such as the ability to "tuck" cards behind the birds, which represents different types of predations. For example, when activating the bird power on the Wedge-Tailed Eagle or the Rufus Owl, the player draws another bird card at random from the deck, and, if the wingspan measured on the card is less than 65 cm, that bird is "tucked" behind the predator to score points at the end of the game. By activating the Wedge-Tailed Eagle, the player also "caches" one rodent resource on the bird for further points, emblematizing a fierce territorial bird that clears the skies of competition to ensure its food supply.

The planarity of the bird card is central to the board game's "engine," with its components featured on the card surface: the bird's wingspan measurement, its illustration, a Latin and common name, a points value, a bird power, a symbol for the type of nest it uses, an icon for the habitat the bird can be played into, and a world map featuring the bird's global habitation. This complex planar canvas of art, iconography, strategic options, and tactical choices is a common feature of tabletop game experiences, both mechanically and strategically. The informational content is part of a long history of the work that game designers must put into their games to avoid negative critiques:

> In past centuries, when card games were considered frivolous, unlawful, or sinful, card designers crowded card faces with moral, religious, or historical lessons, leaving the portion of the card reserved for game-specific information proportionately minuscule. During the mid-90s heyday of CCGs, rule text, game iconography, and statistical cruft dominated the card's surface, sidelining decoration in favour of game-specific information. (Altice 2016, 38)

The "fun facts" at the base of the cards represent a more contemporary synchrony of culture, even featuring a small proportion of colonial and indigenous references. Other facts closely match the bird power effects, demonstrating the harmonization between human knowledge of bird and game mechanics, which Hargrave (2020) reports were a feature of the earliest drafts of the game.

Uniformity

Connected to *Wingspan*'s planar and ordinal design is the uniformity of the game experience, which Altice argues is primarily the industrialized format through which games have cultural and economic affordances (2016, 41). Just as other forms of representational media, from books to cinema and digital games or streaming media, engage in diversity under uniformity, board games, particularly those within the Eurogame category, must meet audience expectations and fit within the affordable limits of production and distribution. *Wingspan* excels in its material construction of the highest quality, but it challenges assumptions about the uniformity of non-random elements in Eurogames. The high number of bird cards and the food generation via a dice mechanic pushes the typical Eurogame format, which is often too strictly formulaic. This change enacts

Foucault's first principle of heterotopia, which describes the shift of these spaces from important categories of crisis, from sacred, privileged, or forbidden places to spaces of deviation, in which behaviors are other than the norm. Here Hargrave deviates from the industrialized design space of the Eurogame, adding elements of risk and randomization that are generally frowned upon by Eurogame purists. Similarly, the heterotopic space of the player's tableau as a bird enclosure departs from the actual lived spaces and behaviors of birds, creating an opportunity for humans to associate with them without the actual lived conditions of reality and the crises of the Anthropocene.

Uniformity in games is crucial to fairness, and while it does not respect the way birds within their species and across them vary dramatically in their looks, experiences, and lives, it is in harmony with the ornithological and common knowledge about birds and typical human encounters with birds. *Wingspan* features more than 250 illustrations of birds, with different powers, effects, and scores. Yet all the cards are uniform in size, quality of production, and illustration. It is the humanness within the uniformity of the scientific illustration that allows these visual representations to express variation and uniqueness. Although it is likely the game would have been enjoyable with photos or even photorealistic digital artwork or overtly stylized graphics, *Wingspan*'s illustrations increase the affective and emotional investment of the human player. In my experience, players make emotional rather than strategic choices, selecting beautiful, well-known, or unusual birds, frequently opting for birds with personal connections to significant events and interests in the players' own lives.

Although the uniform demands of scientific illustration might suggest the necessity for detachment and objectivity, Martínez argues that the images require great care and personal investment. She reports that while there is a core process and means to standardize the image, there is also personal and artistic expression involved in each hand-drawn illustration: "Personally, I prefer the traditional way, because it is the one that reflects the human by means of stroke, pressure, even errors. It is the most primitive way we have to express ourselves and it will be the only one we will always have available" (qtd. in Hook 2019).

For the artist, the images represent human emotional investment in the birds. Similarly, Rojas reports working with the game's publisher, Jamey Stegmaier, to find a unique art style for *Wingspan* bridging scientific uniformity and warmth and expression to attract and communicate clearly with players: "I feel like we found the perfect balance to create illustrations that look alive and realistic but that you can also tell it's a drawing and not a photo" (qtd. in Hook 2019).

The artists' reflections help us see that the heterotopic space of *Wingspan* is produced by the assemblage of the game's mechanic, material, and illustrative design. The result is a ludothematic resonance that does not simulate the experience of birds but represents simulacra of idyllic and utopian existences that players can invest in. It is not necessarily the case that digital photos would afford a more realistic simulation without changes to the ludic structure, although they may cause us to identify in different ways with the humanist expression of the hand-drawn illustrations (Barthes 1980).

Ordinality

In Altice's model, card game platforms can be considered in terms of their ordinality. Cards can be grouped, and they form sets; they can be counted, sorted, ranked, indexed, and ordered. *Wingspan*'s heterotopic simulacra are regulated by the ordinal classifications of the birds into types, habitats, functions, and powers that correspond in part to the representation of the habitats on the tableau and the game mechanics that placing a bird unlocks. As the player introduces a bird into the tableau, they unlock strategic choices, and the habitats become filled with birds and their eggs. Like many Eurogames, bird combinations, locations, and mechanics create statistical complexity through their multiple ordinal systems. Representationally, this complicates the ludothematic resonance, as the number of combinations and strategies threaten to overwhelm the player's sense of theme, expanding the simulacra but effectively decreasing the simulation. However, the benefit of this relationship is the Eurogames' focus on personal choices rather than competitiveness between or among players.

The ordinal frequency means that players can improve their scores through investment in different strategies that have corresponding social-cultural effectiveness as a cultural memory of birds. Wetland birds are associated with drawing cards, increasing the number of drawn cards by adding more birds to the wetland habitat and activating the bird powers. The ludothematic resonance encapsulates the theme of bird knowledge with the player's ability to draw more cards and is represented by the access to water as a necessary ecological fixture. But the flipside of this resonance is the objectification of the birds and their lives, drives, and existences through the human systems of ornithological classification, statistical relevance, and strategic choices leading to likely win conditions.

Ordinality, an important feature of Foucault's third principle, describes the way a heterotopia can juxtapose the incompatibility of multiple sites within a single real place. The botanic garden, with its meticulously managed pathways, garden beds, lawns, greenhouses, and plants from around the globe is "the smallest parcel of the world and then it is the totality of the world" (1984). *Wingspan*'s icons, game mechanics, and food resources present a similarly ordered system designed to universalize birds within an idyllic space that references the real-world locations and habitats of birds but secures them within a precise microcosm. The ordinality of this system is also important for the fourth principle of heterotopias, which is the way they slice time in synchronic symmetry. Ordinality is crucial for heterochrony, which is a break with traditional time, and a function of most tabletop games. *Wingspan* compresses the lifetime of bird experiences, needs, and desires into actions and rounds, while simultaneously structuring the accumulation of human knowledge about these times into strategic choices and actions.

Spatiality

Unlike digital games, which occupy concrete space only in terms of the hardware platforms on which they operate, board games set the boundary of play across a tactile flat surface that can expand and contract depending on the number of players involved. Similarly, unlike the fixed, physical real estate of digital screens, the spatial dimensions of tabletop experiences depend on humans to arrange and display them. The relationship of the human to the game and its spatial density is both mechanically and representationally symbolic; the physical boundary of play on the table is required to enact the virtual heterotopia constructed by the game's ludothematic resonance. The representational qualities of the tableau and the central spatiality of the game have been discussed above. Still, we should note that the representation of virtual space in the tableau is not a reference to specific geography, but rather the idyllic bird *reserve* depicted on the tableau's surface. Spatiality in *Wingspan* enacts the *placeless place* of Foucault's fifth principle, which reminds us that heterotopias are not public places. They might be compulsory locations like prisons or houses of worship that require rites and gestures, or restricted settings like zoos or theatres which demand payment or permission. As a niche-cultural product, *Wingspan* requires a purchase to enter its space. It demands high-level literacies in reading and understanding rules processes, and it relies upon social relations to fully embody its algorithm (although there is a solitaire play option). Games like this also require leisure time. Moreover, this principle also suggests activities of purification, approximating the expulsion of the detrimental effects of the Anthropocene so players might enjoy the birds in artificial isolation from other animals that are not food.

Another important spatial consideration is the cardboard bird feeder (see figure 15.3). The bird feeder, otherwise known as a dice tower, is a cardboard tower with two internal plates against which the food dice bounce off before landing in the tray. The bird feeder resembles a birdhouse, which is a common suburban addition to human-occupied spaces, and the suspended trays of seed that humans make available to birds. The food dice are an unusual

Figure 15.3 The Wingspan Dice Rolling Bird Feeder and Other Game Components.
Source: Photo by author, used by permission from Stonemaier Games.

addition for a predominantly Eurostyle game and represent human understanding of bird dietary needs, including insects, rodents, wheat/seeds, and berries, and have been updated in the Oceania expansion to include nectar. The birdfeeder's materiality and spatiality reinforce both the heterotopia and the game's ludothematic resonance as they represent birds as subject to the taxonomic and cultural knowledge of humans, but also as dependent on human provision of resources. This design is intended to operate within a regime of care as a simulacrum rather than a more educational game that would require simulation-style design, which may be less appealing to *Wingspan*'s broad audience.

Other game spaces in *Wingspan* add to the heterotopia narratively, diegetically, and ludothematically, including the bird powers and the forty wooden action cubes. The cubes structure the emergent narrative of *Wingspan* heterochronologically, helping to pace the game's three-act structure (Tidball 2011), which is divided into four rounds, each with fewer actions than the previous, thus adding pressure to the player decisions. The first step is the human's enactment of the game space: arranging the plastic egg miniatures, setting up the birdfeeder, rolling the dice into it, placing the tableau, shuffling, dealing, and arranging the bird cards. The second act begins as birds are played into the reserve and choices are made about what birds are favored and which ones are tucked and exchanged for eggs and food resources. Strategies and the drama of consequences begin to emerge in the second act. Finally, the third act begins when players perceive the end approaching. This is not necessarily the commencement of the third and final round. Rather, it is the story of the individual playthrough that naturally moves toward its zenith, and the players can more easily plan their final moves. The third act is crowded as the tableau fills with birds and eggs. Resources are frequently more available toward the end of the game as the birds fill up the tableau, which is less harmonious mechanically and thematically.

Texturality

The textural cardware platform of *Wingspan* demonstrates Foucault's sixth and final principle of heterotopias, namely the emergence of a trait that unfolds between two extremes. Foucault argues that the role of the heterotopia is to create a space of illusion that exposes every real space as even more illusory. Or the role is to create a space that is perfect, meticulous, and arranged contrary to our messy and ill-constructed reality, not an illusion but a compensation (Foucault 1984). The latter of these extremes can be mapped onto the final dimension in Altice's model for analyzing card-based platforms, which takes into consideration the texture of the physical and material feel of the tabletop experience: "Cards are made for hands" (Altice 2016, 48). The design and physical manufacture of cards have changed over the centuries better to fit the human hand and play processes, including the rounding of card edges to make shuffling easier and reduce wear. As mentioned, the embossed finish of the *Wingspan* cards gives them a canvas appearance and texture that appeals to the senses of touch and sight (see figure 15.2).

The large food dice have rounded edges and thick wood grain that is distinctively not plastic (see figure 15.3). The relationship between cards and hands has resulted in a linguistic convention: "a hand designates the cards currently in a player's possession" (Altice 2016, 48). However, another convention, the idiom that a "bird in the hand is worth two in the bush," or, in this case the woodland habitat, does not hold true. Rather, the heterotopia compensates for reality because the bird in the habitat is worth points while the bird card in the hand is not. However, the bird cards can be swapped for eggs and other resources, just as the illegal sale of rare and endangered birds, especially from Australia and New Zealand, leads to significant profit and bird mistreatment and deaths. The compensation of *Wingspan*'s ludothematics, where unwanted birds are exchanged freely as commodities, functions as simulacra to expunge the darker side of bird collection from the heterotopia.

Another way to think about the game's cardware is the relationship between its *texturality* and its *textuality*. Interestingly, Altice describes the spatiality of the hand and the discard pile as nondietic; however, this is not the case in the tabletop heterotopia of *Wingspan* and its ludothematic resonance that involves shuffling, drawing, tucking, and discarding birds with both mechanical and symbolic actions and consequences. The Australian Ibis card illustrates this relationship perfectly with its bird power: "When activated: Shuffle the discard pile, then draw 2 cards from it. Choose 1 and tuck it behind this bird or add it to your hand. Discard the other." The Australian Ibis are described as: "The ubiquitous villains of Australia's cities over many decades by snatching our sangas (sausages in a bread sandwich or roll) tossing rubbish around like nobody's business and being generally annoying in every way" (Graham 2020).

As wetlands on the east, southeast, and southwest coastlands were decimated by urbanization and climate change, the ibis migrated and were first seen in Australian cities when conservationists introduced them in the 1970s (Allatson and Connor 2018). The excess of human consumption in cities has proven to be a sustainable niche for the ibis and often a pest for humans as rearticulated in the compensation of the heterotopia as the Australian ibis card's "fun facts."

CONCLUSION

The question of whether *Wingspan* leads to further engagement with bird ecologies and conservation efforts, or if it is a game of avoiding and deferring engagement of a more lasting kind, cannot be answered easily. Altices's model for examining the platform characteristics of card games helps reveal the representational elements of analogue game design, but it does not fully address the performance of heterotopias enacted by players. Just as the emergent narrative of games occurs as players embody the board game algorithm, the heterotopia is formed by the player's understanding of the tabletop platform materially, spatially, culturally, and socially. As Wilson argues, a heterotopia opens a realm of personal interpretation. Given the game's popularity among bird fans, game fans, and new audiences who do not fit either of those two categories, it is possible that *Wingspan*'s ludothematic resonance succeeds as a game design and as a heterotopia that affords great player agency. The game provides a space of freedom, allowing players to gather birds together and take pleasure in encountering birds that would be impossible otherwise. After watching players enjoy the game, I am convinced that Wilsons's observation holds true: players are not simply deferring care but embodying it personally. Furthermore, the reports of player experiences via social media do provide evidence of that passion extending beyond the heterotopia of the tabletop, or at least into the heterotopic spaces of the Internet.

NOTE

1. The artist Ana María Martínez Jaramillo is credited as such on the game *Wingspan* (2019) and its expansions but credited as Ana María Martínez on the book *Celebrating Birds: An Interactive Field Guide Featuring Art from Wingspan* (2021).

REFERENCES

Allatson, Paul, and Andrea Connor. 2018. "Friday Essay: The Rise of the 'Bin Chicken,' a Totem for Modern Australia." *The Conversation*, September 7, 2018. Accessed June 8, 2021. https://theconversation.com/friday-essay-the-rise-of-the-bin-chicken-a-totem-for-modern-australia-100673

Altice, Nathan. 2016. "The Playing Card Platform." In *Analog Game Studies (Volume 1)*, edited by Aaron Trammell, Evan Torner, and Emma Leigh Waldron, 34–54. Pittsburgh: ETC.

Barthes, Roland. 1980. *Camera Lucida: Reflections on Photography*. Translated by Richard Howard. New York: Hill and Wang.

Begy, Jason. 2010. "The History and Significance of Jumping in Games." In *GAME// PLAY//SOCIETY: Contributions to Contemporary Computer Game Studies, Proceedings of the 4th Annual Vienna Games Conference*, edited by C. Swertz and M. Wagner, 83–96. Munich: Kopaed.

———. 2013. "Experiential Metaphors in Abstract Games." *Transactions of the Digital Games Research Association* 1(1). http://todigra.org/index.php/todigra/article/view/3/1.

———. 2017. "Board Games and the Construction of Cultural Memory." *Games and Culture* 12, no. 7–8 (November): 718–738. doi: 10.1177/1555412015600066

BoardgameGeek. n.d. "Wingspan 2019." Accessed June 22, 2021. https://boardgamegeek.com/boardgame/266192/wingspan

Bogost, Ian. 2006. *Unit Operations*. Cambridge, MA: MIT.

———. 2007. *Persuasive Games*. Cambridge, MA: MIT.

Bogost, Ian, and Nick Montfort. 2009. *Raising the Beam: The Atari Video Computer System Platform Studies*. Cambridge, MA: MIT.

Caillois, Roger. 1958. *Man, Play and Games*. Chicago: University of Illinois.

The Cardboard Herald, 2020. "Elizabeth Hargrave on design, community, success and wingspansions—TCbH Interview." *YouTube video*, 30:06 4 December 2020. https://www.youtube.com/watchv=3ZwdKPFdGUs&ab_channel

Evans, Kate. 2020. "The Board Game for Birds." *New Zealand Geographic* 166 (November- December). https://www.nzgeo.com/stories/the-board-game-for-birders/

Frasca, Gonzalo. 2003. "Simulation versus Narrative: Introduction to Ludology." In *The Video Game Theory Reader*, edited by Mark J. P. Wolf and Bernard Perron, 221–235. New York: Routledge.

Field Level Media. 2020. "Report: Gaming Revenue to Top $159B in 2020." *Reuters*, May 12, 2020. https://www.reuters.com/article/esports-business-gaming-revenues-idUSFLM8jkJMl

Foucault, Michel. 1984 [1967]. "Of Other Spaces, Heterotopias." Translated by Jay Miskowiec from *Architecture, Mouvement, Continuité*, no. 5: 46–49. https://foucault.info/documents/heterotopia/foucault.heteroTopia.en/

Graham, Ben. 2020. "Bin Chickens: The Big Myth about Australia's Most Hated Bird," *News.com.au*, November 3, 2020. Accessed June 8, 2021. https://www.news.com.au/technology/science/animals/bin-chickens-the-big-myth-about-australias-most-hated-bird/news-story/353a64d27ead331c0a678e04f78cdf73

Grand View Research, 2019. "Playing Cards and Boardgames Market Size, Share & Trends Analysis Report by Product (board games (chess, scrabble, monopoly, ludo), playing cards), by Distribution Channel, and Segment Forecasts, 2019-2025." *Grand View Research*, September 2019. https://www.grandviewresearch.com/industry-analysis/playing-cards-board-games-market

Hargrave, Elizabeth. 2020. "NYU Game Centre Lecture Series Presents Elizabeth Hargrave." *YouTube*, 1:28:25. October 3, 2020. https://www.youtube.com/watch?v=ZqYXC4_A6KU

Hazan, Susan. 2001. "The Virtual Aura—Is There Space for Enchantment in a Technological World?" Electronic Imaging & the Visual Arts Conference Proceedings. Glasgow, July 24–28, 2001). *Archives & Museum Informatics*. https://www.museumsandtheweb.com/mw2001/papers/hazan.html

Hocking, Clint. 2007. "Ludonarrative Dissonance in Bioshock: The Problem of What the Game is About." *Click Nothing, TypePad.com*, October 7, 2007. Accessed February 25, 2021. http://clicknothing.typepad.com/click_nothing/2007/10/ludonarrative-d.html

Hook, Niklas. 2019. "The Female Artists that Lift *Wingspan* to the Skies." *Unboxing the Art of Board Games*. January 14, 2019. Accessed June 15, 2021. http://www.greenhookgames.com/wingspan-artists/

Howe, Leslie A. 2017. "Ludonarrative Dissonance and Dominant Narratives." *Journal of the Philosophy of Sport* 44, no. 1: 44–54.

Jarvis, Matt. 2020. "Free Time During Lockdown Helped Board Game Sales to Jump in 2020—Report." *Dicebreaker.com*, January 29, 2021. https://www.dicebreaker.com/categories/board-game/news/games-and-puzzles-market-2020-2021

Mizer, Nick. 2016. "'Fun in a Different Way': Rhythms of Engagement and Non-Immersive Play Agendas." In *Analog Game Studies (Volume 2)*, edited by Aaron Trammell, Evan Torner, and Emma Leigh Waldron, 9–14. Pittsburgh: ETC.

Pynenburg, Travis. 2012. *"Games Worth a Thousand Words: Critical Approaches in Ludonarrative Harmony in Interactive Narratives."* Senior Honors Thesis, University of New Hampshire.

rlupion. 2020. "Obligatory post about wingspan and its theme." Board Game Atlas. https://www.boardgameatlas.com/forum/hy9GG84VvB/obligatory-post-about-wingspan-and-its-theme

Stonemaier Games. 2021. "2020 Behind-the-Scenes Stakeholder Report for Stonemaier Games." *Stonemaiergames.com*, April 8, 2021. https://stonemaier-games.com/2020-behind-the-scenes-stakeholder-report-for-stonemaier-games/

Tidball, Jeff. 2011. "Three-Act Structure Just Like God and Aristotle Intended." In *The Kobold Guide to Board Game Design*, edited by Mike Selinker, 11–19. Kirkland, WA: Open Design LLC.

Treanor, Mike. 2013. *Investigating Procedural Expression and Interpretation in Videogames*. Ph.D. dissertation, University of California at Santa Cruz, CA.

Wilson, Devin. 2016. "The Eurogame as Heterotopia." In *Analog Game Studies (Volume 2)*, edited by Aaron Trammell, Evan Torner, and Emma Leigh Waldron, 34–50. Pittsburgh: ETC.

Woods, Stewart. 2012. *Eurogames: The Design, Culture and Play of Modern European Board Games*. Jefferson, NC: McFarland.

Index

Abram, David, 9
Ackerman, Jennifer, 2, 128, 146; *The Bird Way*, 2, 99; *The Genius of Birds*, 10, 99, 146
activism, activist, 121–24, 127, 129, 134, 199, 219, 224
Adams, Douglas, 79
advocacy, 193–94, 206
airship, 53, 59–60, 62, 65, 67, 69
Alaimo, Stacy, 166
Albee, Edward, 75–76
Alcoff, Linda, 3, 106, 109, 111, 118; "The Problem of Speaking for Others," 106
Alter, Robert, 31
Altice, Nathan, 231, 236, 238, 240, 243–44
amusement parks, 58, 60, 62, 65; Coney Island, 55, 59; Luna Park, New York City, 55, 59; Luna Park, Pittsburgh, 59; Steeplechase, 55
animal stories, 89–90, 92–93, 98, 101, 106
Anthropocene, 79, 82, 187, 239, 241
Arnold, Matthew, 9, 105; "Poor Matthias," 105
Asimov, Isaac, 134n3
Atwood, Margaret, 3, 121–34, 192–93, 220; "Act Now to Save Our Birds," 125–26; *Bringing Back the Birds*, 133; *The Complete Angel Catbird*, 3, 122, 126, 130–33; *Dearly*, 133; "Fatal Light Awareness," 133, 192; *For the Birds*, 3, 122, 126–30, 132; *The Handmaid's Tale*, 122; *MaddAddam* trilogy, 122; "Scarlet Ibis," 124; *Surfacing*, 123; *The Year of the Flood*, 125
Audubon, John James, 205, 207
Auerbach, Erich, 14–15
augury, 15, 44
avian, 37; breeding, 132; mind, 99, 101; ontology, 37, 43, 47; other, 80; subjectivity, 205

Babcock, Charles A., 204
Bailey, Florence Merriam, 203
Baird, Alison, 98; *White as Waves*, 98
Baker, John Alec, 3, 139–42, 144, 146–50; *Diaries*, 139–40, 142, 147, 150; *The Hill of Summer*, 139–40, 147–49, 151; "On the Essex Coast," 139, 143, 149; *The Peregrine*, 3, 139, 144–45, 147–48
Balcombe, Jonathan, 98; *What a Fish Knows: The Inner Lives of Our Underwater Cousins*, 98
Ballard, J. G., 2, 37, 39, 42, 50–51; *The Atrocity Exhibition*, 40; *Empire of the Sun*, 42; *Kingdom Come*, 42;

"Memories of the Space Age," 40;
"Myths of the Near Future," 40;
"Storm Bird, Storm Dreamer," 40;
Unlimited Dream Company, 37, 41, 50
Balzac's Coffee, 125
Barbie Chang, 185; "Barbie Chang Can't Stop Watching," 185
Baskin, Leonard, 38, 46–49; "The Interrogator," 48; "The Summoner," 48
bat, 2, 98, 105; Daubenton's, 139; long-tailed, 2
Bate, Jonathan, 49–50
Baudelaire, Charles, 41; "The Albatross," 41–42; *Les Fleurs du mal* [*The Flowers of Evil*], 41
Baxter, Jeanette, 40
Beard, Dan, 205–6, 208; "Let the Eagle Scream!", 206
Beebe, William, 96; *The Bird: Its Form and Function*, 96
Begy, Jason, 235–36
Bekoff, Marc, 98
Bellows, Nathaniel, 190–91; "The Bargain," 190
Benchley, Peter, 114; *Jaws*, 114
Berenstein, Nadia, 183, 193; "Deathtraps in the Flyways: Electricity, Glass and Bird Collisions in Urban North America, 1887–2014," 183
Berger, John, 182; "Why Look at Animals?", 182
Bert, Edmund, 155; *An Approved Treatise of Hawkes and Hawking*, 155
Bialik, Hayyim Nachman, 33
Bird Day, 204
birding: BirdCams, 209; BirdCast, 129; BirdSleuth, 209; Celebrate Urban Birds, 209; Christmas Bird Count, 209; EBird, 209; Great Backyard Bird Count, 209; Habitat Network, 209; history, 199; NestWatch, 209; Project Feederwatch, 209; rhetoric, 4, 199, 203–6, 210–11; youth, 4, 199, 204, 206, 210–11
BirdLife International, 122
birds: albatross, 41, 44, 166, 168, 174–75, 177–78 (Laysan, 165, 176; short-tailed, 177); auk, 78–82; Bald and Golden Eagle Protection Act, 206; bowerbird, 98; butcherbird, grey, 230; cardinal, 215; cassowary, southern, 230; cat predation, 122, 127–28, 130–32; cedar waxwing, 183; chickadee, 189; chicken, 233; crane, 31; crow, 49, 92, 98–101, 183 (American, 100); curlew, 46, 90, 93, 95–97, 101, 150 (Eskimo, 101n2); dodo, 78, 175; dove, 26, 30, 32, 38, 40; duck, 57; dunlin, 150; eagle, 38, 45, 47, 157(bald, 98, 199; wedge-tailed, 237–38); egret, snowy, 187; falcon, merlin, 147; finch, 91; godwit, 150; goose, geese, 27, 38, 57 (graylag, 90, 94); goshawk, 153–56, 161–62; grackle, 184; gray, 100; grebe, little, 150; Gull, 142, 147 (black-backed, 141, 147; blackheaded, 141; common, 141; glaucous, 141; herring, 141; sea, 117, 178); hawk, 44–45, 146, 150, 153–58, 160–62, 189; huia, 78; hummingbird, 190–91; ibis, 10, 124 (Australian, 230, 244); jackdaw, 95, 98, 140; kākāpō, 230; kea, 107, 109–12; kestrel, 140; kioea, 79; kookaburra, 116–17; language of the, 44; lyrebird, 116–17, 230; magpie, 98; martin, purple, 223; mistle, 140; moa, 78; murre, 78; nuthatch, 215; O'ahu nukupu'u, 79; O'ahu 'ō 'ō, 79; osprey, 92; owl, 10, 47, 65, 69, 91, 132, 182, 237 (tawny, 139); oystercatcher, 150; parrot, 91; partridge, 189; pelican, 31; penguin, 76–78, 82, 84; peregrine, 142, 144, 147–48; pheasant, 155; pigeon, 2, 22n1, 26, 28–33, 78, 145, 148, 167, 174, 189, 222; pipistrelle, 139;

protection, protectionists, 199–206, 208, 212; puffins, 78; pūkeko, New Zealand, 230; raven, 47, 98–100; razorbill, 78; redknot, 168–69, 173; redshank, 150; redstart, 140; robin, 215; rook, 47, 98, 140; rooster, 47; shrike, 150; skylark, 14, 46; snipe, 147; sparrow, white-crowned, 222; stork, 31; swallow, 150, 187; swan, 38, 91; swift, 46; tanager, scarlet, 127; tawny frogmouth, 230; teal, 150; thrush, 133, 192; tiercel, 146, 148, 150–51, 157; turkey, 57–58; vulture, 31, 47; warbler, 191; wetland, 240; whimbrel, 150; window collision, 4, 122–23, 132, 181–90, 192–94; wren, 187
Birds Aren't Real [BAR], 4, 215–17, 219, 221, 223–25
Blake, William, 37, 41; *Milton*, 41
Blechman, Andrew, 26
blue humanities, 4, 166–68, 170
Bodsworth, Fred, 3, 90, 93–94; *Last of the Curlews*, 3, 90, 94–96, 101
Bogost, Ian and Nick Montfort, 236
Boke of St. Albans, 156
Booth, Dexter, 184
Bradshaw, David, 11–12
Braun, Alexander, 62
Breton, André, 38, 42; Éluard, Paul, 43; *The Immaculate Conception*, 43
Brown, Dan, 218; *The Da Vinci Code*, 218
Brown, Ruth Mowry, 203; "Frank's Banded Robin," 203
Bugnyar, Thomas, 99
Burgess, Thornton W., 202, 208; *The Burgess Bird Book for Children*, 202
Burroughs, John, 89, 91–93, 200; "Real and Sham Natural History," 89, 91; *Ways of Nature*, 200
Burroughs, William S., 220
Burrows, Steve, 121–22; *A Cast of Falcons*, 121
Butler, Samuel, 107; *A First Year in Canterbury Settlement*, 107

Butter, Michael and Peter Knight, 215, 218
Buxton, Kira, 3, 90, 96, 98–99, 101; *Hollow Kingdom*, 3, 90, 98–101

Canemaker, John, 55
cardware, 236
Carey, John, 130
Carrington, Leonora, 38
Carson, Rachel, 93, 144, 149; *Silent Spring*, 144, 149; *Under the Sea-Wind*, 93
Carwardine, Mark, 79
Caumanns, Ute and Andreas Önnerfors, 222; "Conspiracy Theories and Visual Culture," 222
Chang, Victoria, 185
Chapman, Frank, 203; *Bird-Lore*, 203
citizen science, 209
Cixous, Hélène, 10, 22
Clifton, Lucille, 190; "for the bird who flew against our window one morning and broke his natural neck," 190
climate change, 98, 101, 115, 123, 165, 188, 194, 216, 219, 223, 233
Cocker, Mark, 143–44
cognition, cognitive, 89, 93–94, 98–99, 128
Cohn, Dorrit, 106, 109
Cole, Teju, 188; *Open City*, 188–89
Coleridge, Samuel Taylor, 42, 80, 166, 174; *The Rime of the Ancient Mariner*, 42, 80, 166, 174
Collier, Michael, 188; "Bird Crashing into Window," 188
comparative psychology, 89, 91, 94; avian, 90, 93; ethology, 89–90, 93–94
conspiracy, 4, 215–18; apparel, 215, 217, 222–23; for-profit, 215; Icke, David, 217; Jones, Alex, 217; in literature, 218–19; McIndoe, Peter, 217; McVeigh, Timothy, 219; New York Slave Conspiracy of 1741, 219;

Q: Into the Storm, 219; retail, 215, 217, 223; theories, 215–16, 222–24
Cornell Lab of Ornithology, 125, 129, 209
Cowley, Jason, 142–43, 145
Cramer, Deborah, 4, 166–75; *The Narrow Edge: A Tiny Bird, an Ancient Crab, and an Epic Journey*, 4, 166, 169
Cubbit, Geoffrey, 156
Curthoys, Ann and Anne McGrath, 153; *How to Write History that People Want to Read*, 153

Dalí, Salvador, 38, 40, 42–43
Darwin, Charles, 91, 148; *The Expression of the Emotions in Man and the Animals*, 91
Davies, Bryony, 39
Dee, Tim, 145
DeJong, Meindert, 207–8; *The Wheel on the School*, 207
DeLillo, Don, 218, 220; *Libra*, 218
de Man, Paul, 10
Deniord, Chard, 191–92; "Confession of a Bird Watcher," 191–92
Derrida, Jacques, 19–20
Descartes, René, 81
de Waal, Frans, 98
Dick, Philip K., 220
Dillard, Annie, 153
du Maurier, Daphne, 3, 107, 112, 114–17; "The Birds," 3, 107, 112, 114
Dundas, Deborah, 125
D'Urville, Jules Dumont, 78

Earle, Sylvia, 166; *The World Is Blue*, 166
ecocriticism, ecocritical, 3, 142, 144–45, 149, 168; blue, 168
Eilat, Shuly, 30
Eliade, Mircea, 45
endangered species, 96, 230, 243
Endangered Species Act, 208

Erickson, Laura, 210–11; *Sharing the Wonder of Birds with Kids*, 210
Ernst, Max, 38, 40–41, 47
Evans, E. P., 91
evolution, evolutionary, 90, 92, 96, 98, 100–101, 166
extinction, extinct, 79, 90, 96, 98, 101, 155, 165, 167, 169–70, 175, 188

falconry, 153–55, 157–58, 160
Fanshawe, John, 145–46, 148–49; "Notes on J. A. Baker," 145
Faris, Wendy, 62
Fatal Light Awareness Program [FLAP], 192
Felski, Rita, 121
Fiamengo, Janice, 94
Fink, Louis, 206–7; "Bird Study's Not So Bad," 206
Foucault, Michel, 231, 237, 239–41, 243
France, Anatole, 3, 75, 77, 80–81, 84; *L'Île des Pingouins*, 75; *Penguin Island*, 3, 75–77, 80–81
Fraser, Bill, 84
Freud, Sigmund, 38–39; *The Interpretation of Dreams*, 39
Frost, Robert, 182–83; "Questioning Faces," 182

game, 4, 229, 235, 241; board, 229–30, 232, 236; studies, 230–32
Garnett, David, 159–60
Genette, Gérard, 27–28
Gibson, Graeme, 124–26, 130; *The Bedside Book of Birds*, 130
Glück, Louise, 4
Godfrey-Smith, Peter, 98; *Other Minds: The Octopus, the Sea, and the Deep Origins of Consciousness*, 98
Goodall, Jane, 98
Goodell, Jeff, 172; *The Water Will Come*, 172

Gowdy, Barbara, 98; *The White Bone*, 98
Graham, Edward, 207; "The Story of Wildlife Conservation," 207; and William Van Dersal, 207
Graham, Jorie, 189–90; *Swarm*, 189
graphic novel, 57, 69n4, 122–23, 130
Grennan, Eamon, 191–92; "On a Cape May Warbler Who Flew Against My Window," 191
grief, 99–100, 167
Griffin, Donald, 98, 105
Griffiths, Jay, 18; *Pip Pip: A Sideways Look at Time*, 18
Grinnell, George Bird, 199

Harambam, Jaron, 217
Haraway, Donna, 106, 118
Hargrave, Elizabeth, 229–30, 233, 235, 236, 238–39
Haru, Maija-Liisa, 94
Hasegawa, Hiroshi, 177
Hegel, Georg Wilhelm Friedrich, 156
Heller, Joseph, 220
Herrnstein, Richard J., 94
heterotopia, 231, 233–34, 236–37, 239–44
history, 153–54, 156, 157, 160–61
Hocking, Clint, 231–32
Hofstadter, Richard, 218; "The Paranoid Style in American Politics," 218
Homer, 10
Hopkins, Gerard Manley, 140, 148
Hornaday, William T., 204
Horton, Zach, 174
Howe, Leslie, 231
Hudson, W. H., 141–42; *Land's End: A Naturalist's Impressions of West Cornwall*, 141
Huggan, Graham, 143
Hughes, Ted, 2, 37, 39, 44–47, 49–51, 148; "Bride and Groom Lie Hidden for Three Days," 47; "Cave Birds," 49; *Cave Birds*, 38, 46–48; "A Childish Prank," 50; *Crow*, 38, 45–46, 49–50; "Crow Alights," 50; "Crow and Mama," 50; "Crow Blacker Than Ever," 50; "Crow's Lineage," 50; "Curlews Lift," 46; "The Gatekeeper," 47; "A Green Mother," 47; "The Guide," 47; "Hawk in the Rain," 44–45; *Hawk in the Rain*, 44; "Hawk Roosting," 45; "His Legs Ran About," 47; "The Interrogator," 47; "The Judge," 47; *Lupercal*, 45; *Season Songs*, 46; "skylarks," 46; "swifts," 46; "That Moment," 50

instinct, 90–96, 98, 101, 148
International Ornithological Congress, 126
irony, 215–17, 223–25

Jahn, Manfred, 28
James, William, 13
Jaramillo, Ana María Martínez, 229–30, 239, 244n1; *Celebrating Birds: An Interactive Field Guide Featuring Art from Wingspan*, 230; and Natalia Rojas, 229–30, 239
Jarvis, Brooke, 171
Jefferies, Richard, 140, 142; *The Life of the Fields*, 140
Jenkins, Henry, Sam Ford, and Joshua Green, 217; *Spreadable Media: Creating Value and Meaning in a Networked Culture*, 217
Jung, Carl, 50

Kadar, Marlene, 161
Keats, John, 80, 185; "Ode to a Nightingale," 80, 185
King, Barbara, 100; *How Animals Grieve*, 100
kinship, 165–67, 169–72, 174, 176–78
Kolbert, Elizabeth, 78–79
Kurlansky, Mark, 58

Labio, Catherine, 57
Lanham, J. Drew, 209; *The Home Place: Memoirs of a Colored Man's Love Affair with Nature*, 209
Lavin, Talia C., 219; *Culture Warlords: My Journey into the Dark Web of White Supremacy*, 219
Leber, Jessica, 124
Lejeune, Phillip, 70n7
Lemmon, Robert, 207; *Our Amazing Birds*, 207
Levy, Ceri, 105, 125; and Chris Aldhous, 125; *Ghosts of Gone Birds*, 125
Lobb, Joshua, 3, 107; *The Flight of Birds*, 3, 107, 116, 118
Lockwood, Hazel, 206; *The Golden Book of Birds*, 206
Lockwood, Samuel, 91
Long, William J., 89, 91–93; *School of the Woods*, 89, 92
Lopez, Barry, 79, 84
Lorenz, Konrad, 90, 94–95; "The Companion in the Bird's World," 94
Louv, Richard, 210–11; *Citizen Science*, 211; *Last Child in the Woods: Saving Our Children from Nature-Deficit Disorder*, 210; *Vitamin N: The Essential Guide to a Nature-Rich Life*, 210–11
ludothematic resonance, 4, 229, 231, 233, 236–37, 240–42, 244
Lutwack, Leonard, 123–24, 127, 134; *Birds in Literature*, 123

Macdonald, Helen, 3, 79, 128, 154–62; *H is for Hawk*, 3, 153, 158–59, 161; *Vesper Flights*, 162
magical realism, 29, 31–32, 53, 62, 65, 67
Magritte, Rene, 38, 40
Malebranche, Nicolas, 81
Maresca, Peter, 63
Marra, Peter, 127, 130; and Chris Santella, 128, 130

Marvin, Garry, 106
Marzluff, John, 99–100; *In the Company of Crows and Ravens*, 100; and Tony Angell, 100
Massenet, Jules, 75
McAlpine, Erica, 191; "The Poet's Mistake," 191
McCay, Winsor, 3, 53–71; *The Adventures of Baron Munchausen*, 63; *Little Nemo in Slumberland*, 3, 53–54, 56–64; *A Tale of the Jungle Imps by Felix Fiddle*, 54
McCloskey, Robert, 206; *Make Way for Ducklings*, 206
McCloud, Scott, 62
McHale, Brian, 218
McKibben, Bill, 83, 122; *The End of Nature*, 122–23
Meeker, Joseph W., 145; *The Comedy of Survival: Literary Ecology and a Play Ethic*, 145
Melley, Timothy, 216, 220
Merwin, W. S., 186; "Shore Birds," 186
Middleton, Colin, 41
migration, 95–97, 124, 168, 173, 176, 183, 186, 203, 222–23, 244
Miller, Olive Thorne, 203
Moore, George, 10
Moran, Joe, 143; "A Cultural History of the New Nature Writing," 143
Morrison, Guy, 170; and Brian Harrington, 170, 173
mortality, 165–66, 169–71, 173, 175, 177–78
mourning theory, 165–66, 168
Muir, John, 207

Nabokov, Vladimir, 181–83; *Pale Fire*, 181–82
Nagel, Thomas, 105, 108, 118; "What is it Like to be a Bat?", 105
Nahmanides, 32
Narrative theory, 25; analepsis, 28; focalization, 25, 28, 106, 108; heterodiegetic narrative, 27–29;

homodiegetic narrative, 27–29; paralepsis, 27; sequentiality, 28; temporality, 25, 28
National Aviary, 1
National Wildlife Federation, 208
New Nature Writing, 3, 139, 142–46, 148–49, 151
newspaper comics, 53–54, 59, 69
Newstead, David, 173
Niederhoff, Burkhard, 28
Nielsen, Henrik Scov, 30
Nixon, Richard, 208
Nixon, Rob, 225

Oliver, Mary, 1; "Winter and the Nuthatch," 1
Olmsted, Kathryn S., 216
O'Neal, Sean, 224
O'Neil, Cathy, 221; *Weapons of Math Destruction*, 221
oneiric, 53, 55–56, 60, 63
ordinality, 236, 240–41
Osvath, Mathias, 99
Otto, Stacy, 167

paranoia, 220
Parker, Morgan, 183–85; *Other People's Comfort Keeps Me Up at Night*, 183
Parker, Trey and Matt Stone, 224; *South Park*, 224
Parkins, Kaitlyn, 193
Parkinson Zamora, Lois, 62
Patterson, Virginia Sharpe, 201, 204, 208; *Dickey Downy: The Autobiography of a Bird*, 200–202, 204
Pelee Island Bird Observatory, 124–25
Pendell, Dale, 15; *The Language of Birds: Some Notes on Chance and Divination*, 15
Perkins, David, 79–80
Peterson, Roger Tory, 206; *A Field Guide to the Birds*, 206
Pigott, Andrew, 75–76

planarity, 236–38
Plath, Sylvia, 38, 47, 49
Plumwood, Val, 118
Powers, Richard, 84; *The Overstory*, 84
Pringle, Allen, 91
Pynchon, Thomas, 218, 220; *The Crying of Lot, 49*, 218

Rabelais, 47; *Gargantua and Pantagruel*, 47
Rare Bird Club, 126
Reddy, Srikanth, 187, 190–91; *Underworld Lit*, 187, 190–91
Reed, Ishmael, 218, 220; *Mumbo Jumbo*, 218
Reimink, Keith, 84
Ricoeur, Paul, 218
Ridgely, Steven C., 75
Roader, Katherine, 54
Roberts, Charles G. D., 89, 91–93; *Kindred of the Wild*, 89
Roosevelt, Theodore, 67, 89, 91–93; "Nature Fakers," 92; nature fakers, 89–90
Rosal, Patrick, 184; "Boys' Bodies in Flight (are also a kind of text)," 184
Rose, Alexander, 58
Roth, Philip, 218; *The Plot Against America*, 218
Rowden, Claire, 75
Royal Society for the Protection of Birds, 143
Royle, Nicholas, 12, 22n2; *An English Guide to Bird Watching*, 12–13
Russell, Franklin, 78

Safina, Carl, 4, 98, 166–69, 174–78; *Beyond Words: What Animals Think and Feel*, 98; *Eye of the Albatross*, 4, 166, 168, 174–76; *Song for the Blue Ocean*, 166, 168, 174–75
Sandburg, Carl, 69, 132
Schoolhouse Rock!, 223–24
seabird, 165–66, 169, 174–77
Sethi, Anita, 123

Seton, Ernest Thompson, 89, 91–93; *Wild Animals I Have Known*, 89, 92
Shalev, Meir, 2, 28, 31–33; *A Pigeon and a Boy*, 2, 28–29
Shelley, Percy Bysshe, 80, 186; "To a Skylark," 80
Shiffman, Smadar, 31
shorebird, 165–71, 186
Sicher, Efraim, 30
Siegel, Robert, 98; *Whalesong*, 98
Simondon, Gilbert, 81
Sleigh, Charlotte, 193
Smith, Danez, 184
Smith, Jos, 142; *The New Nature Writing: Rethinking the Literature of Place*, 142
Smithsonian Migratory Bird Center, 125, 127
Soule, Caroline G., 200; "Humanizing the Birds," 200
spatiality, 236, 241
Spiegelman, Art, 69n4
Spielberg, Steven, 220; *Minority Report*, 220
Sproul, William Cameron, 204
Steeves, H. R., 75
Stone, Witmer, 209
stream of consciousness, 13, 15
Strycker, Noah, 82
surrealism, surrealist, 37, 40–42, 48, 50
surveillance, 215, 219–21, 224–25; Amazon Ring, 221; drones, 215, 221, 223; geolocators, 223; Patriot Act, 220; Snowden, Edward, 220–21

Tarr, Joel, 67
Tecumseh, 1
Temple, Philip, 3, 107, 109–11, 116; *Beak of the Moon*, 3, 107, 109–10, 112
Terdiman, Richard, 112–13
Terres, John, 207; *Songbirds in Your Garden*, 207
texturality, 236, 243
Torrey, Bradford, 203

uniformity, 236, 238–39

Vaidhyanathan, Siva, 221
van Dooren, Thom, 1–2, 99, 106, 126, 133, 165, 169; *Flight Ways*, 2; *In The Wake of Crows*, 2, 99

Walker, Jesse, 217; *The United States of Paranoia: A Conspiracy Theory*, 217
Ware, Chris, 69n5
Warner, Sylvia Townsend, 159
Washburn, Margaret, 91; *The Animal Mind*, 91
Wexler, Joyce, 31
White, T. H., 3, 142, 154–56, 158–62; *England Have My Bones*, 159; *The Goshawk*, 3, 142, 154–55, 158, 161; *The Once and Future King*, 158–59, 161; *The Sword and the Stone*, 161–62
Wiese, Anne Pierson, 189; "Birds Hitting Glass," 189
Wilson, Devin, 233, 244
Wilson, Emily, 39
Wilson, Rawdon, 65
Wilson, Robert Anton, 224; *Illuminatus!*, 216; and Robert Shea, 216
Wingspan, 4, 229–30, 232–44
Woessner, Warren, 187–88; "What's An Angel Like?", 187
Wood, Gillen D'Arcy, 78
Wood, Sarah, 19–20
Woolf, Virginia, 2, 10–14, 19; *To The Lighthouse*, 14; *Mrs Dalloway*, 2, 11, 13–16, 19–20, 22

Wright, Mabel Osgood, 200, 204, 208; *Citizen Bird: Scenes from Bird-Life in Plain English for Beginners*, 200, 202, 204–5, 211; and Elliott Coues, 200, 204

Yeats, William Butler, 186

Zim, Herbert and Ira Gabrielson, 206; *Birds*, 206

Zuboff, Shoshana, 221

About the Editors and Contributors

ABOUT THE EDITORS

Danette DiMarco is professor of English at Slippery Rock University. She has published in the journals *Mosaic*, *Papers on Language and Literature*, *College Literature*, and *Teaching English in the Two-Year College*, and in the collections *Teaching Literature Online*, *The Sea and the Literary Imagination*, *Misfit Children*, *Teaching Multiethnic American Literatures*, *Inhabited by Stories*, and *Eloquent Images*. She teaches across levels in British, world, and environmental literatures, and is a past recipient of her university's President's Awards for Excellence in Teaching and Scholarly and Creative Achievement.

Timothy Ruppert is an assistant professor of English at Slippery Rock University. He received his PhD in Nineteenth-Century British Literature from Duquesne University in 2008. Since then, he has published about authors such as Mary Shelley, Lord Byron, Louisa Stuart Costello, and Anne Bannerman. He has also authored ten book reviews for various periodicals and, with Danette DiMarco and Jason T. Hilton, coedited *Pandemic University: Teaching and Learning in a Global Crisis* (2020). He writes plays as well; titles within the last five years include *Vicious Lands: A Colonial Comedy*, *Vivienne*, and *The Consorts*, which received a nomination for the Pulitzer Prize in Drama in 2017.

ABOUT THE CONTRIBUTORS

Debarati Bandyopadhyay is professor of English at Visva-Bharati, a Central University in India. She was a Post-Doctoral Fellow (2011–2012; Rabindranath Tagore Centre for Human Development Studies jointly under Calcutta University and the Institute of Development Studies Kolkata), International Visiting Fellow (2017; Essex University), Visiting Fellow (2018; Glasgow University), and Visiting Scholar (2018; Scottish Centre of Tagore Studies, Edinburgh Napier University). She studies ecocriticism and new nature writing, and is author of the ecobiography *Rabindranath Tagore: A Life of Intimacy with Nature* (2019).

Louis J. Boyle is professor of English and chair of the Department of Art, Communication and English at Carlow University in Pittsburgh, Pennsylvania. He is the author of *T. H. White's Reinterpretation of Malory's* Le Morte Darthur and has published articles and presented numerous papers on Malory, T. H. White, and other topics. He is a winner of Carlow University awards for teaching and also for student advising, both of which are chosen by students.

Jemma Deer is a researcher-in-residence at the Rachel Carson Center for Environment and Society and author of *Radical Animism: Reading for the End of the World*. She cohosts *EcoCast*, the official podcast of the Association for the Study of Literature and Environment (ASLE) and is narrator and associate producer of *Shakespeare for All*.

Declan Lloyd lectures in areas of literature, art, and film at Lancaster University, UK. His research looks primarily at the intersections of art and literature from the Modern period onward. Some previously published work has looked to depictions of temporality in contemporary Surrealism, ekphrastic engagements with the visual art of Francis Bacon, and the advertising art experiments of J. G. Ballard.

Joshua Lobb teaches creative writing at the University of Wollongong, Australia. His "novel in stories" about grief and climate change, *The Flight of Birds*, was shortlisted for the 2019 Readings Prize for New Australian Fiction and the 2020 Mascara Literary Review Avant Garde Awards for Best Fiction. He is also part of the multiauthored project *100 Atmospheres: Studies in Scale and Wonder*. His creative and scholarly interest is in the interaction between narrative and climate change.

Laura Major is head of the English Department at Achva Academic College in Israel and lectures there and at Hemdat Hadarom College in the field of literature. Her research interests include pedagogy, women's narratives, crime fiction, creative writing, and Holocaust literature.

Laura McGrath is a professor of rhetoric and professional writing in the English Department at Kennesaw State University. She joined the faculty in 2004, after earning her PhD in English from The University of Georgia and holding a Brittain Postdoctoral Fellowship at Georgia Tech. Her research focuses primarily on digital rhetoric and culture. Publications include *Collaborative Approaches to the Digital in English Studies* (Utah State, 2011) and articles in *Res Rhetorica, Literacy in Composition Studies*, and *Computers and Composition*.

Calista McRae is an assistant professor of English at the New Jersey Institute of Technology, in Newark, NJ. She is the author of *Lyric as Comedy: The Poetics of Abjection in Postwar America* (2020) and coeditor of *The Selected Letters of John Berryman* (2020). Her current book project, *Other Species and Our Feelings: Animal Ethics in Contemporary Lyric,* centers on how recent English-language poets represent human interventions in nonhuman lives.

Christopher Moore is a senior lecturer and academic program director in Media and Communication at the University of Wollongong, Australia. He is a researcher in Internet and fan studies, analogue and digital games and online persona. He is the coauthor of *Persona Studies: An Introduction* and a coeditor of the *Journal of Persona Studies.*

Mark O'Connor is an associate professor of English at Slippery Rock University where he teaches creative writing, literature, and composition. He is the assistant chair and faculty advisor on *SLAB*. In addition to receiving a Pennsylvania Arts Fellowship for Creative Nonfiction and a CACHH grant, his writing has been published in *The Massachusetts Review, Creative Nonfiction, Gulf Coast*, and elsewhere. His chapter on Lynda Barry is forthcoming in *Critical Approaches to Comics Artists.*

Jennifer Schell is professor of English at the University of Alaska Fairbanks. Her specialties include North American literature, animal studies, circumpolar writing, and environmental humanities. Her book, *"A Bold and Hardy Race of Men": The Lives and Literature of American Whalemen* was published in 2013. She has written numerous articles on ecogothic themes involving endangered or extinct species. She is currently working on a monograph entitled *Ghost Species: North American Extinction Writing and the Ecogothic.*

Lauren Shoemaker is an assistant professor of English at Slippery Rock University. Her research explores intersections of race, gender, sexuality, and environment in Caribbean literature and occasionally in US popular culture. Her recent publications include "Femme Finales: Gender, Violence and Nation in Marlon James' Novels" in *The Journal of West Indian Literature* and "A Structure of Terror in Jamaica Kincaid's *A Small Place*" in *Meridians: Feminism, Race, Transnationalism*.

Keri Stevenson is an assistant professor of English at the University of New Mexico-Gallup. She specializes in research relating to birds and animal kinship in Victorian literature and animal memoirs; her latest publication is a book chapter about kinship with birds as proto ecofeminism in George Meredith's novel *The Egoist*. She is the area chair for Eco-criticism and the Environment at the Southwest Popular/American Culture Association annual conference.